Henry Brooke, Charlotte Brooke

Poetical Works

Vol. II

Henry Brooke, Charlotte Brooke

Poetical Works
Vol. II

ISBN/EAN: 9783744677868

Printed in Europe, USA, Canada, Australia, Japan

Cover: Foto ©Thomas Meinert / pixelio.de

More available books at **www.hansebooks.com**

THE
POETICAL WORKS
OF
HENRY BROOKE, Esq.

AUTHOR OF GUSTAVUS VASA, FOOL OF QUALITY, &c.

IN FOUR VOLUMES OCTAVO.

Revised and corrected by the

ORIGINAL MANUSCRIPT;

WITH A

PORTRAIT OF THE AUTHOR,

AND HIS

LIFE.

BY MISS *BROOKE*.

THE THIRD EDITION.

VOL. II.

DUBLIN;

PRINTED FOR THE *EDITOR*.

1792.

FABLES:

THE TEMPLE OF HYMEN.

THE SPARROW AND THE DOVE.

THE FEMALE SEDUCERS.

LOVE AND VANITY.

THE

TEMPLE of HYMEN.

AS on my couch ſupine I lay,
Like others, dreaming life away;
Methought, expanded to my ſight,
A temple rear'd its ſtately height,
All ready built, without omitting
One ornament, for temples fitting.

Large look'd the pile, ſublime and fair;
But "Who the Godhead worſhip'd there?"
This to inquire, appearing meet,
Imagination lent me feet,
And thither, without further cavil,
I fairly undertook to travel.

At once, in bright proceſſion ſpied,
The Female World was at my ſide,

Mingled, like many colour'd patterns,
Nymphs, mes dames, trollops, belles, and ſlatterns,
From point, and ſaucy ermine, down
To the plain coif, and ruſſet gown;
All, by inquiry as I found,
On one important errand bound.

Their van, to either tropick ſpread,
Forerunning Expectation led;
Pleaſure the Female-ſtandard bore,
And Youth danced lightly on before;
While Prudence, Judgment, Senſe, and Taſte,
The few Directing Virtues, placed
To form and guide a woman's mind,
Diſcarded, ſigh'd and ſlunk behind.

At length, in jubilee, arriving,
Where dwelt the jolly God of Wiveing,
All preſt promiſcuouſly to enter,
Nor once reflected on the venture.
But here, the Muſe, affecting ſtate,
Beckon'd her clamorous ſex to wait,
Leſt ſuch a rendezvous ſhould hinder
To ſay what paſt, the while, within door.

Againſt

Againſt the portal, full in ſight,
His ſable veſture ſtarr'd like night,
High throned upon an ebon ſeat,
Beneath a canopy of ſtate,
That o'er his duſky temples nodded,
Was fix'd the Matrimonial Godhead.

Low at his feet, in pomp diſplay'd,
The world's collected wealth was laid;
Where bags of mammon, piled around,
And cheſts on cheſts, o'erwhelm'd the ground,
With bills, bonds, parchments, the appointers
Of doweries, ſettlements, and jointures;
From whence, in juſt proportion weigh'd,
And down, by ſpecial tail, convey'd,
The future progenies inherit
Taſte, beauty, virtue, ſenſe, and merit.

Whatever titles here may ſuit us
For this ſame God, HYMEN, or PLUTUS,
Who, from his trade of a gold-finder,
Might now become a marriage-binder,
And, haply, uſe that precious meta
To ſolder ſexes, like a kettle;
No earthly God, in my opinion,
Claim'd ſuch an abſolute dominion.

To prove his right to adoration
Through every age, and every nation,
Around the ſpacious dome, diſplay'd
By many a fabled light and ſhade,
Was emblematically told
The great Omnipotence of Gold. . . .

And firſt, in yonder panel ſeen,
A lad, call'd Paris, ſtrolled the green,
Poor, hungry, witleſs, and dejected,
By country, and by kin, neglected;
Till Fortune, as ſhe croſs'd the plain,
Conceived a crotchet in her brain,
And, laughing at the baſhful blockhead,
Took a huge pippin from her pocket,
Of the true glittering tempting kind,
And gold throughout from core to rind;
This, in a whim, the Dame beſtow'd,
Then, ſmiling, turn'd, and went her road.

The neighbours, now, when Fame had ſhewn 'em
The youth had got the Summum Bonum,
From many a hut and hamlet croud,
And, duly, at his levy bow'd.

His

His reputation ſpreads apace—
O, ſuch a ſhape, and ſuch a face!
His mouth he opens, and they ſwear
The Delphic oracle is there.

Now, ſee the king of Troy aſpire
To be the wealthy ſhepherd's ſire.
For him, the brighteſt nymphs contended;
To him, three Goddeſſes deſcended,
And ſhew'd, in fair and open day,
Where honour, wit, and beauty lay,
O'er which, our poem, to conceal
From vulgar opticks, drops a veil.

In the next panel, you diſcover
Olympic Jove, that thundering lover,
Who, charm'd with old Acriſius' daughter,
In many a ſhape had vainly ſought her,
And run the round of all his tricks,
Yet ſtill was doubtful where to fix;
Till, by ſome wiſer head inclined,
To caſt his bluſtering bolt behind,
His duller lightning to withhold,
And wear the brighter form of Gold,
He took the hint, he ſtorm'd the tower,
And dropt in yon omnific ſhower.

In the next board, the tale ſo common is,
'Twixt Atalanta and Hippomenes,
I ſhall but ſlightly ſtop a minute,
To drop one obſervation in it;
Remarking, that howe'er prefer'd to
Their ſex, for many a courſe in virtue,
The bright allurement, well applied,
May tempt good nymphs to turn aſide.

Next, Lybia's golden orchard grew
Blooming temptation to the view,
In which a dragon, call'd The Law,
Kept conſcientious fools in awe:
Yet, Power ſuperior to the crime,
And tall Ambition ſkill'd to climb,
With traitors of a new invention,
Who ſell their country for a penſion,
Through many a thicket won their way,
And ſpoil'd the grove, and ſhared the prey.

On the ſame golden ſyſtem laid,
The world was in the fifth diſplay'd:
The earth a golden axis turn'd;
The heavens, with golden planets, burn'd;
And thence, as aſtrologians know,
Derived their influence below:

A girdle,

A FABLE.

A girdle, call'd the Zodiac, graced
The glittering round of Nature's waſte,
Whoſe myſtic charm from Gold ariſes,
For this the Cæſtus of the ſkies is:
And as in Homer's works, we read
(And Homer is the poet's creed)
Of a well twiſted golden tether,
That tied the heavens and earth together,
Such was the cord, or ſuch the cable,
That tied the ſpheres within this table;
By which, the artiſt, underhand,
Would give the wiſe to underſtand,
That Intereſt, in every creature,
Throughout religion, law, and nature,
From eaſt to weſt, and pole to pole,
Moves, binds, ſuſpends, and turns the whole.

While thus, in paſſing ſlightly o'er, I
Surveyed the ſcenes of ancient ſtory;
Or eyed, with more minute attention,
What Prudence, here, forbids to mention;
The Muſe my ſhoulder tapp'd, to mind me
Of things that paſs'd, the while, behind me.

I turn'd, and view'd, with deep ſurprize,
The phantom that aſſail'd my eyes:

His hinder-head diſrobed of hair,
His ſapleſs back, and ſhoulders bare,
Confeſt the wrinkles of a ſage
Who paſt ten Neſtors in his age;
But cloathed before, with decent grace,
And infant ſweetneſs in his face,
Not Smintheus with ſuch vigour ſtrung,
Nor blooming Hebe look'd ſo young.

On his left hand a palette lay,
With many a teint of colours gay;
While, guided with an eaſy flight,
The flying pencil graced his right.

Unnumber'd canvaſſes appear'd,
Before the moving artiſt rear'd,
On whoſe inſpirited expanſe he
Expreſt the creatures of his fancy;
So touch'd, with ſuch a ſwift command,
With ſuch a magic power of hand,
That Nature, did, herſelf, appear
Leſs real than her ſemblance here,
And, not a mortal, ſo betray'd,
Could know the ſubſtance from the ſhade!

Whate'er

Whate'er the world conceives, in life,
Worth toil, anxiety, and ſtrife;
Whate'er by Ignorance is bought,
By Madneſs wiſh'd, or Folly ſought,
The mitres, coronets, and garters,
To which Ambition leads his martyrs;
With every joy, and toy, that can
Amuſe the various child of man,
Was painted here in many a ſcene,
A trifling, tranſient, charming train!

Awhile I ſtood, in thought ſuſpended,
To gueſs what theſe affairs intended;
When, lo, the Muſe, in whiſpers, told,
"'Tis Father Time whom you behold;
"In part diſcovered to the Wiſe,
"In part conceal'd from human eyes.
"A ſlave to yon Gold-giving Power,
"For him he ſpends each reſtleſs hour;
"The product of his toil intends
"As gifts to thoſe his God befriends,
"And paints what other mortals view
"As ſubſtances, though ſhades to you."

She ceas'd, and turning to the ſentry,
Deſired he'd give the Ladies entry;

And ſtraight the portal opened wide,
And in they deluged like a tide.
So, to ſome grove, by ſtreſs of weather,
Faſt flock the fowl of every feather;
A mighty, pretty, prating rabble,
Like Iris rigg'd, and tongued like Babel;
Then crowding toward the nuptial throne,
By bags of ſtrong attraction known,
Low bending to their God they bow'd,
And vented thus their prayer aloud:

" Great Power! in whom our ſex confides,
" Who ruleſt the turns of female tides,
" Who kenſt, while varying Fancy ranges
" Through all its doubles, twirles, and changes,
" To what a Woman's heart is prone,
" A ſecret to ourſelves unknown—
" O, give us, give us, Mighty Power!
" The wedded joy of every hour:
" Aſſign thy favourites, in marriage,
" To coaches of diſtinguiſh'd carriage;
" To all the frippery of dreſſing,
" A nameleſs, boundleſs, endleſs bleſſing;
" To drums, ridottos, ſights and ſounds;
" To viſits in eternal rounds;

" To card and counter, rake and rattle;
" To the whole lust of tongue and tattle;
" And all the dear delightful trances
" Of countless frolicks, fits, and fancies.
" You have heard, that men, unpolish'd boors!
" Lay naughty passions at our doors;
" 'Tis your's to contradict the lyar,
" Who are, yourself, our chief desire.
" O then, as widow, or as wife,
" To you we yield each choice in life;
" Or would you every prayer fulfil,
" Wed us! O! wed us, to our will!"

They ceas'd, and, without more addition,
The God confirm'd their full petition:
To Time he beckon'd, and desired
He'd give the good each nymph required;
And, from his visionary treasure,
Wed every woman to her pleasure.

The first, who came, resolv'd to fix
Upon a gilded coach and six;
The suit was granted her on sight,
The nymph with ardour seiz'd her right.
A wonder! by possession banish'd,
The coach and dappled coursers vanish'd;

And a foul waggon held the Fair
Full laden with a weight of care:
She ſigh'd; her ſiſters caught the ſound,
And one inſulting laugh went round.

The ſecond was a dame of Britain,
Who by a coronet was ſmitten;
With boldneſs ſhe advanced her claim,
Exulting in ſo juſt a flame.
But ah, where bliſs alone was patent,
What unſuſpected miſchief latent!
The worſt in all Pandora's box,
Her coronet contain'd a ——.

With this example in her eye,
The third, a widow'd dame, drew nigh,
And fix'd her ſight and ſoul together
Upon a raking hat and feather;
Nor ſigh'd in vain, but ſeiz'd her due,
And claſp'd old age in twenty-two.

Thus, through the difference and degrees
Of ſword-knots, mitres, and toupees,
Prim bands, pert bobs, and well hung blades,
Long robes, ſmart jackets, fierce cockades,

And

And all the fooleries in fashion,
Whate'er became the darling passion,
The good for which they did importune,
Was straight revers'd into misfortune;
And every woman, like the first,
Was, at her own entreaty, curst.

At length, was introduced a Fair,
With such a face, and such an air.
As never was, on earth, I ween,
Save by poetic organs, seen.

With decent grace, and gentle cheer,
The bright Adventurer drew near;
Her mild approach the Godhead spied,
And, " Fairest," with a smile, he cried,
" If aught you seek in HYMEN's power,
" You find him in a happy hour."

At this, the Virgin, half amazed,
As round the spacious dome she gazed,
With caution every symbol eyed,
And, blushing, gracefully replied.

" If you are he, whose power controuls
" And knits the sympathy of souls,

" Then,

" Then, whence this pomp of worthleſs geer,
" And why this heap of counters here?
" Is this vain ſhew of glittering ore,
" The bliſs, that HYMEN has in ſtore?
" Love ſees the folly, with the gloſs,
" And laughs to ſcorn thy uſeleſs droſs.

" Where are the ſymbols of thy reign?
" And where thy robe of Tyrian grain,
" Whoſe teint, in virgin-colours dyed,
" Derives its bluſhing from the bride?
" Where is thy torch, ſerenely bright,
" To lovers yielding warmth and light,
" That from the heart derives its fire,
" And only can, with life, expire?

" Will this unactive maſs impart
" The ſocial feelings of the heart?
" Or can material fetters bind
" The free affections of the mind?
" Through every age, the Great, and Wiſe,
" Behold thee with ſuperior eyes;
" Love ſpurns thy treaſures with diſdain,
" And Virtue flies thy hoſtile reign.

" By

"By Love, congenial souls embrace,
"Celestial source of human race!
"From whence, the cordial sense within,
"The bosom'd amities of kin,
"The call of nature to her kind,
"And all the tunings of the mind,
"That, winding Heaven's harmonious plan,
"Compose the brotherhood of man."

She said, and gracefully withdrew;
Her steps the Muse and I pursue.
Along an unfrequented way
The Virgin led, nor led astray;
Till, like the first, in form and size,
A second Fabric struck our eyes:
We enter'd, guided by the Fair,
And saw a second HYMEN there.

A silken robe, of saffron hue,
About his decent shoulders flew;
While a fair taper's virgin light
Gave Ovid to his soul and sight.

An hundred Cupids wanton'd round,
Whose useless quivers strow'd the ground;

While, carelefs of their wonted trade,
They with the Smiling Graces play'd.

Along the wall's extended fide,
With teints of varying nature dyed,
In needled tapeftry, was told
The tale of many a love of old.

In groves, that breathed a citron air,
Together walk'd the wedded pair;
Or toy'd upon the vernal ground,
Their beauteous offspring fporting round;
Or, lock'd in fweet embracement, lay,
And flept, and loved, the night away.

There fat Penelope in tears,
Befieged, like Troy, for ten long years:
Her fuitors, in a neighbouring room,
Wait the long promife of the loom,
Which fhe defers, from day to day,
Till death, determin'd to delay.
With thoughts of fond remembrance wrung,
Deep forrowing, o'er her work fhe hung;
Where, in the fields, at Ilium fought,
The labours of her lord fhe wrought,

The

The toil, the duſt, the flying foe,
The rallied hoſt, the inſtant blow;
Then, ſighing, trembled at the view,
Scared at the dangers which ſhe drew.

There too, ſuſpended o'er the wave,
Alcione was ſeen to rave,
When, as the foundering wreck ſhe ſpied,
She on her ſinking Ceÿx cried:
Her Ceÿx, though by ſeas oppreſt,
Still bears her image in his breaſt;
And, with his fondeſt lateſt breath,
Murmurs, "Alcione!" in death.

Panthea there, upon a bier,
Laid the ſole lord of her deſire:
His limbs were ſcatter'd through the plains;
She join'd, and kiſs'd, the dear remains.
Too ponderous was her weight of woe,
For ſighs to riſe, or tears to flow;
On the loved corſe ſhe fix'd her view,
Nor other uſe of ſeeing knew;
While high and ſtedfaſt as ſhe gazed,
Her ſnowy arm a poniard raiſed,
Nor yet the deſperate weapon ſtaid,
But, for a longer look, delayed,

Till, plunged within her beauteous breaſt,
She on his boſom ſunk to reſt.

But, O, beyond whate'er was told
In modern tales, or truths of old,
One Pair, in form and ſpirit twined,
Out loved the loves of human kind;
She Hero, he Leander, named,
For mutual faith, as beauty, famed!
Their ſtory, from its ſource, begun,
And, to the fatal period, run.

While, bow'd at Cytherea's ſhrine,
The Youth adores her power divine,
He ſees her blooming prieſteſs there,
Beyond the ſea-born goddeſs, fair:
She, as ſome God, the ſtripling eyes,
Juſt lighted from his native ſkies—
The God, whoſe chariot guides the hour;
Or haply, Love's immortal power.

At once, their conſcious glances ſpoke,
Like fate, the ſtrong and mutual ſtroke;
Attracted by a ſecret force,
Like currents meeting in their courſe,

That, thence, one ſtream for ever rolls,
Together ruſh'd their mingling ſouls,
Too cloſe for fortune to divide,
For each was loſt in either tide.

In vain, by ruthleſs parents torn,
Their bodies are aſunder born,
And towering bulwarks intervene,
And envious ocean rolls between;
Love wings their letters o'er the ſea,
And kiſſes melt the ſeals away.

And now the ſable night impends,
Leander to the ſhore deſcends,
Exults at the appointed hour,
And marks the ſignal on the tower—
A torch, to guide the Lover's way,
Endear'd beyond the brighteſt day!

At once, he plunges in the tide;
His arms the Helleſpont divide;
The danger and the toil he braves,
And daſhes the contending waves.

While near, and nearer to his ſight,
The taper darts a ruddier light,

Recruited at the view, he glows;
Aside the whelming billow throws:
The winds and seas oppose in vain;
He spurns, he mounts, he skims the main.

Now, from the tower, where Hero stood,
And threw a radiance o'er the flood,
Leander, in the deep, she spied,
And would have sprung to join his side;
Howe'er, her wishes make essay,
And clasp and warm him on his way.

The main is cross'd, the shore is gain'd,
The long wish'd hour, at last, attain'd.
But, lovers, if there e'er arose
A pair, so form'd and fond as those,
So loved, so beauteous, and so blest,
Alone can speak or think the rest;
Nor will the weeping muse unfold
The close, too tragic to be told!

Long were the loving list to name,
With Portia's faith, that swallow'd flame;
But much the longer list were those
Whose joys were unallay'd by woes;

Whose

Whoſe bliſs no cruel parents croſt,
Whoſe love not ages could exhauſt,
Where not a cloud did intervene,
Or once o'er-caſt their bright ſerene,
But, through the ſummer's day of life,
The huſband tender as the wife,
Like Henry and his Nut-brown Maid,
Their faith nor ſhaken nor decay'd,
Together ran the bliſsful race,
Together lived, and ſlept in peace.

Long time, the much inquiring Maid,
From ſtory, on to ſtory ſtray'd;
Joy'd in the joys that lovers know,
Or wept her tribute to their woe;
Till HYMEN, with a placid air,
Approaching, thus addreſt the Fair.

" Hail to the Nymph, whoſe ſacred train
" Of virtues ſhall reſtore my reign!
" Whate'er the wiſhes of thy ſoul,
" But ſpeak them, and poſſeſs the whole."

" Thanks, gentle Power," the Maid replied;
" Your bounty ſhall be amply tried.

" I ſeek not titles, rank, or ſtate,
" Superfluous to the truly great;
" Nor yet, to ſordid wealth inclined,
" The pooreſt paſſion of the mind;
" But, ſimply fix'd to nature's plan,
" I ſeek the ASSOCIATE in the MAN.

" Yet, O beware! for much depends
" On what that ſyllable intends.

" Give him a form that may delight
" My inward ſenſe, my mental ſight;
" In every outward act, deſign'd
" To ſpeak an elegance of mind.

" In him, by ſcience, travel, taſte,
" Be nature poliſh'd, not defaced;
" And ſet, as is the brilliant ſtone,
" To be, with double luſtre, ſhewn.

" Sweet be the muſic of his tongue,
" And, as the lyre of David, ſtrung,
" To ſteal, from each delighted day,
" Affliction, care, and time, away.

" Within his comprehenſive ſoul
" Let Heaven's Harmonious Syſtem roll;

" There

"There let the Great, the Good, the Wiſe,
"Of famed antiquity ariſe;
"From every age and every clime,
"Eluding death, and circling time!
"There let the SACRED VIRTUES meet,
"And range their known and native ſeat!
"There let the Charities unite,
"And Human Feelings weep Delight!"

"Kind POWER! if Such a Youth you know,
"He's all the Heaven I aſk, below."

So wiſh'd the much aſpiring Maid;
Pale turn'd the POWER, and, ſighing, ſaid:

"Alas! like him you fondly claim,
"Through every boaſted form and name,
"That graces Nature's varying round,
"A SECOND is not to be found!
"Your ſuit, Fair Creature, muſt miſcarry,
"Till CHARLEMONT reſolves to marry."

THE

SPARROW and the DOVE.

IT was, as learn'd traditions ſay,
Upon an April's blithſome day,
When Pleaſure, ever on the wing,
Return'd companion of the ſpring,
And chear'd the birds with amorous heat,
Inſtructing little hearts to beat;
A Sparrow, frolic, gay, and young,
Of bold addreſs, and flippant tongue,
Juſt left his lady of a night,
Like him, to follow new delight.

The youth, of many a conqueſt vain,
Flew off to ſeek the chirping train;
The chirping train he quickly found,
And with a ſaucy eaſe bow'd round.

‡ For

For every ſhe his boſom burns,
And this, and that, he wooes by turns;
And here a ſigh, and there a bill,
And here—" thoſe eyes, ſo form'd to kill!"
And now, with ready tongue, he ſtrings
Unmeaning, ſoft, reſiſtleſs things;
With vows and dem-me's ſkill'd to woo,
As other pretty fellows do.
Not that he thought this ſhort eſſay
A prologue needful to his play;
No, truſt me, ſays our learned letter,
He knew the virtuous ſex much better:
But theſe he held as ſpecious arts,
To ſhew his own ſuperior parts;
The form of decency to ſhield,
And give a juſt pretence to yield.

Thus finiſhing his courtly play,
He mark'd the favourite of a day;
With careleſs impudence drew near,
And whiſper'd hebrew in her ear;
A hint, which, like the maſon's ſign,
The conſcious can alone define.

The fluttering nymph, expert at feigning,
Cried, " Sir—pray, ſir, explain your meaning—

" Go,

" Go, prate to thoſe that may endure ye—
" To me this rudeneſs!—I'll aſſure ye!"——
Then off ſhe glided, like a ſwallow,
As ſaying—you gueſs where to follow.

To ſuch as know the party ſet,
'Tis needleſs to declare they met;
The parſon's barn, as authors mention,
Confeſt the fair had apprehenſion.
Her honour there ſecure from ſtain,
She held all further trifling vain,
No more affected to be coy,
But ruſh'd licentious on the joy.

" Hiſt, love!"—the male companion cried;
" Retire a while, I fear we are ſpied."
Nor was the caution vain; he ſaw
A Turtle ruſtling in the ſtraw,
While o'er her callow brood ſhe hung,
And fondly thus addreſt her young.

Ye tender objects of my care!
Peace, peace, ye little helpleſs pair!
Anon he comes, your gentle ſire,
And brings you all your hearts require.

ℵ For

For us, his infants, and his bride,
For us, with only love to guide,
Our lord aſſumes an eagle's ſpeed,
And like a lion dares to bleed.
Nor yet by wintry ſkies confined,
He mounts upon the rudeſt wind;
From danger tears the vital ſpoil,
And with affection ſweetens toil.
Ah ceaſe, too venturous! ceaſe to dare;
In thine, our dearer ſafety ſpare!
From him, ye cruel falcons, ſtray;
And turn, ye fowlers, far away!

Should I ſurvive to ſee the day,
That tears me from myſelf away,
That cancels all that Heaven could give,
The life by which alone I live;
Alas, how more than loſt were I,
Who, in the thought, already die!

Ye Powers, whom men and birds obey,
Great rulers of your creatures, ſay,
Why mourning comes, by bliſs convey'd,
And even the ſweets of love allay'd?
Where grows enjoyment, tall, and fair,
Around it twines entangling care;

While

While fear for what our ſouls poſſeſs,
Enervates every power to bleſs:
Yet friendſhip forms the bliſs above;
And, life! what art thou, without Love?

Our Hero, who had heard apart,
Felt ſomething moving in his heart;
But quickly, with diſdain, ſuppreſt
The virtue riſing in his breaſt:
And firſt he feign'd to laugh aloud;
And next, approaching, ſmiled and bow'd.

"Madam, you muſt not think me rude;
" Good manners never can intrude.
" I vow I come thro' pure good nature—
" Upon my ſoul, a charming creature!—
" Are theſe the comforts of a wife?
" This careful, cloiſter'd, moaping life?
" No doubt, that odious thing, call'd duty,
" Is a ſweet province for a beauty.
" Thou pretty ignorance! thy will
" Is meaſured to thy want of ſkill;
" That good old-faſhion'd dame, thy mother,
" Has taught thy infant years no other—
" The greateſt ill in the creation,
" Is ſure the want of education!

" But

" But think ye?—tell me without feigning,
" Have all theſe charms no further meaning?
" Dame nature, if you don't forget her,
" Might teach your ladyſhip much better.
" For ſhame, reject this mean employment;
" Enter the world, and taſte enjoyment,
" Where time, by circling bliſs, we meaſure;
" Beauty was form'd alone for pleaſure!
" Come, prove the bleſſing, follow me;
" Be wiſe, be happy, and be free."

" Kind ſir," replied our Matron chaſte,
" Your zeal ſeems pretty much in haſte.
" I own, the fondneſs to be bleſt,
" Is a deep thirſt in every breaſt:
" Of bleſſings too I have my ſtore;
" Yet quarrel not, ſhould Heaven give more.
" Then prove the change to be expedient,
" And think me, ſir, your moſt obedient."

Here turning, as to one inferior,
Our Gallant ſpoke, and ſmiled ſuperior.
" Methinks, to quit your boaſted ſtation,
" Requires a world of heſitation!
" Where brats and bonds are held a bleſſing,
" The caſe, I doubt, is paſt redreſſing.

" Why,

" Why, child, ſuppoſe the joys I mention,
" Were the mere fruits of my invention,
" You've cauſe ſufficient for your carriage,
" In flying from the curſe of marriage;
" That ſly decoy, with varied ſnares,
" That takes your widgeons in by pairs;
" Alike to huſband, and to wife,
" The cure of love, and bane of life;
" The only method of forecaſting,
" To make misfortune firm and laſting;
" The ſin, by heaven's peculiar ſentence,
" Unpardon'd, through a life's repentance:
" It is the double ſnake, that weds
" A common tail to different heads,
" That lead the carcaſs ſtill aſtray,
" By dragging each a different way.
" Of all the ills that may attend me,
" From marriage, mighty gods, defend me!

" Give me frank nature's wild demeſne,
" And boundleſs tract of air ſerene,
" Where Fancy, ever wing'd for change,
" Delights to ſport, delights to range.
" There, Liberty! to thee is owing
" Whate'er of bliſs is worth beſtowing:

" Delights, still varied, and divine,
" Sweet goddeſs of the hills! are thine.

" What ſay you now, you pretty pink you?
" Have I for once ſpoke reaſon, think you?
" You take me now for no romancer—
" Come, never ſtudy for an anſwer;
" Away, caſt every care behind ye,
" And fly where joy alone ſhall find ye."

" Soft yet," return'd our female fencer,
" A queſtion more, or ſo—and then, ſir.
" You have rallied me with ſenſe exceeding,
" With much fine wit, and better breeding:
" But pray, ſir, how do you contrive it?
" Do thoſe of your world never wive it?"

No, no—" How then?"—Why dare I tell?—
What does the buſineſs full as well.

" Do you ne'er love?"—An hour at leiſure.
" Have you no friendſhips?"—Yes, for pleaſure.
" No care for little ones?"—We get 'em;
The reſt the mothers mind, and let 'em.

" Thou wretch," rejoin'd the kindling Dove,
" Quite loſt to life, as loſt to love!

" Whene'er

"Whene'er misfortune comes, how just!
"And come misfortune surely must;
"In the dread season of dismay,
"In that your hour of trial, say,
"Who then shall prop your sinking heart?
"Who bear affliction's weightier part?

"Say, when the black-brow'd welkin bends,
"And winter's gloomy form impends,
"To mourning turns all transient chear,
"And blasts the melancholy year;
"For times, at no persuasion, stay,
"Nor vice can find perpetual May;
"Then where's that tongue, by folly fed?
"That soul of pertness, whither fled?
"All shrunk within thy lonely nest,
"Forlorn, abandon'd, and unblest!
"No friends, by cordial bonds allied,
"Shall seek thy cold unsocial side;
"No chirping prattlers, to delight
"Shall turn the long-enduring night;
"No bride her words of balm impart,
"And warm thee at her constant heart.

"Freedom, restrained by Reason's force,
"Is as the sun's unvarying course,

 "Benignly

" Benignly active, ſweetly bright,
" Affording warmth, affording light;
" But torn from Virtue's ſacred rules,
" Becomes a comet, gazed by fools,
" Foreboding cares, and ſtorms, and ſtrife,
" And fraught with all the plagues of life.

" Thou fool! by Union, every creature
" Subſiſts through univerſal nature;
" And this, to beings void of mind,
" Is wedlock of a meaner kind.

" While womb'd in ſpace, primæval clay
" A yet unfaſhion'd embryo lay,
" The Source of Endleſs Good above
" Shot down his ſpark of kindling Love:
" Touch'd by the all-enlivening flame,
" Then motion firſt exulting came;
" Each atom ſought its ſeparate claſs,
" Through many a fair enamour'd maſs;
" Love caſt the central charm around,
" And with eternal nuptials bound.
" Then form and order, o'er the ſky,
" Firſt train'd their bridal pomp on high;

" The

" The sun display'd his orb to sight,
" And burnt with hymeneal light.

" Hence nature's virgin-womb conceived,
" And with the genial burden heaved:
" Forth came the oak, her first born heir,
" And scaled the breathing steep of air;
" Then infant stems, of various use,
" Imbibed her soft maternal juice;
" The flowers, in early bloom disclosed,
" Upon her fragrant breast reposed;
" Within her warm embraces grew,
" A race of endless form and hue;
" Then pour'd her lesser offspring round,
" And fondly cloath'd their parent ground.

" Nor here alone the virtue reign'd,
" By matter's cumbering form detain'd;
" But thence, subliming, and refined,
" Aspired, and reach'd its kindred Mind:
" Caught in the fond, celestial fire,
" The mind perceived unknown desire;
" And now with kind effusion flow'd,
" And now with cordial ardours glow'd;

" Beheld the ſympathetic Fair,
" And loved its own reſemblance there;
" On all with circling radiance ſhone,
" But, centering, fix'd on one alone;
" There claſp'd the heaven-appointed Wife,
" And doubled every joy of life.

" Here ever bleſſing, ever bleſt,
" Reſides this beauty of the breaſt;
" As from his palace, here the God
" Still beams effulgent bliſs abroad;
" Here gems his own eternal round,
" The ring, by which the world is bound;
" Here bids his ſeat of empire grow,
" And builds his little Heaven below.

" The bridal partners thus allied,
" And thus in ſweet accordance tied,
" One body, heart, and ſpirit, live,
" Enrich'd by every joy they give;
" Like echo, from her vocal hold,
" Return'd in muſic twenty fold.
" Their union firm, and undecay'd,
" Nor time can ſhake, nor power invade;
" But as the ſtem and ſcion ſtand,
" Ingrafted by a ſkilful hand,

" They

" They check the tempest's wintry rage,
" And bloom and strengthen into age.
" A thousand amities unknown,
" And powers, perceiv'd by Love alone,
" Endearing looks, and chaste desire,
" Fan and support the mutual fire,
" Whose flame, perpetual as refined,
" Is fed by an immortal mind.

" Nor yet the nuptial sanction ends;
" Like Nile it opens, and descends,
" Which, by apparent windings led,
" We trace to its celestial head:
" The sire, first springing from above,
" Becomes the source of life and love,
" And gives his filial heir to flow,
" In fondness down on sons below.
" Thus roll'd in one continued tide,
" To time's extremest verge they glide;
" While kindred streams, on either hand,
" Branch forth in blessings o'er the land.

" Thee, wretch! no lisping babe shall name,
" No late-returning brother claim,
" No kinsman on thy road rejoice,
" No sister greet thy entering voice,

" With partial eyes no parents see,
" And bless their years restored in thee.

" In age rejected, or declined,
" An alien even among thy kind,
" The partner of thy scorn'd embrace
" Shall play the wanton in thy face;
" Each spark unplume thy little pride,
" All friendship fly thy faithless side;
" Thy name shall like thy carcass rot,
" In sickness spurn'd, in death forgot.

" All-giving Pow'r! great Source of Life!
" O hear the parent! hear the wife!
" That life thou lendest from above,
" Though little, make it large in love!
" O bid my feeling heart expand
" To every claim, on every hand;
" To those from whom my days I drew,
" To these in whom those days renew;
" To all my kin, however wide,
" In cordial warmth, as blood allied;
" To friends, with steelly fetters twined,
" And to the cruel not unkind!

" But chief, the lord of my desire,
" My life, myself, my soul, my sire,
" Friends, children, all that wish can claim,
" Chaste passion clasp, and rapture name;
" O spare him, spare him, Gracious Power!
" O give him to my latest hour!
" Let me my length of life employ,
" To give my sole enjoyment joy;
" His love, let mutual love excite;
" Turn all my cares to his delight;
" And every needless blessing spare,
" Wherein my darling wants a share.
" When he with graceful action wooes
" And sweetly bills, and fondly cooes,
" Ah! deck me, to his eyes alone,
" With charms attractive as his own;
" And in my circling wings carest,
" Give all the lover to my breast.
" Then in our chaste, connubial bed,
" My bosom pillow'd for his head,
" His eyes with blisful slumbers close,
" And watch, with me, my lord's repose;
" Your peace around his temples twine,
" And love him, with a love like mine.

" And, for I know his generous flame,
" Beyond whate'er my ſex can claim,
" Me too to your protection take,
" And ſpare me for my huſband's ſake.
" Let one unruffled calm delight
" The loving, and beloved unite;
" One pure deſire our boſoms warm,
" One will direct, one wiſh inform;
" Through life, one mutual aid ſuſtain;
" In death, one peaceful grave contain!"

While, ſwelling with the darling theme,
Her accents pour'd an endleſs ſtream,
The well-known wings a ſound impart,
That reach'd her ear, and touch'd her heart:
Quick dropp'd the muſic of her tongue,
And forth, with eager joy, ſhe ſprung;
As ſwift her entering conſort flew,
And plumed and kindled at the view;
Their wings their ſouls embracing meet,
Their hearts with anſwering meaſure beat;
Half loſt in ſacred ſweets, and bleſt
With raptures felt, but ne'er expreſt.

Straight to her humble roof ſhe led
The partner of her ſpotleſs bed:

Her

Her young, a fluttering pair, arise,
Their welcome sparkling in their eyes;
Transported, to their sire they bound,
And hang with speechless action round.
In pleasure wrapt, the parents stand,
And see their little wings expand;
The sire, his life sustaining prize
To each expecting bill applies,
There fondly pours the wheaten spoil,
With transport given, tho' won with toil;
While, all collected at the sight,
And silent through supreme delight,
The Fair high Heaven of bliss beguiles,
And on her lord and infants smiles.

The Sparrow, whose attention hung
Upon the Dove's enchanting tongue,
Of all his little slights disarm'd,
And from himself, by VIRTUE, charm'd;
When now he saw, what only seem'd,
A fact, so late a fable deem'd,
His soul to envy he resigned,
His hours of folly to the wind;
In secret wish'd a Turtle too,
And sighing to himself withdrew.

Her young, a flutt'ring pair, arise,
Their welcome sparkling in their eyes;
Transported, to their sire they bound,
And hang with speechless action round.
In pleasure wrapt, the parents stand,
And see their little wings expand;
The sire, his life-sustaining prize
To each expecting bill applies;
There fondly pours the wheaten spoil,
With transport given, tho' won with toil;
While, all collected at the sight,
And silent through supreme delight,
The Fair high Heaven of bliss beguiles,
And on her lord and infants smiles.

The Sparrow, whose attention hung
Upon the Dove's enchanting tongue,
Of all his little slights disarm'd,
And from himself, by Virtue, charm'd,
When now he saw, what only seem'd,
A fact, so late a fable deem'd,
His soul to envy he resign'd,
His hours of folly to the wind;
In secret wish'd a Turtle too,
And sighing to himself withdrew.

THE

FEMALE SEDUCERS.

'TIS ſaid of widow, maid, and wife,
That Honour is a woman's life:
Unhappy ſex! who only claim
A being, in the breath of Fame,
Which tainted, not the quickening gales
That ſweep Sabæa's ſpicy vales,
Nor all the healing ſweets reſtore,
That breathe along Arabia's ſhore.

The traveller, if he chance to ſtray,
May turn uncenſured to his way;
Polluted ſtreams again are pure,
And deepeſt wounds admit a cure:
But woman no redemption knows;
The wounds of Honour never cloſe!

Tho'

Tho' diſtant every hand to guide,
Nor ſkill'd on life's tempeſtuous tide,
If once her feeble bark recede,
Or deviate from the courſe decreed,
In vain ſhe ſeeks the friendleſs ſhore—
Her ſwifter folly flies before;
The circling ports againſt her cloſe,
And ſhut the wanderer from repoſe;
'Till, by conflicting waves oppreſt,
Her foundering pinnace ſinks to reſt.

" Are there no offerings to atone,
" For but a ſingle error?"—None.
Tho' woman is avow'd, of old,
No daughter of celeſtial mould,
Her tempering not without allay,
And form'd but of the finer clay,
We challenge from the mortal dame
The ſtrength angelic natures claim;
Nay more; for ſacred ſtories tell,
That even Immortal Angels fell.

" Whatever fills the teeming ſphere
" Of humid earth, and ambient air,

" With

" With varying elements endued,
" Was form'd to fall, and riſe renew'd.

" The ſtars no fix'd duration know;
" Wide oceans ebb, again to flow;
" The moon repletes her waining face,
" All-beauteous, from her late diſgrace;
" And ſuns, that mourn approaching night,
" Refulgent riſe with new-born light.

" In vain may Death and Time ſubdue,
" While Nature mints her race anew,
" And holds ſome vital ſpark apart,
" Like Virtue, hid in every heart:
" 'Tis hence, reviving warmth is ſeen
" To cloath a naked world in green;
" No longer barr'd by winter's cold,
" Again the gates of life unfold;
" Again each inſect tries his wing,
" And lifts freſh pinions on the ſpring;
" Again, from every latent root,
" The bladed ſtem and tendril ſhoot,
" Exhaling incenſe to the ſkies,
" Again to periſh, and to riſe.

" And muſt weak woman then diſown
" The change, to which a world is prone?
" In one meridian brightneſs ſhine,
" And ne'er like evening ſuns decline?
" Reſolved and firm alone?—Is this
" What we demand of woman?"—Yes.

" But ſhould the ſpark of veſtal fire,
" In ſome unguarded hour expire;
" Or ſhould the nightly thief invade
" Heſperia's chaſte and ſacred ſhade,
" Of all the blooming ſpoil poſſeſt,
" The dragon Honour charm'd to reſt;
" Shall Virtue's flame no more return?
" No more with virgin ſplendor burn?
" No more the ravaged garden blow
" With ſpring's ſucceeding bloſſom?"—No:
Pity may mourn, but not reſtore;
And woman falls, to riſe no more!

WITHIN this ſublunary ſphere,
A country lies—no matter where;
The clime may readily be found,
By all who tread poetic ground.

A ſtream,

A ſtream, call'd Life, acroſs it glides,
And equally the land divides:
And here, of Vice the province lies;
And there, the hills of VIRTUE riſe!

Upon a mountain's airy ſtand,
Whoſe ſummit look'd to either land,
An Ancient Pair their dwelling choſe,
As well for proſpect, as repoſe;
For mutual faith they long were famed,
And Temperance, and Religion, named.

A numerous progeny divine,
Confeſt the honours of their line:
But in a little Daughter fair,
Was center'd more than half their care;
For Heaven, to gratulate her birth,
Gave ſigns of future joy to earth:
White was the robe this infant wore,
And Chaſtity the name ſhe bore.

As now the Maid in ſtature grew,
A flower juſt opening to the view!
Oft thro' her native lawns ſhe ſtray'd,
And wreſtling with the lambkins play'd:

Her looks diffusive sweets bequeath'd,
The breeze grew purer as she breath'd;
The morn her radiant blush assumed,
The spring with earlier fragrance bloom'd;
And Nature yearly took delight,
Like her, to dress the world in white.

But when her rising form was seen
To reach the crisis of fifteen,
Her parents up the mountain's head,
With anxious step their darling led;
By turns they snatch'd her to their breast,
And thus the fears of age exprest.

" O joyful cause of many a care!
" O daughter, too divinely fair!
" Yon world, on this important day,
" Demands thee to a dangerous way;
" A painful journey all must go,
" Whose doubtful period none can know;
" Whose due direction who can find,
" Where Reason's mute, and Sense is blind?
" Ah, what unequal leaders these,
" Thro' such a wide perplexing maze!
" Then mark the warnings of the wise,
" And learn what love and years advise.

" Far

" Far to the right thy prospect bend,
" Where yonder towering hills ascend:
" Lo, there the arduous path's in view,
" Which VIRTUE, and her sons pursue;
" With toil o'er lessening earth they rise,
" And gain, and gain, upon the skies!
" Narrow's the way her children tread;
" No walk for pleasure smoothly spread,
" But rough, and difficult, and steep,
" Painful to climb, and hard to keep.

" Fruits immature those lands dispense,
" A food indelicate to sense,
" Of taste unpleasant; yet from those
" Pure health with chearful vigour flows,
" And strength unfeeling of decay,
" Throughout the long laborious way.

" Hence, as they scale that Heavenly road,
" Each limb is lightened of its load;
" From earth refining still they go,
" And leave the mortal weight below:
" Then spreads the strait, the doubtful clears,
" And smooth the rugged path appears;
" For custom turns fatigue to ease,
" And, taught by VIRTUE, pain can please.

"At length, the toilsome journey o'er,
"And near the bright celestial shore,
"A gulph, black, fearful, and profound,
"Appears, of either world the bound,
"Thro' darkness leading up to light:
"Sense backwards shrinks, and shuns the sight;
"For there the transitory train,
"Of time, and form, and care, and pain,
"And matter's gross incumbering mass,
"Man's late associates, cannot pass,
"But sinking, quit the immortal charge,
"And leave the wondering soul at large;
"Lightly she wings her obvious way,
"And mingles with eternal day.

"Thither, O thither, wing thy speed,
"Tho' Pleasure charm, or Pain impede!
"To such the ALL-BOUNTEOUS POWER has given,
"For present earth, a future Heaven;
"For trivial loss, unmeasured gain;
"And endless bliss, for transient pain.

"Then fear, ah! fear to turn thy sight,
"Where yonder flowery fields invite;
"Wide on the left the path-way bends,
"And with pernicious ease descends:

" There ſweet to ſenſe, and fair to ſhow,
" New-planted Edens ſeem to blow,
" Trees that delicious poiſon bear,
" For death is vegetable there.

" Hence is the frame of health unbraced,
" Each ſinew ſlackening at the taſte;
" The ſoul to paſſion yields her throne,
" And ſees with organs not her own;
" While, like the ſlumberer in the night,
" Pleaſed with the ſhadowy dream of light,
" Before her alienated eyes,
" The ſcenes of fairy land ariſe;
" The puppet world's amuſing ſhow,
" Dipt in the gayly colour'd bow,
" Scepters, and wreaths, and glittering things,
" The toys of infants, and of kings,
" That tempt, along the baneful plain,
" The idly wiſe, and lightly vain;
" Till verging on the gulphy ſhore,
" Sudden they ſink, and riſe no more.

" But liſt to what thy fates declare;
" Tho' thou art Woman, frail as fair,
" If once thy ſliding foot ſhould ſtray,
" Once quit yon Heaven-appointed way,

" For thee, loſt Maid, for thee alone,
" Nor prayers ſhall plead, nor tears atone:
" Reproach, ſcorn, infamy, and hate,
" On thy returning ſteps ſhall wait;
" Thy form be loathed by every eye,
" And every foot thy preſence fly."

Thus arm'd with words of potent ſound,
Like guardian-angels placed around,
A charm by Truth divinely caſt,
Forward, our young Adventurer paſt:
Forth from her ſacred eye-lids ſent,
Like morn, fore-running radiance went;
While Honour, hand-maid late aſſigned,
Upheld her lucid train behind.

Awe-ſtruck the much admiring crowd
Before the Virgin Viſion bow'd,
Gazed with an ever new delight,
And caught freſh virtue at the ſight:
For not of earth's unequal frame
They deem the Heaven-compounded dame;
If matter, ſure the moſt refined,
High wrought, and temper'd into mind!
Some darling daughter of the day,
And bodied by her native ray!

Where

Where e'er ſhe paſſes, thouſands bend;
And thouſands, where ſhe moves, attend;
Her ways obſervant eyes confeſs,
Her ſteps purſuing praiſes bleſs;
While to the elevated Maid
Oblations, as to Heaven, are paid.

'Twas on an ever blithſome day,
The jovial birth of roſy May,
When genial warmth, no more ſuppreſt,
New melts the froſt in every breaſt,
The cheek with ſecret fluſhing dyes,
And looks kind things from chaſteſt eyes;
The ſun with healthier viſage glows,
Aſide his clouded 'kerchief throws,
And dances up the etherial plain,
Where late he uſed to climb with pain;
While Nature, as from bonds ſet free,
Springs out, and gives a looſe to glee.

And now, for momentary reſt,
The Nymph her travell'd ſtep repreſt;
Juſt turn'd to view the ſtage attain'd,
And gloried in the height ſhe had gain'd.

Out-ſtretch'd before her wide ſurvey,
The realms of ſweet perdition lay,
And pity touch'd her ſoul with woe,
To ſee a world ſo loſt below;
When ſtraight the breeze began to breathe
Airs gently wafted from beneath,
That bore commiſſion'd witchcraft thence,
And reach'd her ſympathy of ſenſe;
No ſounds of diſcord, that diſcloſe
A people ſunk and loſt in woes,
But as of preſent good poſſeſt,
The very triumph of the bleſt.
The Maid in rapt attention hung,
While thus approaching Sirens ſung.

"Hither, Faireſt, hither haſte!
"Brighteſt Beauty, come and taſte
"What the powers of bliſs unfold,
"Joys too mighty to be told!
"Taſte what extaſies they give—
"Dying raptures taſte and live.

"In thy lap, diſdaining meaſure,
"Nature empties all her treaſure;
"Soft deſires that ſweetly languiſh,
"Fierce delights that riſe to anguiſh!

"Faireſt,

"Faireſt, doſt thou yet delay?
"Brighteſt Beauty, come away!

"Liſt not, when the froward chide,
"Sons of pedantry and pride;
"Snarlers, to whoſe feeble ſenſe
"April's ſunſhine is offence;
"Age and envy will adviſe,
"Even againſt the joy they prize.

"Come, in Pleaſure's balmy bowl,
"Slake the thirſtings of thy ſoul,
"Till thy raptured powers are fainting,
"With enjoyment paſt the painting:
"Faireſt, doſt thou yet delay?
"Brighteſt Beauty, come away!"

So ſung the Sirens, as of yore,
Upon the falſe Auſonian ſhore;
And O! for that preventing chain,
That bound Ulyſſes on the main,
That ſo our Fair One might withſtand
The covert ruin now at hand.

The ſong her charm'd attention drew,
When now the Tempters ſtood in view—

Curioſity,

Curiosity, with prying eyes,
And hands of busy bold emprise;
Like Hermes, feather'd were her feet,
And, like fore-running Fancy, fleet:
By search untaught, by toil untired,
To novelty she still aspired;
Tasteless of every good possest,
And but in expectation blest.

With her, associate, Pleasure came,
Gay Pleasure, frolic-loving dame;
Her mien all swimming in delight,
Her beauties half revealed to sight;
Loose flowed her garments from the ground,
And caught the kissing winds around.
As erst Medusa's looks were known
To turn beholders into stone,
A dire reversion here they felt,
And in the eye of Pleasure melt.
Her glance with sweet persuasion charm'd,
Unnerv'd the strong, the steel'd disarm'd;
No safety even the flying find,
Who, venturous, look but once behind.

Thus was the much-admiring Maid,
While distant, more than half betray'd.

With

With ſmiles, and adulation bland,
They join'd her ſide, and ſeiz'd her hand:
Their touch envenom'd ſweets inſtill'd,
Her frame with new pulſations thrill'd;
While half conſenting, half denying,
Reluctant now, and now complying,
Amidſt a war of hopes and fears,
Of trembling wiſhes, ſmiling tears,
Still down, and down, the winning Pair
Compell'd the ſtruggling yielding Fair.

As when ſome ſtately veſſel, bound
To bleſt Arabia's diſtant ground,
Borne from her courſes, haply lights
Where Barca's flowery clime invites,
Conceal'd around whoſe treacherous land,
Lurk the dire rock, and dangerous ſand;
The pilot warns, with ſail and oar
To ſhun the much ſuſpected ſhore—
In vain; the tide, too ſubtly ſtrong,
Still bears the wreſtling bark along;
Till foundering, ſhe reſigns to fate,
And ſinks o'erwhelm'd with all her freight.

So, baffling every bar to ſin,
And Heaven's own Pilot placed within,

Along

Along the devious ſmooth deſcent,
With powers increaſing as they went,
The Dames, accuſtom'd to ſubdue,
As with a rapid current drew;
And o'er the fatal bounds convey'd
The loſt the long reluctant Maid.

Here ſtop, ye Fair Ones, and beware,
Nor ſend your fond affections there:
Yet, yet, your Darling, now deplored,
May turn, to you, and Heaven, reſtored;
Till then, with weeping Honour wait,
The ſervant of her better fate,
With Honour left upon the ſhore,
Her friend and handmaid now no more;
Nor, with the guilty world, upbraid
The fortunes of a wretch betray'd,
But o'er her failing caſt a veil,
Remembring you yourſelves are frail.

And now, from all-enquiring light,
Faſt fled the conſcious ſhades of night;
The Damſel, from a ſhort repoſe,
Confounded at her plight, aroſe.

As when, with ſlumberous weight oppreſt,
Some wealthy miſer ſinks to reſt,
Where felons eye the glittering prey,
And ſteal his hoard of joys away;
He, borne where golden Indus ſtreams,
Of pearl and quarry'd diamond dreams;
Like Midas, turns the glebe to oar,
And ſtands all wrapt amidſt his ſtore;
But wakens, naked, and deſpoil'd
Of that, for which his years had toil'd.
So fared the Nymph—her treaſure flown,
And turn'd, like Niobe, to ſtone;
Within, without, obſcure and void,
She felt all ravaged, all deſtroy'd:
And, " O thou curs'd, inſidious coaſt!
" Are theſe the bleſſings thou can'ſt boaſt?
" Theſe, VIRTUE! theſe the joys they find,
" Who leave thy heaven-topt hills behind?
" Shade me ye pines, ye caverns hide,
" Ye mountains cover me!" ſhe cried.

Her trumpet Slander raiſed on high,
And told the tidings to the ſky;
Contempt diſcharged a living dart,
A ſide-long viper to her heart;

Reproach

Reproach breathed poisons o'er her face,
And soil'd and blasted every grace:
Officious Shame, her handmaid new,
Still turn'd the mirror to her view,
While those, in crimes the deepest dyed,
Approach'd to whiten at her side,
And every lewd insulting dame
Upon her folly rose to fame.

What should she do?—attempt once m'
To gain the late-deserted shore?
So trusting, back the Mourner flew;
As fast the train of fiends pursue.

Again the farther shore's attain'd,
Again the land of VIRTUE gain'd;
But echo gathers in the wind,
And shows her instant foes behind.
Amazed, with headlong speed she tends,
Where late she left an host of friends;
Alas! those shrinking friends decline,
Nor longer own that form divine:
With fear they mark the following cry,
And from the lonely Trembler fly;
Or backward drive her on the coast,
Where peace was wreck'd, and honour lost.

From

From earth thus hoping aid in vain,
To Heaven not daring to complain,
No truce by hoſtile clamour given,
And from the face of friendſhip driven;
The Nymph ſunk proſtrate on the ground,
With all her weight of woes around.

Enthroned within a circling ſky,
Upon a mount, o'er mountains high,
All radiant ſate, as in a ſhrine,
VIRTUE, Firſt Effluence Divine,
Far, far above the ſcenes of woe,
That ſhut this cloud-wrapt world below;
Superior Goddeſs, eſſence bright,
Beauty of Uncreated Light,
Whom ſhould mortality ſurvey,
As doom'd upon a certain day,
The breath of frailty muſt expire;
The world diſſolve in living fire;
The gems of Heaven, and ſolar flame,
Be quench'd by her eternal beam;
And Nature, quickening in her eye,
To riſe a new-born phœnix, die.

Hence, unreveal'd to mortal view,
A veil around her form ſhe threw,

Which three ſad ſiſters of the ſhade
Pain, Care, and Melancholy made.

Thro' this her all-enquiring eye,
Attentive from her ſtation high,
Beheld, abandon'd to deſpair,
The ruins of her Favourite Fair;
And with a voice, whoſe awful ſound
Appall'd the guilty world around,
Bid the tumultuous winds be ſtill,
To numbers bow'd each liſtening hill,
Uncurl'd the ſurging of the main,
And ſmooth'd the thorny bed of pain;
The golden harp of Heaven ſhe ſtrung,
And thus the tuneful Goddeſs ſung.

" Lovely Penitent, ariſe!
" Come, and claim thy kindred ſkies;
" Come, thy Siſter Angels ſay,
" Thou haſt wept thy ſtains away.

" Let experience now decide,
" 'Twixt the good, and evil tried:
" In the ſmooth, enchanted ground,
" Say, unfold the treaſures found?—

" Structures

" Structures raised by morning dreams,
" Sands that trip the flitting streams,
" Down that anchors on the air,
" Clouds that paint their changes there!
" Seas that smoothly dimpling lie,
" While the storm impends on high,
" Showing, in an obvious glass,
" Joys that in possession pass;
" Transient, fickle, light, and gay,
" Flattering, only to betray!
" What, alas, can Life contain?
" Life, like all it's circles, vain!

" Will the stork, intending rest,
" On the billow build her nest?
" Will the bee demand his store
" From the bleak and bladeless shore?
" Man alone, intent to stray,
" Ever turns from Wisdom's way;
" Lays up wealth in foreign land,
" Sows the sea, and plows the sand.

" Soon this elemental mass,
" Soon the incumbering world shall pass,
" Form be wrapt in wasting fire,
" Time be spent, and life expire.

" Then, ye boasted works of men,
" Where is your asylum then?
" Sons of pleasure, sons of care,
" Tell me mortals, tell me where?
" Gone, like traces on the deep,
" Like a scepter grasp'd in sleep,
" Dews exhaled from morning glades,
" Melting snows, and gliding shades!

" Pass the world, and what's behind?—
" VIRTUE's gold, by fire refined;
" From an universe depraved,
" From the wreck of nature saved:
" Like the life-supporting grain,
" Fruit of patience, and of pain,
" On the swain's autumnal day,
" Winnowed from the chaff away.

" Little Trembler, fear no more!
" Thou hast plenteous crops in store,
" Seed by genial sorrows sown,
" More than all thy scorners own.

" What tho' hostile earth despise,
" Heaven beholds with gentler eyes;

" Heaven

" Heaven thy friendleſs ſteps ſhall guide,
" Chear thy hours, and guard thy ſide.
" When the fatal trump ſhall ſound,
" When the immortals pour around,
" Heaven ſhall thy return atteſt,
" Hail'd by myriads of the bleſt.

" Little Native of the ſkies,
" Lovely Penitent, ariſe!
" Calm thy boſom, clear thy brow,
" VIRTUE is thy ſiſter now.

" More delightful are my woes,
" Than the rapture pleaſure knows;
" Richer far the weeds I bring,
" Than the robes that grace a king.

" On my wars of ſhorteſt date,
" Crowns of endleſs triumph wait;
" On my cares, a period bleſt;
" On my toils, Eternal Reſt.

" Come, with VIRTUE at thy ſide,
" Come, be every bar defied,
" Till we gain our Native Shore:
" Siſter, come, and turn no more!"

LOVE AND VANITY.

THE breezy morning breathed perfume,
The wakening flowers unveil'd their bloom;
Up with the ſun, from ſhort repoſe,
Gay Health, and luſty Labour roſe;
The milkmaid carol'd at her pail,
And ſhepherds whiſtled o'er the dale;
When LOVE, who led a rural life,
Remote from buſtle, ſtate, and ſtrife,
Forth from his thatch'd-roof'd cottage ſtray'd,
And ſtrolled along the dewy glade.

A Nymph, who lightly trip'd it by,
To quick attention turn'd his eye:
He mark'd the geſture of the Fair,
Her ſelf-ſufficient grace and air,
Her ſteps that mincing meant to pleaſe,
Her ſtudied negligence and eaſe;

And curious to enquire what meant
This thing of prettineſs and paint,
Approaching ſpoke, and bow'd obſervant;
The Lady, ſlightly,—" Sir, your ſervant."

" Such beauty in ſo rude a place!
" Fair one, you do the country grace:
" At court, no doubt, the public care—
" But Love has ſmall acquaintance there!"

" Yes, ſir," replied the fluttering Dame,
" This form confeſſes whence it came:
" But dear variety, you know,
" Can make us pride and pomp forego.
" My name is Vanity. I ſway
" The utmoſt iſlands of the ſea:
" Within my court all honour centers;
" I raiſe the meaneſt ſoul that enters;
" Endow with latent gifts and graces,
" And model fools for poſts and places.

" As Vanity appoints at pleaſure,
" The world receives its weight, and meaſure;
" Hence all the grand concerns of life,
" Joys, cares, plagues, paſſions, peace and ſtrife.

Reflect

" Reflect how far my power prevails,
" When I step in, where Nature fails,
" And every breach of sense repairing,
" Am bounteous still, where Heaven is sparing.

" But chief, in all their arts and airs,
" Their playing, painting, pouts, and prayers,
" Their various habits and complexions,
" Fits, frolicks, foibles, and perfections,
" Their robing, curling, and adorning,
" From noon 'till night, from night 'till morning,
" From six to sixty, sick or sound,
" I rule the Female Word around."

" Hold there a moment," Cupid cried,
" Nor boast dominion quite so wide.
" Was there no province to invade,
" But that by LOVE and Meekness sway'd?
" All other empire I resign;
" But be the Sphere of Beauty mine.
" For in the downy lawn of rest,
" That opens on a Woman's breast,
" Attended by my peaceful train,
" I chuse to live, and chuse to reign.

" Far-ſighted Faith I bring along;
" And Truth, above an army ſtrong;
" And Chaſtity, of icy mould,
" Within the burning tropics cold;
" And Lowlineſs, to whoſe mild brow,
" The power and pride of nations bow;
" And Modeſty, with downcaſt eye,
" That lends the morn her virgin dye;
" And Innocence, array'd in light;
" And Honour, as a tower upright;
" With ſweetly winning Graces, more
" Than poets ever dreamt of yore,
" In unaffected conduct free,
" All ſmiling ſiſters, three times three;
" And roſy Peace, the cherub bleſt,
" That nightly ſings us all to reſt.

" Hence, from the bud of Nature's prime,
" From the firſt ſtep of infant time,
" Woman, the world's appointed light,
" Has ſkirted every ſhade with white;
" Has ſtood for imitation high,
" To every heart and every eye;
" From antient deeds of fair renown,
" Has brought her bright memorials down;

" To

" To Time affix'd perpetual youth,
" And form'd each tale of love and truth.

" Upon a new Promethean plan,
" She moulds the eſſence of a man,
" Tempers his maſs, his genius fires,
" And, as a better ſoul, inſpires.

" The Rude ſhe ſoftens, warms the Cold,
" Exalts the Meek, and checks the Bold;
" Calls Sloth from his ſupine repoſe;
" Within the Coward's boſom glows;
" Of Pride unplumes the lofty creſt;
" Bids baſhful Merit ſtand confeſt;
" And, like coarſe metal from the mines,
" Collects, irradiates, and refines.

" The gentle ſcience ſhe imparts,
" All manners ſmooths, informs all hearts:
" From her ſweet influence are felt,
" Paſſions that pleaſe, and thoughts that melt;
" To ſtormy rage ſhe bids controul,
" And ſinks ſerenely on the ſoul;
" Softens Deucalion's flinty race,
" And tunes the warring world to peace.

" Thus,

" Thus, arm'd to all that's light and vain,
" And freed from thy fantastic chain,
" She fills the sphere, by Heaven assigned,
" And ruled by me, o'er-rules mankind."

He spoke. The Nymph impatient stood;
And laughing, thus her speech renew'd.

" And pray, sir, may I be so bold
" To hope your pretty tale is told;
" And next demand, without a cavil,
" What new Utopia do you travel?—
" Upon my word, these high flown fancies
" Shew depth of learning—in romances.

" Why, what unfashion'd stuff you tell us,
" Of buckram dames, and tiptoe fellows!
" Go, child; and when you're grown maturer,
" You'll shoot your next opinion surer.

" O such a pretty knack at painting!
" And all for softening, and for fainting!
" Guess how, who can, a single feature,
" Thro' the whole piece of Female Nature!
" Then mark! my looser hand may fit
" The lines, too coarse for Love to hit.

" 'Tis said that Woman, prone to changing,
" Thro' all the rounds of folly ranging,
" On life's uncertain ocean riding,
" No reason, rule, nor rudder guiding,
" Is like the comet's wandering light,
" Eccentric, ominous, and bright;
" Trackless, and shifting, as the wind;
" A sea, whose fathom none can find;
" A moon, still changing, and revolving;
" A riddle, past all human solving;
" A bliss, a plague, a heaven, a hell,
" A—something, that no man can tell.

" Now learn a secret from a friend;
" But keep your counsel, and attend.

" Tho' in their tempers thought so distant,
" Nor with their sex, nor selves consistent,
" 'Tis but the difference of a name,
" And every Woman is the same.
" For as the world, however varied,
" And through unnumber'd changes carried,
" Of elemental modes, and forms,
" Clouds, meteors, colours, calms and storms,

" Tho'

" Tho' in a thousand suits array'd,
" Is of one subject matter made;
" So, sir, a Woman's constitution,
" The world's enigma, finds solution;
" And let her form be what you will,
" I am the Subject Essence still.

" With the first spark of Female Sense,
" The speck of being, I commence;
" Within the womb make fresh advances,
" And dictate future qualms and fancies;
" Thence in the growing form expand,
" With childhood travel hand in hand,
" And give a taste of all their joys,
" In gewgaws, rattles, pomp, and noise.

" And now, familiar, and unaw'd,
" I send the fluttering soul abroad.
" Prais'd for her shape, her face, her mein,
" The little goddess, and the queen,
" Takes at her infant shrine oblation,
" And drinks sweet draughts of adulation.

" Now blooming, tall, erect, and fair,
" To dress, becomes her darling care:

" The

" The realms of Beauty then I bound;
" I ſwell the hoop's enchanted round,
" Shrink in the waiſt's deſcending ſize,
" Heaved in the ſnowy boſom riſe,
" High on the floating lappet ſail,
" Or curl'd in treſſes kiſs the gale.
" Then to her glaſs I lead the Fair,
" And ſhew the lovely idol there;
" Where, ſtruck as by divine emotion,
" She bows with moſt ſincere devotion;
" And, numbering every beauty o'er,
" In ſecret bids the world adore.

" Then all for parking, and parading,
" Coquetting, dancing, maſquerading;
" For balls, plays, courts, and crouds, what paſſion!
" And churches, ſometimes—if the faſhion:
" For Woman's ſenſe of right, and wrong,
" Is ruled by the almighty throng;
" Still turns to each meander tame,
" And ſwims the ſtraw of every ſtream.
" Her ſoul intrinſic worth rejects,
" Accompliſh'd only in defects;
" Such excellence is her ambition;
" Folly, her wiſeſt acquiſition;

" And even, from pity, and disdain,
" She'll cull some reason to be vain.

" Thus, sir, from every form, and feature,
" The wealth, and wants of female nature,
" And even from vice, which you'd admire,
" I gather fewel to my fire;
" And, on the very base of shame,
" Erect my monument of fame.

" Let me another truth attempt,
" Of which your Godship has not dreamt.

" Those shining virtues, which you muster,
" Whence think you they derive their lustre?
" From native honour, and devotion?—
" O yes, a mighty likely notion!
" Trust me, from titled dames to spinners,
" 'Tis I make saints, whoe'er makes sinners;
" 'Tis I instruct them to withdraw,
" And hold presumptuous man in awe;
" For female worth, as I inspire,
" In just degrees still mounts the higher,
" And Virtue, so extremely nice,
" Demands long toil, and mighty price:
" Like Sampson's pillars, fix'd elate,
" I bear the Sex's tottering state;

" Sap

" Sap these, and, in a moment's space,
" Down sinks the fabric to its base.

" Alike from titles, and from toys,
" I spring, the fount of Female Joys;
" In every widow, wife, and miss,
" The sole artificer of bliss.
" For them each tropic I explore;
" I cleave the sand of every shore;
" To them uniting Indias sail,
" Sabæa breathes her farthest gale:
" For them the bullion I refine,
" Dig sense and virtue from the mine;
" And from the bowels of invention,
" Spin out the various arts you mention.

" Nor bliss alone my powers bestow,
" They hold the sovereign balm of woe:
" Beyond the stoic's boasted art,
" I sooth the heavings of the heart;
" To pain give splendor and relief,
" And gild the pallid face of grief.

" Alike the palace, and the plain,
" Admit the glories of my reign:

"Thro' every age, in every nation,
"Taste, talents, tempers, state, and station,
"Whate'er a Woman says, I say;
"Whate'er a Woman spends, I pay:
"Alike, I fill and empty bags,
"Flutter in finery and rags,
"With light coquets thro' folly range,
"And with the prude disdain to change.

"And now you'd think, 'twixt you and I,
"That things were ripe for a reply—
"But soft; and, while I'm in the mood,
"Kindly permit me to conclude,
"Their utmost mazes to unravel,
"And touch the farthest step they travel.

"When every pleasure's run aground,
"And folly tired thro' many a round,
"The Nymph, conceiving discontent hence,
"May ripen to an hour's repentance,
"And vapours, shed in pious moisture,
"Dismiss her to a church, or cloyster:
"Then on I lead her, with devotion
"Conspicuous in her dress, and motion;
"Inspire the heavenly-breathing air,
"Roll up the lucid eye in prayer,

"Soften

" Soften the voice, and in the face
" Look melting harmony and grace.

" Thus far extends my friendly power,
" Nor quits her in her lateſt hour:
" The couch of decent pain I ſpread,
" In form recline her languid head,
" Her thoughts I methodize in death,
" And part not, with her parting breath:
" Then do I ſet, in order bright,
" A length of funeral pomp to ſight,
" The glittering tapers and attire,
" The plumes that whiten o'er her bier;
" And laſt, preſenting to her eye
" Angelic fineries on high,
" To ſcenes of painted bliſs I waft her,
" And form the heaven ſhe hopes hereafter."

" In truth," rejoin'd LOVE's gentle god,
" You have gone a tedious length of road:
" And ſtrange, in all the toilſome way,
" No houſe of kind refreſhment lay;
" No Nymph, whoſe virtues might have tempted,
" To hold her from her ſex exempted."

" For one, we'll never quarrel, man;
" Take her; and keep her,—if you can:
" And pleafed I yield to your petition,
" Since every Fair, by fuch permiffion,
" Will hold herfelf the one felected;
" And fo my fyftem ftands protected."

" O deaf to virtue, deaf to glory,
" To truths divinely vouch'd in ftory!"—
The Godhead in his zeal return'd,
And kindling at her malice burn'd:
Then fweetly raifed his voice, and told
Of Heavenly Nymphs, revered of old—
Hypfipyle, who faved her fire;
And Portia's love, approved by fire;
Alike Penelope was quoted,
Nor laurel'd Daphne paft unnoted;
Nor Laodamia's fatal garter,
Nor famed Lucretia, honour's martyr;
Alcefte's voluntary fteel,
And Catherine fmiling on the wheel!
But who can hope to plant conviction,
Where cavil grows on contradiction?
Some fhe evades, or difavows;
Demurs to all, and none allows—

" A kind

" A kind of ancient things, call'd Fables!"
And thus the Goddeſs turn'd the tables.

Now both in argument grew high,
And choler flaſh'd from either eye;
Nor wonder each refuſed to yield
The conqueſt of ſo fair a field.
When happily arrived in view
A Goddeſs, whom our grandames knew;
Of aſpect grave, and ſober gaite,
Majeſtic, aweful, and ſedate;
As heaven's autumnal eve ſerene,
When not a cloud o'ercaſts the ſcene;
Once PRUDENCE call'd, a matron famed,
And in old Rome Cornelia named.
Quick at a venture, both agree
To leave their ſtrife to her decree.

And now by each the facts were ſtated,
In form and manner as related.
The caſe was ſhort. They craved opinion,
" Which held o'er Females chief dominion?"
When thus the Goddeſs, anſwering mild,
Firſt ſhook her gracious head, and ſmiled:

"Alas, how willing to comply,
"Yet how unfit a judge am I!
"In times of golden date, 'tis true,
"I ſhared the Fickle Sex with you;
"But from their preſence long precluded,
"Or held as one whoſe form intruded,
"Full fifty annual ſuns can tell,
"PRUDENCE has bid the Sex farewell."

In this dilemma what to do,
Or who to think of, neither knew;
For both, ſtill biaſs'd in opinion,
And arrogant of ſole dominion,
Were forced to hold the caſe compounded,
Or leave the quarrel where they found it.

When in the nick, a Rural Fair,
Of inexperienced gaite and air,
Who ne'er had croſs'd the neighbouring lake,
Nor ſeen the world beyond a wake,
With cambrick coif, and kerchief clean,
Tript lightly by them o'er the green.

"Now, now!" cried Love's triumphant Child,
And at approaching conqueſt ſmiled;

"If

" If Vanity will once be guided,
" Our difference may be ſoon decided:
" Behold yon Wench! a fit occaſion
" To try your force of gay perſuaſion.
" Go you, while I retire aloof,
" Go, put thoſe boaſted powers to proof;
" And if your prevalence of art,
" Tranſcends my yet unerring dart,
" I give the favourite conteſt o'er,
" And ne'er will boaſt my empire more."

At once, ſo ſaid, and ſo conſented,
And well our Goddeſs ſeem'd contented;
Nor pauſing, made a moment's ſtand,
But tript, and took the Girl in hand.

Meanwhile the Godhead, unalarm'd,
As one to each occaſion arm'd,
Forth from his quiver cull'd a dart,
That erſt had wounded many a heart;
Then bending, drew it to the head—
The bow-ſtring twang'd, the arrow fled;
And, to her ſecret ſoul addreſt,
Transfix'd the whiteneſs of her breaſt.

But here the Dame, whoſe guardian care
Had to a moment watch'd the Fair,
At once her pocket mirrour drew,
And held the wonder full in view;
As quickly, ranged in order bright,
A thouſand beauties ruſh to ſight,
A world of charms till now unknown,
A world revealed to her alone!
Enraptured ſtands the Love-ſick Maid,
Suſpended o'er the Darling Shade;
Here only fixes to admire,
And centers every fond deſire.

THE LAST SPEECH OF JOHN GOOD,

VULGARLY CALLED

Jack the Giant-Queller;

WHO

Was condemned on the Firſt of April 1745,

AND

Executed on the Third of May following.

THE

LAST SPEECH

OF

JOHN GOOD.

Countrymen and Fellow Chriſtians!

AN Order hath iſſued for my being TURNED OFF THE STAGE of this Tranſitory Life; and, in theſe my laſt moments, it would no longer become me, to contend with UNRIGHTEOUSNESS, or to diſpute againſt POWER.

For the preſent, I barely mean to give you a brief account of my Family and Education; to recollect ſuch of my Actions and Sentiments, as were moſt likely to have haſtened this melancholy hour; and to adviſe and exhort you all againſt ſuch a Courſe of Life, as, by my example, may bring you to this Untimely End.

Perhaps

Perhaps it may appear wonderful to you, my Brethren, that a perſon of my reputed Proweſs and Spirit, ſhould thus tamely ſubmit to this Shameful Period of my Labours.

Let it ſuffice to be told you, that, throughout the Hiſtory of my Progenitors, our Proweſs hath rather ſubſiſted in the Weight of our Arguments, than in the Force of our Arms; and that VIRTUE and SUFFERING, have ever been the diſtinguiſhing characteriſtics of our Family.

Indeed, when I look back to the unſearchable Wiſdom of my Accuſers, from the penetration of whoſe Authority I could not conceal my intentions, and who have fathomed all depths by the Lead of their own Genius; were I diſpoſed to be merry on an occaſion ſo ſolemn, I could turn your tears into glee, and your mourning into peals of laughter: but this BLAZON muſt not be for the preſent; you will find it annexed to the Hiſtory of my Life, and ſpare not to be merry when I am departed.

It has long been a received opinion, that "All "men are Brothers; All Branches, however "warped, of the Same Stock; All Sketches, "however bungled, of the Same Original."

Wherefore, when I come to ſhew, that it is not from One Houſe, but from Two Separate

Houſes, that the inhabitants of the earth are derived; when I demonſtrate, that the Generation of The Goods was from Principles eternally oppoſite to that of The Giants; when I prove, that thoſe Lubbards were created the natural Vaſſals of my Progenitors, and that it is the Servant who is thus exalted above his Lord; let not your faith be alarmed, neither hold me for a ſetter-forth of new doctrines.

I ſtand here, my friends, as a culprit, convicted before the world, touching a late Hiſtory of my Life and Adventures. The Crimes, that are charged to this Hiſtory, are not of a light or venial nature: they are no other than Blaſphemy, Treaſon, Sedition, Faction, Diſaffection to Majeſty and good Government, and Univerſal Malevolence to Mankind.

But how, my brethren, will ye be aſtoniſhed to hear, how will the Enemies of our Houſe be abaſhed to diſcover, that this Hiſtory, ſo diſcountenanced by the caution of expectants, ſo ſuppreſſed by * was Stolen, almoſt word for word, from an Opera that was acted near ſix thouſand years ago, and penned by the Author of Nature!

Had not the confeſſion, that is expected from all perſons in my unhappy ſituation, extorted from me an acknowledgment of this Theft, it might possibly have remained a secret to the end of things: for, in fact, the Tables and Characters of the DIVINE ORIGINAL, are so erased by Time, and blotted by Interpolations, and the Enemies of our Family are such utter Strangers both to the Text and the Comment; that they would never have conjectured at the TRUTH, till The Day wherein Giantism shall appear as a Midge, and my Judges shall themselves be brought to their Audit.

This DIVINE OPERA, of which I speak, was opened on the sixth day of creation; the AUTHOR was himself the Conductor of the drama; the entrance was Human Life; and the theatre was the Bosom of the First Man that ever breathed.

And the two first characters, who were appointed to make their appearance, were the embryon Giants of AMBITION and APPETITE, who thereafter grew up into POWER and VIOLENCE: and, as they were formed of the gross elements of matter, they retained the tempestuous nature of their principles; fiery, indeed, and devouring, when unreined; but, therefore, more active for service, when duly subjected, and tempered to government.

And when these Vassals were thus prepared to usher in the state of their Masters; the breath of life came into this microcoſm of nature, and inſtantly THREE CHARACTERS of Divine Similitude made their entrance; to wit, Prime Vizier GOODNESS, Princely WISDOM, and Imperial WILL: and the province of Vizier GOODNESS was, to influence and incline; and the province of Prince WISDOM was, to remonſtrate and enlighten; and the province of King WILL was, to order and impel thoſe Inferior and Elementary Raſcals to their Duty.

And while Prime Vizier GOODNESS was retained in the heart and ſeat of influence, all was ſmooth, all was joyous, all was happy: for he was not an enemy to the Paſſions; he was not the Killer, but the Queller of thoſe Giants; and indulged them to the Capacity of their Nature, which was only ſuſceptible of Benefit within the ſphere of their Obedience.

And Imperial WILL liſtened with a pleaſed attention to the remonſtrances of Princely WISDOM, and he was illuminated thereby; and a ſecret and inexpreſſible Delight aroſe within him from every Impulſe of Prime Vizier GOODNESS: and while his Orders, ſo influenced, rather won a ſpontaneous Obedience, than exacted a reluctant Submiſſion, all motions within the world of man became eaſy; every action was free, every wiſh was gratified, every capacity was filled; no ſymmetry in Beauty,

no

no consonance in harmony could rival the music of a Government so tuned; and in this Subordination of Faculties, this Symphony of Powers, consisted the Original Rectitude, the Perfection of human kind.

AND THUS ENDED THE FIRST ACT.

NOW the Giants of AMBITION and APPETITE began to grow apace, and they became mighty in their own eyes; and they ſaid, "We "will form a WILL unto ourſelves, we will have a "monarch of our own election, and we will dic-"tate our deſires unto him; and we will be in the "place of this Prince and Prime Vizier, and will "rule over him."

And while they thus caballed between themſelves, they turned away their eyes from the Enlightenings of WISDOM, and grew enraged at the Reproofs and Goadings of GOODNESS; and they began to ſay unto King WILL, "Thou art bur-"dened by thy counſellors, thou haſt no need of "theſe thy haughty adviſers; for thou art ſuffi-"cient unto Thyſelf; thou art a God, wiſe and "free from eternity; and we are ſubjects and "vaſſals unto thee alone; and we will exalt thy "ſtate, and be miniſters unto thy pleaſure for "ever."

And by their inſinuations they won upon the inclination of this King, and by their obſequiouſneſs they attached him to their party: and theſe Two Giants, together with King WILL, roſe up in in arms as by one consent; and they drove out Prime Vizier GOODNESS from the kingdom, and they put Prince WISDOM in chains. And from this unnatural coalition and intimacy of these rebels with their King, a Third GIANT, called INIQUITY or WRONG, arose; and these Three Varlets waxed great in power, and absolute in authority; and they issued a proclamation, whereby it became "High Treason in any to lift up his voice "against Giants." And they laid violent hands on King WILL whom they had seduced; and they put out his eyes, so that he should not see his way for ever; and they placed a pageant scepter in his hand, and he became their vassal. And a thick darkness fell upon The World of Man, and uproar and tumult was heard therein.

AND THUS ENDED THE SECOND ACT.

NOW, had this Opera ended here, forasmuch as the period would have been sudden, the conduct imperfect, and the catastrophe extremely tragical, and very different from the Original Design; the Author called the banished Prime Vizier, and appointed him to make his Second Entrance on the stage; and He gave him a Scorpion, called Conscience, in his hand, and said unto him,

"Inasmuch as The World of Man is become "a Chaos; and that those of thy Family, to "whom the Government was appointed, are them-"selves conquered and quelled therein.

"Inasmuch as, The Giants are increased in "number, and grown absolute in authority, and "have enslaved their Prince, and blinded the "understanding of their Sovereign."

"Do thou re-enter among them, and deliver "Prince Wisdom from prison, and take King "Will into thy leading; for thou shalt not as "yet be able to restore sight to the King, neither "wholly to rescue the Prince from his shackles. "And do thou kindle A New Light in The

" World of Man, that ſhall invade and contend " with the Darkneſs thereof: and be thou watch- " ful and mighty, and enter into perpetual war " with The Giants, and ſtrive to ſubdue them; " and when they riſe up in arms againſt thee, " take this Scorpion in thy hand, and ſpare " not to ſting their guilt, and to laſh their re- " bellions.

" But foraſmuch as thy Enemies are filled with " POWER, and VIOLENCE, and WRONG, and can " neither be ſhamed by foils, nor wholly ſlain by " woundings; they ſhall be able to prevail againſt " thee for ſix thouſand years: and during this " Combat, thou thyſelf ſhalt be ſubject to many " diſcomfitures, and inflictions, and confuſions of " face; but in the end thou ſhalt overcome. And " thou ſhalt take the Third of the Giants and " ſhalt ſlay him; and the other Two Giants thou " ſhalt reſtore as at the firſt: and that they be " able no more to rebel, thou thyſelf ſhalt take " the Government upon thee; and thou ſhalt give " New Eyes and Underſtanding to King WILL, " and ſhalt deliver Prince WISDOM to perfect " Freedom; and they ſhall rejoice to become thy " Servants, and ſhall walk the foremoſt in thy " Train for ever."

And Prime Vizier GOODNESS did as he was commanded: and he entered upon his new commiſſion; and he ſpoke Peace to the tumult, and Silence to the uproar in Man; and New Light ſprung up in his hemiſphere, and the Form of Order was reſtored therein; and thoſe, who had not known the Firſt World, were delighted at the Beauty of the Second.

AND THUS ENDED THE THIRD ACT.

NOW, as the Fourth Act was appointed to fill a long Parenthesis, called Time, and yet was only susceptible of a single action, to wit, the Combat between the Family of The Goods and the Family of The Giants; as this Fourth Act was solely intended to recapitulate and illustrate the Three former Acts, and was of no further importance than as it was preparatory to the Fifth and Last Act of this Great Drama; The Author, in order to introduce his grand catastrophe, with all the dignity and variety that the nature of his plan would admit, determined to enlarge his Theatre, and increase the number of his Actors, without increasing his Characters, or deviating a tittle from his Original Model.

Wherefore HE spread out this earth for his Stage, and the skies for his Curtain; and his scenes were wrought from the several elements, and in them was hieroglyphically designed and incyphered each emblem of the Future Combat; and The Spirit of Giantism spread throughout, and was prevalent and exalted therein.

Hence the Earth, by nature sluggish and stupid, grew animated and convulsed through its internal

internal vacuities; and, through its emptineſs, it became overſwoln and overweening; and, in its pride, it ſhook and made war upon its kindred elements, and it ingulphed the Water, and belched forth the Flame.

And the AIR began to murmur; and, changing from its native ſerenity and ſweetneſs, it roſe into wrath, and exclaimed loudly againſt the Economy and Beauty of Nature; and it attempted to throw the Ocean from its ſeat, and to diveſt the Earth of its cloathing and ornaments.

And the SEA was moved thereat; and it combated the Winds, and foamed againſt the Earth; and, in its fury, it would have ſcaled the very Heavens, for it was enraged that any Limits ſhould be ſet to its Ambition.

And through theſe violent commotions the FLAME was enkindled; and it fell on the ripened corn, and on the ſhrubs, and on the foreſts; and oppoſition but ſerved to adminiſter to its violence, and it ſeized on the ſhelter of cattle, and on the aſylums and little neſts of the choiring inhabitants, and ravaged and laid all waſte without mercy.

And while the Noiſy thus bluſtered, and the Empty uttered ſounds of terror, the Barren Mountains were ſwelled in their Pride, and elated and hardened in the Opinion of their Dignity; and they arose above the Fertility of the humble and refreshing Vales, and in their nakedness they assumed pre-eminence, and claimed the skies in right of their Insignification.

For the AUTHOR had appointed, in the FERMENTATION of GIANTISM, that the Mean and Inconsiderable should get uppermost; and that the Light, and the Despicable, and the Detestable, should ascend.

Wherefore the Vapour, and the Dross, and the Scum of Nature, sprung aloft; and the Stench and the Nuisance of the earth were exalted; and they condensed their powers, and rode sublime, and intercepted the benignity of the sun-beams; and they looked down with contempt on all fruits, and on all fragrance; and they blasted the fields with their lightnings, and with their thunders they terrified the living. And All that was Valuable lay low; and the Gold, and the Gems, and the Riches of the Earth sunk from sight, and were hid in the depth, and in the bosom thereof.

And THE SPIRIT OF GIANTISM entered into the beasts, and the fowl, and the fish, and into the very insects, and crawling reptiles of nature: and the Pard began to glare, and the Lion to roar in the forest; and the Whale drew the fish

by

by ſhoals into his maw; and the Shark ſaid, "In "voraciouſneſs conſiſteth dominion." And the Hawk, and the Eagle, and the Vulture, ſoared on high; and they looked down, with indignation, on THE SPIRIT OF GOODNESS, where it bleated in the Fields, and made muſic in the Groves; and they marked the Lamb, and the Suckling, and the Gentle Robin, and the Cooing Dove, and the Matin Lark, for their Prey.

And when this Great Theatre was thus prepared, the DIVINE AUTHOR called forth two characters from The Boſom of ADAM, and appointed them to make their entrance; and the one was called CAIN, and the other was called ABEL: and the Firſt was the Repreſentative of the Family of The GIANTS, and the Second was the Repreſentative of the Family of The GOODS; and the Elder, from the Principles of his Generation, was called THE SON OF MAN; and the Younger, from the Principles of his Generation, was called THE SON OF GOD.

And The Elder roſe up againſt The Younger, and ſlew him; and he ruled alone, and begot a Race of GIANTS: and all the Sons of Enmity, and of Avarice, and of Ambition, and of Violence, and of Luſt, and of Senſuality, and The Mighty in Shew, and The Little in Signification, are the Deſcendents of the ſaid Giant unto this day.

 Wherefore,

Wherefore, in order to give ſome Poiſe to the Scale of Iniquity, The AUTHOR appointed a Second Repreſentative of the Family of the GOODS, who ſhould ſtand in the place of his brother who was ſlain, and he called his name SETH. And he alſo proſpered, and begot a numerous iſſue, who multiplied through ſeveral centuries; and all the Sons of Love, and of Candour, and of Fortitude, and the Generous, and the Honourable, and the Humane, and the Great of Soul, and the Little of Oſtentation, are the Deſcendents of the ſaid ANCESTOR unto this day.

And in proceſs of time it came to paſs, that theſe The Children of GOD beheld the Daughters of the Giants, and ſaw that they were fair; and they ſaid, "We will no longer wage war "againſt the Giants, but will enter into league "and into affinity with them; and we will be as "One Family, and as One Houſe:" and Female Beauty became to them as a ſecond kind of Forbidden Fruit; they taſted, they communicated with the Enemies of Virtue; nature felt a Second Wound; every imagination grew incarnate and corrupt; it repented The AUTHOR that he had brought man upon the ſtage, and he determined to ſweep him from the ſurface thereof.

And in thoſe days there was a certain Poet called NOAH, who refuſed to liſten to the enchantments

ments of his wife: and growing bold in his integrity, he lifted up his voice against a world, and he warned them to deprecate the impending judgment; and he preached to the Giants, "That "All should become Little in their own eyes." And his sermon appeared as a Farce, or as a matter of Mummery, and they laughed at the Man; but though "the earth was then filled with violence," they declined to lay a hand on the Preacher.

And the waters descended, and the floods arose, and this Poet was lifted thereon above the heads of the GIANTS: and the pride of their stature did not avail them for wading; and the fire of their lusts was quenched, and their offences and their filth and their impurities were washed away, and all their sins were covered. And this Poet with his household alone remained, to renew the Present World, and to carry Tidings of the Former to Posterity.

Now the earth, thus delivered of her foul and monstrous burden, began to smile afresh, and to rejoice as in the First Morning and Spring-Tide of Innocence. But forasmuch as, in the house of NOAH, there still remained of the blood of The GIANTS; forasmuch as this world, an irksome passage to The Progeny of the GOODS, is yet the proper nursery and province, the Sole Heaven and Native

Native Element of GIANTISM: nature began anew to aſſert her own; the two families again became diſtinguiſhed; they reſumed their animoſity; the war was renewed; and The Giants, as in old times, were crowned with ſucceſs.

And they built themſelves Babels, and erected monuments to their own glory; and they formed new governments, and new ſtates, and new religions; and they became Mighty Hunters, and Emperors, and Rulers, and Potentates, and High-Prieſts, and Grandees, and Judges, and Juſtices, and Taxgatherers, and Catchpoles, and Jailers, and Executioners: and fear fell upon all men; and they ſaid, "Surely the hand of Heaven doth "fight for The Giants, for with them alone is "Omnipotence!" and they paid divine honours unto them, and worſhipped, and bowed down before them to the duſt; and ſcarce refrained from ſuffocating thoſe their idols with the ſtench of their adulations.

And The GIANTS enacted new laws, and new habits, and new cuſtoms, and new faſhions: and they reverſed Nature and Reaſon from the bottom to the top; and they appointed to all men, that Good ſhould become Evil, and Evil become Good, and that the Great ſhould appear Little, and the Little appear Great; and it was ſo. And, as Gods, they created new happineſs, and new pleaſures,

pleasures, and new appetites, and new opinions; and the Substance of Dignity was turned into Shew, and the Simplicity of Honour into Gaud and Equipage. And they ordered, that all Virtue should be dug from the Bowels of the Earth, and that all Merit should be weighed in Scales of Bullion; and it was so. And Power was denominated from the capacity of Mischief, and Wealth from the issues of Fraud and Depredation. And Truth and Wisdom were levelled with the dust; and the Traitor, and the Pander, and the Buffoon, were exalted. And hymns were sung to the Deities of Rioting and Drunkenness, and anthems to the arm of Inhumanity and Devastation.

Thus did GIANTISM prosper, and grow, and rise in stature, and spread abroad in bulk, till it attained to Universal Dominion; so that OUR FAMILY did not dare to shew their heads throughout the earth, and scarce the appearance of contest remained between us. For though I can quote a few instances, as of HERCULES, JOSHUA, DAVID, and the first BRUTUS, where our House have prevailed; yet the MILTIADES's, the SOCRATES's, the ARISTIDES's, the PHOCIONS, the SCIPIO's, the CICERO's, the PETUS's, the AGRICOLA's, the &c. of our Family, have been imprisoned by Practice, devoted by Superstition, proscribed by Envy, murdered by Faction, exiled by Ingratitude, sacrificed by Ambition, stabbed by Malice, doomed ed by Tyranny—SACRED VICTIMS TO LIBERTY! MARTYRS TO TRUTH!

At length The PRINCE and GREAT PRINCIPLE OF OUR FAMILY, The LIGHT from whence ALL VIRTUE hath received Illumination, The SEED of our Growth, The ESSENCE of our Effluence, deſcended; and the Heavens bowed down to give HIM way, and the earth ſprung forward to receive HIM.

And HE came, not arrayed in the Fool's Coat of GIANTISM, nor in the Weakneſs of their Power, nor in the Meanneſs of their Dignity; but, over his IMMENSITY, HE threw the appearance of Limitation, and with Time HE inveſted his ETERNITY; and his OMNIPOTENCE put on Frailty, and his SUPREMACY put on Subjection; and with the Veil of Mortality he ſhrouded his BEAUTY, leſt degenerate nature ſhould ſhrivel at his Sight, and creation, through its depravity, be annihilated in HIS PRESENCE.

And in HIS WORD was Life, and in HIS BREATH there was Healing; and Death fled before him, and Sickneſs grew ſound at his Sight; and the Lame ran, and the Blind gazed, and the Deaf liſtened; and all the elements were huſhed; and the earth trembled with Reverence beneath the Foot of her CREATOR.

And

And THE POWERS OF GIANTISM were ſhaken, and they greatly feared for their State, and for their Kingdom; and they murmured that this their hour had fallen unawares; and they ſaid, "Art "thou come to torment us before our day?"

And THE Prince of the Giants took this The PRINCE of our Family apart, and held before him the Magnifying Perſpective of the Dreamer; and he ſhewed him the Whole Toy-houſe of the Children of men, their diſtinctions, and their properties, and cares, and concerns, and amuſements, and privileges, and ſtars, and ribbons, and trinkets, and hobbies, and go carts, and revellings, and wailings. And through This Glaſs they appeared as of reality and importance; and they ſhewed like kingdoms, and policies, and dominion, and glory, and honour, and pomp, and acquiſitions worthy of triumph, and loſſes worthy of lamentation.

And The Prince of the Family of the Giants ſaid unto the The PRINCE of the Family of the GOODS; "HERE alone is true exiſtence, and true power, and "true pleaſure, and true poſſeſſion; and this is the "world of high thoughts, and of happy atchieve- "ments; and All Theſe Things are MINE, and "whoſoever deſireth the ſame doth Homage to "My Supremacy; and I give them to my mini-

"ons,

" ons, and to my votaries, and I will conſtitute " Thee the Prince and the Ruler thereof."

And The Prince of Our Family beheld, and the Perſpective was not able to endure His Regard: The Glaſs ſhivered at THE BEAM OF HIS EYE,—and All the Shew vaniſhed!

And HE looked abroad, to ſee who of his Kindred remained on the earth, and to know which of them would acknowledge The POWER OF HIS REDEMPTION. But all had ſtrayed as in a foreign land, and luſted after the fleſh-pots of their taſkmaſters. And The Giants had taken them captive, and had made them hewers of wood, and drawers of water, and caterers for their tables, and fiſhers for their delicacies. And Our Family had become as Aſſes, to carry the burdens of GIANTISM; and as Oxen, to plow a ſoil, " wherein they had no Inheritance."

And their PRINCE had compaſſion upon them, and HE called them unto him, and looſed them from the Chains of their Luſts; and with the Balm of his Breath he healed their Wounds, and with the Robe of his Mercy he cloathed their infirmities. And HE widened their Capacity, HE ſtretched out their Exiſtence; HE carried them backward where Time was not, and forward through the Tracts of Eternity. And HE gave them

them Dominion over the clamours of appetite, and a Scepter over the tumult of paſſions, and Power over The Principalities of Giantiſm, and over Weakneſs, and over Sin, and over Pain. And HE gave them GOODNESS to drink as morning's milk, and WISDOM for food as at a feſtival. And HE lifted them on high, whence they looked, and beheld this world as a Molehill, and The Giants as Reptiles thereon; and they ſmiled at all beneath, as at the impertinence of a dream that had paſſed; for they diſcovered Human Life as a ſhort though thorny paſs, and Death but as a portal that opened on Immortality. And he poured Affection into their hearts, and Exultation into their boſoms; and their ſouls were expanded in Delight, and they became as GODS; for each drank in the Happineſs of All, and with the arms of their Love they embraced the Univerſe, as though it had been the work of their own creation.

And the Thrones, and the Sanhedrims, and the Potentates, and the Rulers, and the High-Prieſts, and the Elders, and the Judges, and the Placemen, and the Miniſters through Earth and through Hell, aroſe; and All The Powers of Giantiſm took council together. And they ſummoned their armies of tipſtaves, and bailiffs, and bravoes, and ruffians, and with a Mortal Arm they laid hold on OMNIPOTENCE, and they brought THE JUDGE OF QUICK AND DEAD before the Tribunal

Tribunal of Iniquity. And they accuſed Him of miſdemeanors, and of high crimes againſt the State; for they proved that RIGHTEOUSNESS was a paradox to Human Policy, and that TRUTH was high treaſon againſt their Statutes and againſt their Ordinances. Wherefore, for his Good Works He ſtood impeached; he was convicted according to the Fullneſs of Law; he was appointed to the Croſs by the Equity of their Adminiſtration; and THE PRINCE OF PARDON was condemned, THE FOUNTAIN OF HONOUR was ſpit upon; and they ſcourged THE HEALER, and put to torture THE DISPENSER OF DELIGHTS.

And all the elements ſtood aghaſt, and the rocks were rent with Remorſe, and the earth ſweat drops of Anguiſh; and the Sun withdrew his face, and the ſtars refuſed to behold, leſt THE LAMP THAT FED THEIR LIGHTS ſhould be extinguiſhed.

Then did Heaven pluck the Rein from the muzzle of GIANTISM, that it might rage without check or limitation: and it gnaſhed upon GOODNESS; as a Vulture it caught THE BEAUTY OF ETERNITY in its talons, and it ſtabbed at THE SOURCE OF LIFE, and in its Wrath would have annihilated INFINITUDE. Yet it ſerved but to rend in twain the Veil of his Mortality, that his DIVINITY might thereby become apparent. Wherefore

fore HE permitted the utmoſt of their malice, that HE might ſhew to all his Houſe, and to all his Kindred, how impotent, how inconſiderable, how wholly deſpicable, is GIANTISM; that its Strength is Weakneſs, its Wiſdom Folly, its Wealth Poverty; its Honours an Indignity, its Pride a Ridicule, its Pomp a Sneer; its Judgment a Lie, its Pleaſures a Dream, its Triumphs a Defeat; its Hopes an Illuſion, its Purſuits an Error, its Poſſeſſions a Phantom; its Ornaments Nakedneſs, its Beauty a Blemiſh, its Health a Diſeaſe:—And that nothing is ſtrong, nothing is wiſe, nothing is wealthy; nothing is decent, nothing is ornamental, nothing is honourable; nothing is pleaſant, nothing is true, nothing is real; nothing is hopeful, nothing is beautiful, nothing is deſirable—but GOODNESS.

Thus, my friends, although it was expected, that the CHIEF of our Family as at that time ſhould deſcend, in order to make an end at once with Giantiſm: yet this The PRINCE of our progeny did himſelf declare, that he came not to accompliſh but reinforce the combat; that "he "came not to bring peace but a ſword upon "earth," and to put new weapons for war into the hands of his failing Fraternity, whereby we are enabled to wage truceleſs and irreconcileable conflict with Giants, whether they be of the World, or of the Fleſh, or of that

 Spirit

Spirit who is the Power of both—till time ſhall draw to its final period, till this Cerberean Dog of Giantiſm ſhall have fulfilled his day; when The Captain of our Warfare ſhall himſelf return, to commence the fifth and laſt act of his Almighty Drama; when the hugeneſs, and the ſeeming almightineſs of Giantiſm, ſhall be caſt to mockery, and to ſpurnings, and to annihilation; and to the Little, and to the Low, and to the Abaſed of our Houſe, ſhall be rendered enlargement, and elevation, and glory, for ever.

And now, my brethren, foraſmuch as I have ſhewn you, that the Giants of my late Hiſtory, ſo variouſly and ſhrewdly applied by the Ingenious, to Modern Miniſters, Juſtices, Privy Counſellors, Judges, Mayors, Sheriffs, Aldermen, &c. &c. were no other than the Original Giants of the Great Drama I have recited; that our Firſt Parent fell by their rebellion, that on his ruins they erected their dominion, that in his reſtoration they were combated but not quelled, and that the appointed warfare ſtill ſubſiſts between us: had I proceeded thus far only, had I limited my Opera to Nature and to Truth as ſet down and preſcribed in the Divine Original, that power is not on earth who could have called me to queſtion. But, inaſmuch as I added a fifth and untimely act thereto, inaſmuch as I carried the preſent times into futurity, and untruly and injuriouſly and audaciouſly ſet forth, that the might of Giantiſm was already conquered, and that GOODNESSS was prevalent and triumphant among us, I juſtly ſuffer the penalty of this my error and my arrogance.

However, I would not have you be ignorant, that I am the leaſt of many writers, both modern and ancient, both ſacred and profane, who have undertaken to treat of theſe things. And you will find throughout the pages of Authentic Holineſs, that all of this Reprobate and Enormous Race have ever been the Enemies of VIRTUE and Opponents of the ALMIGHTY; and that no Giant whatever, whether of Cain or of Nimrod, a ſon of Amalek or of Philiſtim, hath yet drawn a ſword in favour of EQUITY; or hath at any time ariſen, from the beginning until now, a PATRON OF LIBERTY, or CHAMPION FOR TRUTH.

And in the gigantic days of Rome and of Cæſar, two Seers aroſe who propheſied of theſe matters; and the firſt was called Virgilius, and the ſecond was called Ovidius. And the firſt took his parable from foreign parts, and ſaid,

That in Sicily there dwelled a nation of tremendous inhabitants, whoſe inſtitution was Iniquity, and whoſe prey was Man. And their ſtature was lifted up in the height of Ambition, and their arms ſtretched forth to the extent of Power. And their taſk was, in the forge of infernal operations, to frame thunders for the ſpreading of death and of terror, and weapons for hoſtility, and implements for miſchief. But, foraſmuch as their Hands did outnumber their Optics, this prophet did thereby give his readers to underſtand, that the Authority of Giantiſm did ſurpaſs its Intellects, and that its Force was twofold the extent of its Diſcernment. Moreover, he tells us, that under the appearance of Ulyſſes and his train, Knowledge came upon this land, and Wiſdom viſited this people: and that, in the ſemblance of Æneas and the Gods of his Hearth, Piety and Hoſpitality would have intruded among them. But they looked upon Wiſdom as an enemy to their policy, and on Piety as an enemy to the idols of their worſhip. And ſome of theſe meſſengers they prohibited their ſhores, and others they ſlaughtered, and others they devoured; and the chiefs of theſe ambaſſies with difficulty eſcaped, to carry to other climates the benefits of their viſitation. And foraſmuch as this prophet, in this his hiſtory of the Cyclopes, did according to the nature and veracity of things, and gave glory and honour and conqueſt to Giantiſm, he was approved by the Wealthy, and careſſed by the Great, and received praiſe and remuneration from the Mighty ones of his country.

And the other Seer, even as I have done, took up his parable from ancient times. And he lift up his

his voice and cried aloud to all people, that "Giantiſm was Iniquity; and that GOODNESS "was richer than Gold, and more honourable "than Power."

And he ſung, that in the days of old there were Giants in the land, who were the ſons of the earth and the boiſterous progeny of the elements; and they were a people of magnitude, and enormity, and renown throughout the world, and of prodigious deeds, and of peſtilentious atchievements; and they graſped the Eaſt with their right hand, and with their left they laid hold upon the Weſt; and with their head they appeared to puſh the ſtars from their ſeats, ſo highly did they move in the Pride of their Exaltation. Yet their ſteps were not formed to the ways of Humanity, for they walked upon the feet of the Dragon and of the Old Serpent; and they ſeized upon the earth with all its inhabitants, and moved countries to and fro, and transferred nations at pleaſure. And they ſaid among themſelves, "What is Heaven "that we ſhould fear, and what is Righteouſneſs "that we ſhould obſerve? Our will is the law, "and our pleaſure is the end, and our power is "the compaſs and execution thereof." And foraſmuch as they had heard that there was Equity above, and vengeance in the Hands of ONE ſtiled the ALMIGHTY; they proclaimed loud war againſt government and againſt order, and attempted the throne and the habitation of SUPREMACY: and they rent the hills and the promontories from their ancient foundations, and piled Oſſa upon Olympus, and Pelion upon Oſſa; and they ſcaled the Heavens, and belched forth their blaſphemies in the face of ETERNAL TRUTH, and hurled up the weapons of enmity and defiance. But JUPITER ſent forth Minerva and Aſtræa, the THUNDERER gave commiſſion to the diſpenſers of Wiſdom and of Equity; and Wiſdom was cloathed with power, and Equity with terror; and the Giants were diſcomfited, and the mountains which they had reared were caſt upon their heads; they were buried and entombed under their own operations; and the gulph opened its depth and its vaſtneſs beneath, and received them to that final and irremeable place which from the beginning was appointed for the habitation of Giantiſm.

"So ſung this unhappy and ill-adviſed Bard." For, inaſmuch as he gave honour and excellence to GOODNESS, and diſcomfiture and abaſement to the Sons of the Earth; he became an offence to Dignities, and a nuiſance to Station, and they caſt him forth from among them; and he was forbidden to tune his voice, "Save unto mourning," for ever.

And I alſo, in theſe the days of Degeneracy, being the Leaſt of all the Prophets, was tempted to viſit the fallen off of our kindred. And there came Giants from the eaſt and from the ſouth, and invaded the north of theſe kingdoms; and in my zeal I aroſe, and I preached againſt the aſſailers of our Liberty and the enemies of our Law; and my ſermon was heard through many nations, and all thoſe of our Houſe and of our Lineage united as one man, and prepared to the battle. And the abettors of Giantiſm were greatly amazed thereat, and their courage was apalled, and their machinations were confounded; and Heaven fought on our ſide, and defeated the hoſt of their confidence, that a Remnant of our Family might yet be left upon the earth.

And I exulted at this the prevalence and triumph of VIRTUE, and I ſaid within myſelf, "Surely the hour approaches and is even now "arrived, when Giantiſm ſhall be trodden as dirt, "and ſwept away from among us, and to my "brethren alone ſhall be granted dominion with-"out end." And I bid my Kinsfolk and my Aſſociates to look abroad, and remark, how the Dews of Good Government were diſpenſed as from above, and how all baſked in the Sunſhine of a Happy Adminiſtration.

And, thereupon, I opened my mouth with boldneſs, and I exalted myſelf againſt iniquity; for, I ſaid, that POWER is with GOODNESS, and will prove a ſhield unto thoſe who combat the guilty, and a patron to the exposers and scourgers of unrighteousness.

And I took my text from the sixth chapter of Genesis and onward, and I preached unto all people, that, "In those days there were Giants "in the earth, and also after that; and the same "became mighty men, which were of old men of "renown; and GOD saw that their wickedness was "great upon the earth, and that every imagina- "tion of the thoughts of their heart was only evil "continually." And thereafter I set forth the History of the Generation and Adventures of Giantism, and the History of the Generation and Adventures of GOODNESS, as you will shortly find it written, being a transcript of the DIVINE DRAMA above recited; saving that I added thereto an Act of Supererogation, wherein I did unjustly and unadvisedly aver, that the day of appointed Retribution was come, wherein Giantism was wholly stripped of dignity and station, and was become a pigmy to the eyes of the laughing beholders; and that Wealth, Power, and Pre-eminence, were with GOODNESS alone, who should dispose the same in Equity, and dispense the fruits thereof in Beneficence without end.

And while I yet spake, all the people shouted; and they cried, "Amen, so be it!" and they rent their sides with merriment, and the air with acclamations.

mations. When, lo! a Power, whence I leaſt expected, aroſe; and a Giantiſm, that I looked not for, came upon me; and the Stature thereof was ſtupendous, and it appeared high over Property, and over Liberty, and over Law. And while I ſtood aſtoniſhed at the ſuddenneſs of the viſion, it ruſhed and ſtopped my mouth before I could make my Appeal; it cenſured me untried, unheard, and unimpeached, neither ſuffered me to plead againſt my condemnation; and I was appointed unto Reproof where Applauſe had been prepared, and unto Death on the very ſpot where I attempted Immortality.

And now, my beloved brethren, foraſmuch as the grave is a mocker of mortal malice; and that I have nothing further to fear touching what Giants can do unto me; my only concern is for the Safety of my Kinsfolk, and my panic for the Defenceleſs among my Fraternity.

Wherefore, that you may not be ſurpriſed through your ignorance of the Adverſary, I will give you certain Marks and Criterions of Giantiſm, that may ſerve as a rattle to warn you when the Snake approacheth; that you may flee if you have not the courage to contend, or prepare to the combat if ſuch is your virtue.

Giantiſm is a bugbear, a monſter, a monopoly; as where the Head hath ingulphed the Limbs, or the

the Members abſorbed the Underſtanding. In the natural world, it is Deformity; in the moral world, it is Wickedneſs; in the political world, Miſrule: Flattery is the harbinger, and Fear the trainbearer thereof; it is worſhipped becauſe of its violence, it is praiſed becauſe of its fangs: though diveſted of right, yet it is cloathed with power; though it is deſpicable, yet is it terrible.

Take heed therefore that ye blaſpheme not Vice, neither open your lips againſt Vanity or Riches; and when ye ſee Folly in the ſeat of Judgment, or Infamy lifted on high, beware that ye look not up,—leſt ye be tempted to laughter.

In patience then poſſeſs ye your ſpirit; be ſtill and contemplate, be ye ſilent and remark; for the force of Giantiſm is as the hurricane of an hour, and its ſplendour is that of a meteor which paſſeth away: as a cloud that thickeneth upon the face of the morning, it is laden with tempeſts, it is big of its thunders; yet in the Pride of its Utterance ſhall it ſuddenly be brought down, it ſhall be diſſipated by the miſchief which it beareth within its Bowels.

But foraſmuch as it is not in man to compaſs this matter, neither in the arm of any mortal to bring it to paſs; thus ſaith The Blessed and only Potentate, Who mocketh at all Pride as the

ſwelling

ſwelling of a frog, and at Giantiſm as a cricket who exalteth himſelf in his corner.

" Men of high degree are a lie; pride com-
" paſſeth them about as a chain, violence covereth
" them as a garment; their quiver is an open
" ſepulchre, they are all mighty men. Their
" land alſo is full of ſilver and gold, neither is
" there any end of their treaſures; their land alſo
" is full of horſes, neither is there any end of their
" chariots.

" Shall I not viſit for theſe things, ſaith the
" Lord, and ſhall not my ſoul be avenged on ſuch
" a nation as this? For the oppreſſion of the
" poor, for the ſighing of the needy, now will I
" ariſe, ſaith the Lord, I will ſet him in ſafety
" from him that puffeth at him; for the ſpoil of
" the poor is in their houſes, upon a lofty and
" high mountain have they ſet their bed; but
" though thou exalt thyſelf as the eagle, and
" though thou ſet thy neſt among the ſtars,
" thence will I bring thee down, ſaith the Lord.

" Hear then the word of the Lord, ye ſcornful
" men! Becauſe ye have ſaid we have made a co-
" venant with death, and with hell are we at
" agreement; when the overflowing ſcourge ſhall
" paſs thro' it ſhall not come unto us; for we have
" made lies our refuge, and under falſehood have

" we

" we hid ourselves: but thus saith the Lord, " your covenant with death shall be disannulled, " and your agreement with hell shall not stand. " For the day of their calamity is at hand, and " the things that shall come upon them make " haste. Therefore hell hath enlarged herself, " and opened her mouth without measure, and " their glory, and their multitude, and their pomp, " shall descend into it: for the triumphing of the " wicked is short; though his excellency mount " up to the Heavens, and his head reach unto the " clouds, he shall be chased away as a vision of " the night, and the eye which saw him shall see " him no more.

" But the Lord is a strength to the poor, a " strength to the needy in his distress, a refuge " from the storm, a shadow from the heat. He " strengtheneth the spoiled against the strong, He " shall turn the shadow of their death into mourn- " ing; and his judgment shall run down as waters, " and his righteousness as a mighty stream.

" But howl ye wicked, for the day of the " Lord is at hand! it cometh cruel both with " wrath and fierce anger, to lay the land desolate; " and He shall destroy the sinners thereof out of it.

" For that day is a day of wrath, a day of " trouble and distress, a day of wasteness and

" desolation,

" desolation, a day of darkness and gloominess, a " day of clouds and thick darkness; a day of the " trumpet and alarm against the fenced cities, and " against the high towers; neither their silver nor " their gold shall be able to deliver them in the " day of the Lord's wrath.

" And every mountain and island shall be mov- " ed out of their places; and all whose habita- " tions are on high, and the kings of the earth, " and the great men, and the rich men, and the " chief captains, and the mighty men, shall hide " themselves in the dens, and in the rocks of the " mountains, and shall say unto the rocks and " the mountains, Fall on us! and hide us from " the face of HIM that sitteth on the throne! for " the great day of his wrath is come, and who " shall be able to stand?

" And the LORD himself shall descend from " Heaven with a shout, with the voice of the " arch-angel, and with the trump of GOD. Then " shall the Heavens depart as a scroll when it is " rolled together; and the elements shall melt " with fervent heat, and the earth shall reel to and " fro like a drunkard, and shall be removed like " a cottage.

" And having spoiled Principalities and Powers, " HE shall make a shew of them openly. And

" Death

"Death ſhall be ſwallowed up of VICTORY, and "Mortality ſhall be ſwallowed up of LIFE."

WHO IS LIKE UNTO THEE, O LORD! AMONGST THE GODS? WHO IS LIKE UNTO THEE? GLORIOUS IN HOLINESS, FEARFUL IN PRAISES, DOING WONDERS? WHEREFORE, BLESSING, AND GLORY, AND THANKSGIVING, AND HONOUR, AND POWER, AND MIGHT, BE UNTO OUR GOD ALONE FOR EVER AND EVER! AMEN.

GUSTAVUS VASA,

THE

Deliverer of his COUNTRY.

A

TRAGEDY.

AS IT WAS TO HAVE BEEN ACTED AT THE

THEATRE-ROYAL IN DRURY-LANE.

PRINTED, MDCCXXXIX.

A

PREFATORY DEDICATION

TO THE

SUBSCRIBERS.

AS I esteemed it my happiness to live under a government, where NATIONAL LIBERTY was established by LAW, and the RIGHTS of Subjects were interwoven with their ALLEGIANCE; so I ever thought it my safety to act with such allowable freedom, as did not contradict any of our written and known regulations.

Though inconsiderable in myself, I am yet a subject of Great Britain; and the privileges of her meanest member are dear to the whole constitution.

Among those privileges, I claim that of justifying my conduct, I claim that of defending my property; and wiſh I could do both, without giving diſguſt even to thoſe by whoſe cenſures I am a ſufferer.

When I wrote the following ſheets I had ſtudied the ancient laws of my country, but was not converſant with her preſent political ſtate. I did not conſider things minutely: in the general view I liked our conſtitution, and zealouſly wiſhed that the religion, the laws, and liberties of England, might ever be ſacred and ſafe. I had nothing to fear or hope from party or preferment; my attachments were only to TRUTH: I was conſcious of no other principles, and was far from apprehending that ſuch could be offenſive.

I took my ſubject from the Hiſtory of Sweden, one of thoſe Gothic and glorious nations, from whom our form of government is derived; from whom Britain has inherited thoſe unextinguiſhable SPARKS OF LIBERTY and PATRIOTISM, that were Her LIGHT through the ages of ignorance and ſuperſtition; her FLAMING SWORD turned every way againſt invaſion; and that VITAL HEAT, which has ſo often preſerved her, ſo often reſtored her from inteſtine malignities.

Thoſe

Thoſe are the SPARKS, the GEMS, that alone give true ornament and brightneſs to the CROWN of a Britiſh monarch; that give him freely to reign over the free; and ſhall ever ſet him above the princes of the earth, till corruption grow univerſal; till ſubjects wiſh to be ſlaves, and kings know not how to be happy.

I was pleaſed with this ſimilitude between the principles, and, as I may ſay, between the natural conſtitutions of Sweden and Britain. I looked no further for ſentiments, than as they aroſe from facts; and for the facts I am indebted to hiſtory: nay, I ingenuouſly confeſs, I was ſo far from a view of merit with the diſaffected, that I looked on this performance as the higheſt compliment I could pay the preſent eſtabliſhment—Such was my ignorance, or ſuch is my misfortune!

Many are the difficulties a new author has to encounter in introducing his play on the ſtage: I had the good fortune to ſurmount them. This piece was about five weeks in rehearſal, the day was appointed for acting, I had diſpoſed of many hundred tickets, and imagined I had nothing to fear but from the weakneſs of the performance.

But then it was, that where I looked for approbation, I met with repulſe. I was condemned and puniſhed in my works, without being accuſed of any crime; and made obnoxious to the government under which I live, without having it in my power to alter my conduct, or know in what inſtance I had given offence.

However ſingular and unprecedented this treatment may appear, had I conceived it to be the intention of the legiſlature, I ſhould have ſubmitted without complaining: or had any, among hundreds who have peruſed the manuſcript, obſerved but a ſingle line that might inadvertently tend to Sedition or Immorality, I would then have been the firſt to ſtrike it out, I would now be the laſt to publiſh it.

Had the dignity of the Lord Chamberlain's office condeſcended, as ſome would inſinuate, to a Theatrical examination of the Drama; to a critical inquiſition of the conduct, the unities, and tricks of ſcenery; even ſo I might

have

have hoped for equal indulgence with farces, pantomimes, and other performances of like taſte and genius.

But this is not the caſe: the Lord Chamberlain's office is alone concerned in thoſe reaſons, which gave birth to the ſtatute; it is to guard againſt ſuch repreſentations, as He may conceive to be of pernicious influence in the commonwealth. This is the only point to which his prohibitions are underſtood to extend; and his prohibition lays me under the neceſſity of publiſhing this piece, to convince the public, that, though of no valuable conſequence, I am at leaſt INOFFENSIVE.

PATRIOTISM, or THE LOVE OF COUNTRY, is the great and ſingle MORAL which I had in view through this play. This LOVE (ſo ſuperior in its nature to all other intereſts and affections) is perſonated in the character of GUSTAVUS. It is the love of NATIONAL WELFARE; national welfare is NATIONAL LIBERTY; and he alone can be conſcious of it, he alone can contribute to the ſupport of it, who is PERSONALLY FREE.

By PERSONAL FREEDOM, I mean that ſtate reſulting from VIRTUE; or REASON ruling in the breaſt ſuperior to appetite and paſſion: and by NATIONAL FREEDOM, I mean a ſecurity (ariſing from the nature of a well-ordered conſtitution) for thoſe advantages and privileges that each man has a right to, by contributing as a member to the weal of that community.

The monarch or head of ſuch a conſtitution, is as the FATHER of a large and well regulated family; his ſubjects are not Servants, but SONS; their care, their affections, their attachments, are reciprocal; and their intereſt is ONE, is not to be divided.

This is truly to reign; this, only, is to reign. How glorious, how extenſive is the prerogative of ſuch a monarch! He is ſuperior to ſubjects, each of whom is equal to any monarch, who is only ſuperior to ſlaves. He is ſceptered in the HEARTS of his people, from whence he directs their hands with double force and energy. His office partakes of the DIVINE INCLINATION, by being exerted to no other end, but The Happineſs of a People.

O, never may any ſubtleties, any inſinuations raiſe groundleſs jealouſies in a people ſo governed!

governed! Never may they be influenced to imagine, that ſuch a prince is invading their rights, while he is only ſolicitous to confirm and preſerve them!

And never may any miniſtry, any adulation, ſeduce ſuch a prince from that his true intereſt and honour!

I ſhould not have had the aſſurance to ſoli cit a ſubſcription in favour of ſentiments, that any circumſtance could ever make me retract· Theſe, and theſe only, are the principles of which you are patrons; and the honourable names* prefixed to this performance, lay me under ſuch a future obligation of conduct, as ſhall ever make me cautious of forfeiting the advantages I receive from them. They are alſo to me a laſting memorial of that gratitude with which I am,

Your moſt Obliged, moſt Faithful,

and moſt Humble Servant,

HENRY BROOKE.

* Amounting to near one thouſand.

PROLOGUE.

BRITONS! this night presents a ſtate diſtreſt:
Tho' brave, yet vanquiſh'd; and tho' great, oppreſt.
Vice, ravening vulture, on her vitals prey'd;
Her peers, her prelates, fell corruption ſway'd:
Their rights, for power, the ambitious weakly ſold;
The wealthy, poorly, for ſuperfluous gold.
Hence waſting ills, hence ſevering factions roſe,
And gave large entrance to invading foes:
Truth, juſtice, honour, fled the infected ſhore;
For Freedom, Sacred Freedom, was no more.

Then, greatly riſing in his country's right,
Her hero, her deliverer, ſprung to light:
A race of hardy northern ſons he led,
Guiltleſs of courts, untainted, and unread;
Whoſe inborn ſpirit ſpurn'd the ignoble fee,
Whoſe hands ſcorn'd bondage, for their hearts were free.

Aſk ye, what law their conquering cauſe confeſt?—
Great nature's law, the law within the breaſt;
Form'd by no art, and to no ſect confined,
But ſtamp'd by Heaven upon the unletter'd mind.

Such, ſuch, of old, the firſt born natives were,
Who breathed the virtues of Britannia's air,

Their

Their realm when mighty Cæſar vainly ſought;
For Mightier Freedom againſt Cæſar fought,
And rudely drove the famed invader home,
To tyrannize o'er poliſhed—venal Rome,

Our bard, exalted in a freeborn flame,
To every nation would transfer this claim:
He, to no ſtate, no climate, bounds his page,
But bids the moral beam thro' every age.
Then be your judgment generous as his plan;
Ye ſons of freedom!—ſave the friend of man.

The PERSONS represented.

MEN.

CRISTIERN, King of Denmark and Norway, and usurper of Sweden,	Mr. WRIGHT.
TROLLIO, A Swede, archbishop of Upsal, and vicegerent to Cristiern,	Mr. CIBBER.
PETERSON, A Swedish nobleman, secretly of the Danish party, and friend to Trollio,	Mr. TURBUTT.
LAERTES, A young Danish nobleman, attendant on Cristina,	Mr. WOODWARD.
GUSTAVUS, Formerly general of the Swedes, and first cousin to the deceased king,	Mr. QUIN.
ARVIDA, Of the royal blood of Sweden, friend and cousin to Gustavus,	Mr. MILWARD.
ANDERSON, Chief lord of Dalecarlia,	Mr. MILLS.
ARNOLDUS, A Swedish priest, and chaplain in the copper-mines of Dalecarlia,	Mr. HAVARD.
SIVARD, Captain of the Dalecarlians,	Mr. RIDOUT.

WOMEN.

CRISTINA, Daughter to Cristiern,		Mrs. GIFFARD.
AUGUSTA, Mother to Gustavus,	Prisoners in Cristiern's camp,	Mrs. BUTLER.
GUSTAVA, Sister to Gustavus, a Child,	Prisoners in Cristiern's camp,	Miss COLE.
MARIANA, Attendant and confident to Cristina,		Mrs. CHETWOOD.

Soldiers, Peasants, Messengers, and Attendants.

SCENE DALECARLIA, a Northern Province in SWEDEN.

GUSTAVUS VASA,

THE

Deliverer of his COUNTRY.

ACT I. SCENE I.

The Inside of the Copper Mines in Dalecarlia.

Enter ANDERSON, ARNOLDUS, and Servants with Torches.

AND. YOU tell me wonders.
ARN. Soft—behold, my lord,
Behold him ſtretch'd, where reigns eternal night;
The flint his pillow, and cold damps his covering!
Yet bold of ſpirit, and robuſt of limb,
He throws inclemency aſide, nor feels
The lot of human frailty.
AND. What horrors hang around!—The ſavage race
Ne'er hold their den, but where ſome glimmering ray
May bring the chear of morn. What then is he?—
His dwelling marks a ſecret in his ſoul,
And whiſpers ſomewhat more than man about him.

ARN.

ARN. Draw but the veil of his apparent wretchedneſs,
And you ſhall find, his form is but aſſumed
To hoard ſome wondrous treaſure, lodged within.
AND. Let him bear up to what thy praiſes ſpeak him,
And I will win him ſpite of his reſerve;
Bind him with ſecret friendſhip to my ſoul,
And make him half myſelf.
ARN. 'Tis nobly promiſed;
For worth is rare, and wants a friend in Sweden.
And yet I tell thee, in her age of heroes,
When, nurſed by Freedom, all her ſons grew great,
And every peaſant was a prince in virtue;
I greatly err, or this abandoned ſtranger
Had ſtept the firſt for fame—tho' now he ſeeks
To veil his name, and cloud his ſhine of virtues;
For there is danger in them.
AND. True, ARNOLDUS:
Were there a prince throughout the ſcepter'd globe,
Who ſearch'd out merit for its due preferment,
With half that care our tyrant ſeeks it out
For ruin; happy, happy were that ſtate,
Beyond the golden fable of thoſe pure
And earlieſt ages—Wherefore this, good Heaven?
Is it of fate, that he who aſſumes a crown
Throws off humanity?
ARN. So CRISTIERN holds.
He claims our country as by right of conqueſt,
A right to every wrong. Even now 'tis ſaid,
The tyrant envies what our mountains yield
Of health or aliment; he comes upon us,

Attended

Attended by a numerous hoſt, to ſeize
Theſe laſt retreats of our expiring liberty.
AND. Say'ſt thou?
ARN. This riſing day, this inſtant hour,
Thus chaced, we ſtand upon the utmoſt brink
Of ſteep perdition; and muſt leap the precipice,
Or turn upon our hunters.
AND. Now, GUSTAVUS!
Thou prop and glory of inglorious Sweden,
Where art thou mightieſt man?—Were he but here!—
I'll tell thee, my ARNOLDUS, I beheld him,
Then when he firſt drew ſword, ſerene and dreadful,
As the brow'd evening 'ere the thunder break;
For ſoon he made it toilſome to our eyes,
To mark his ſpeed, and trace the paths of conqueſt:
In vain we followed, where he ſwept the field;
'Twas death alone could wait upon GUSTAVUS.
ARN. He was, indeed, whate'er our wiſh could form him.
AND. Array'd and beauteous in the blood of Danes,
The invaders of his country, thrice he chaced
This CRISTIERN, this fell conqueror, this uſurper,
With route and foul diſhonour at his heels,
To plunge his head in Denmark.
ARN. Nor ever had the tyrant known return,
To tread our necks, and blend us with the duſt,
Had he not dared to break thro' every law
That ſanctifies the nations; ſeized our hero,
The pledge of ſpecious treaty; tore him from us,
And led him chained to Denmark.

AND.

AND. Then we fell.—
If ſtill he lives, we yet may learn to riſe;
But never can I dare to reſt a hope
On any arm but his.

ARN. And yet I truſt,
This ſtranger that delights to dwell with darkneſs,
Unknown, unfriended, compaſt round with wretchedneſs,
Conceals ſome mighty purpoſe in his breaſt,
Now labouring into birth.

AND. When came he hither?

ARN. Six moons have changed upon the face of night,
Since here he firſt arrived, in ſervile weeds,
But yet of mien majeſtic. I obſerved him;
And ever, as I gazed, ſome nameleſs charm,
A wondrous greatneſs not to be concealed,
Broke thro' his form, and awed my ſoul before him.
Amid theſe mines he earns the hireling's portion;
His hands out-toil the hind, while on his brow
Sits patience, bathed in the laborious drop
Of painful induſtry—I oft have ſought,
With friendly tender of ſome worthier ſervice,
To win him from his temper; but he ſhuns
All offers, yet declined with graceful act,
Engaging beyond utterance: and at eve,
When all retire to ſome domeſtic ſolace,
He only ſtays, and, as you ſee, the earth
Receives him to her dark and cheerleſs boſom.

AND. Has no unwary moment e'er betray'd
The labours of his ſoul; ſome favourite grief,
Whereon to raiſe conjecture?

ARN.

ARN. I ſaw, as ſome bold peaſants late deplored
Their country's bondage, ſudden paſſion ſeized
And bore him from his ſeeming. Straight his form
Was turn'd to terror; ruin fill'd his eye;
And his proud ſtep appeared to awe the world:
When check'd as thro' an impotence of rage,
Damp ſadneſs ſoon uſurp'd upon his brow,
And the big tear roll'd graceful down his viſage.

AND. Your words imply a man of much importance.

ARN. So I ſuſpected; and at dead of night
Stole on his ſlumbers. His full heart was buſy;
And oft his tongue pronounced the hated name
Of—bloody CRISTIERN!—there he ſeem'd to pauſe:
And recollected to one voice, he cried,
O Sweden! O my country! Yet I'll ſave thee.

AND. Forbear—he riſes—Heavens, what majeſty!

SCENE II.

Enter GUSTAVUS.

AND. Your pardon, ſtranger, if the voice of virtue,
If cordial amity from man to man,
And ſomewhat that ſhould whiſper to the ſoul,
To ſeek and chear the ſufferer, led me hither
Impatient to ſalute thee. Be it thine
Alone to point the path of friendſhip out;
And my beſt power ſhall wait upon thy fortunes.

GUST. Yes, generous man! there is a wondrous test,
The truest, worthiest, noblest cause for friendship;
Dearer than life, than interest, or alliance,
And equal to your virtues.

AND. Say—unfold.

GUST. Art thou a soldier, a chief lord in Sweden,
And yet a stranger to thy country's voice
That loudly calls the hidden patriot forth?
But what's a soldier? What's a lord in Sweden?
All worth is fled, or fallen—Nor has a life
Been spared, but for dishonour; spared to breed
More slaves for Denmark, to beget a race
Of new-born virgins for the unsated lust
Of our new masters. Sweden! thou art no more!
Queen of the north! thy land of liberty,
Thy house of heroes, and thy seat of virtues,
Is now the tomb, where thy brave sons lie speechless,
And foreign snakes engender.

AND. O 'tis true.
But wherefore? To what purpose?—

GUST. Think of Stockholm!
When CRISTIERN seized upon the hour of peace,
And drench'd the hospitable floor with blood;
Then fell the flower of Sweden, mighty names!
Her hoary senators, and gasping patriots.
The tyrant spoke, and his licentious band
Of blood-trained ministry were loosed to ruin.
Invention wanton'd in the toil of infants
Stabb'd on the breast, or reeking on the points
Of sportive javelins. Husbands, sons, and sires,

With

With dying ears drank in the loud deſpair
Of ſhrieking chaſtity. The waſte of war
Was peace and friendſhip to this civil maſſacre.
O heaven and earth! Is there a cauſe for this?
For ſin without temptation, calm, cool villainy,
Deliberate miſchief, unimpaſſioned luſt,
And ſmiling murder?—Lie thou there, my ſoul!—
Sleep, ſleep upon it—image not the form
Of any dream but this, 'till time grows pregnant,
And thou canſt wake to vengeance.

AND. Thou haſt greatly moved me. Ha! thy tears ſtart forth.
Yes, let them flow, our country's fate demands them:
I too will mingle mine, while yet 'tis left us
To weep in ſecret, and to ſigh with ſafety.
But wherefore talk of vengeance? 'Tis a word
Should be engraven on the new fallen ſnow,
Where the firſt beam may melt it from obſervance.
Vengeance on CRISTIERN?—Norway and the Dane,
The ſons of Sweden, all the peopled north
Bend at his nod: my humbler boaſt of power
Meant not to cope with crowns.

GUST. Then what remains,
Is briefly this—your friendſhip has my thanks,
But muſt not my acceptance: never—no—
Firſt ſink thou baleful manſion to the center,
And be thy darkneſs doubled round my head;
'Ere I forſake thee for the bliſs of Paradiſe,
To be enjoyed beneath a tyrant's ſcepter!
No, that were wilful ſlavery—Freedom is

The brilliant gift of Heaven; 'tis reaſon's ſelf,
The kin of Deity—I will not part wi't.

AND. Nor I, while I can hold it; but alas!
That is not in our choice.

GUST. Why?—where's that power whoſe engines are of force
To bend the brave and virtuous man to ſlavery?
Baſe fear, the lazineſs of luſt, groſs appetites,
Theſe are the ladders, and the groveling footſtool,
From whence the tyrant riſes on our wrongs,
Secure and ſcepter'd in the ſoul's ſervility.
He has debauch'd the genius of our country;
And rides triumphant, while her captive ſons
Await his nod, the ſilken ſlaves of pleaſure,
Or fetter'd in their fears.

AND. I apprehend you:
No doubt, a baſe ſubmiſſion to our wrongs
May well be term'd a voluntary bondage.
But think, the heavy hand of power is on us;
Of power, from whoſe impriſonment and chains
Not all our free-born virtue can protect us.

GUST. 'Tis there you err, for I have felt their force;
And had I yielded to enlarge theſe limbs,
Or ſhare the tyrant's empire, on the terms
Which he propoſed—I were a ſlave indeed.
No—in the deep and deadly damp of dungeons
The ſoul can rear her ſceptre, ſmile in anguiſh,
And triumph o'er oppreſſion.

AND. O glorious ſpirit!—Think not I am ſlack
To reliſh what thy noble ſcope intends;

But

But then the means! the peril! and the consequence!
Great are the odds, and who shall dare the trial?

GUST. I dare.—
O wer't thou still that gallant chief
Whom once I knew! I could unfold a purpose,
Would make the greatness of thy heart to swell,
And burst in the conception,

AND. Give it utterance.
Perhaps there lie some embers yet in Sweden,
Which, wakened by thy breath, might rise in flames,
And spread vindictive round—You say you know me;
But give a tongue to such a cause as this,
And if you hold me tardy in the call,
You know me not—But thee I have surely known;
For there is somewhat in that voice and form,
Which has alarm'd my soul to recollection;
But 'tis as in a dream, and mocks my reach.

GUST. Then name the man, whom it is death to know,
Or knowing to conceal—and I am he.

AND. GUSTAVUS!—Heavens! 'Tis he! 'tis he himself!

SCENE III.

Enter ARVIDA, Speaking to a Servant.

ARV. I thank you, friend, he is here; you may retire.

AND. Good morning to my noble guest, you are early! [GUSTAVUS walks apart.

ARV. I come to take a ſhort and haſty leave:
'Tis ſaid, that from the mountain's neighbouring brow,
The canvas of a thouſand tents appears,
Whitening the vale—Suppoſe the tyrant there;
You know my ſafety lies not in the interview—
Ha! What is he, who in the ſhreds of ſlavery
Supports a ſtep, ſuperior to the ſtate
And inſolence of ermine?

GUST. Sure that voice,
Was once the voice of friendſhip and ARVIDA!

ARV. Ha! Yes—'tis he!—ye powers! it is GUSTAVUS.

GUST. Thou brother of adoption! in the bond
Of every virtue wedded to my ſoul—
Enter my heart, it is thy property.

ARV. I am loſt in joy and wondrous circumſtance.

GUST. But, wherefore, my ARVIDA, wherefore is it,
That in a place, and at a time like this,
We ſhould thus meet? Can CRISTIERN ceaſe from cruelty?—
Say, whence is this, my brother? How eſcaped you?
Did I not leave thee in the Daniſh dungeon?

ARV. Of that hereafter. Let me view thee firſt—
How graceful is the garb of wretchedneſs,
When worn by virtue! Faſhions turn to folly;
Their colours tarniſh, and their pomps grow poor
To her magnificence.

GUST.

GUST. Yes, my ARVIDA;
Beyond the ſweeping of the proudeſt train
That ſhades a monarch's heel, I prize theſe weeds,
For they are ſacred to my country's freedom.
A mighty enterprize has been conceived,
And thou art come auſpicious to the birth,
As ſent to fix the ſeal of Heaven upon it.

ARV. Point but thy purpoſe—let it be to bleed——

GUST. Your hands, my friends!

ALL. Our hearts.

GUST. I know they are brave—
Of ſuch the time has need, of hearts like yours,
Faithful and firm; of hands inured and ſtrong;
For we muſt ride upon the neck of danger,
And plunge into a purpoſe big with death.

AND. Here let us kneel and bind us to thy ſide.
By all——

GUST. No, hold—if we want oaths to join us,
Swift let us part, from pole to pole aſunder.
A cauſe like ours is its own ſacrament:
Truth, juſtice, reaſon, love, and liberty,
The eternal links that claſp the world, are in it;
And he, who breaks their ſanction, breaks all law,
And infinite connection.

ARN. True, my lord,

AND. And ſuch the force I feel.

ARV. And I.

ARN. And all.

GUST. Know then, that 'ere our royal STENON fell,
While this my valiant couſin and myſelf,

By chains and treachery, lay detained in Denmark,
Upon a dark and unſuſpected hour,
The bloody CRISTIERN ſought to take my head.
Thanks to the ruling power, within whoſe eye
Imboſom'd ills and mighty treaſons roll,
Prevented of their blackneſs!—I eſcaped,
Led by a generous arm, and ſome time lay
Conceal'd in Denmark: for my forfeit head
Became the price of crowns; each port and path
Was ſhut againſt my paſſage; 'till I heard
That STENON, valiant STENON fell in battle,
And freedom was no more. O then, what bounds
Had power to hem the deſperate? I o'erpaſt them,
Travers'd all Sweden, thro' ten thouſand foes,
Impending perils, and ſurrounding tongues
That from himſelf enquired GUSTAVUS out.
Witneſs my country, how I toil'd to wake
Thy ſons to liberty! In vain—for fear,
Cold fear had ſeiz'd on all—Here laſt I came,
And ſhut me from the ſun, whoſe hateful beams
Serv'd but to ſhew the ruins of my country.
When here, my friends, 'twas here at length I found,
What I had left to look for, gallant ſpirits,
In the rough form of untaught peaſantry.

AND. Indeed they once were brave: our Dalecarlians
Have oft been known to give a law to kings;
And as their only wealth has been their liberty,
From all the unmeaſured graſpings of ambition
Have held that gem untouch'd—tho' now 'tis fear'd—

GUST.

GUST. It is not fear'd—I ſay they ſtill ſhall hold it.
I have ſearch'd theſe men, and find them like the ſoil,
Barren without, and to the eye unlovely;
But they have their mines within; and this the day
In which I mean to prove them.
ARN. O GUSTAVUS!
Moſt aptly haſt thou caught the paſſing hour,
Upon whoſe critical and fated hinge
The ſtate of Sweden turns.
GUST. And to this hour
I have therefore held me in this darkſome womb,
That ſends me forth as to a ſecond birth
Of freedom, or thro' death to reach eternity.
This day return'd with every circling year,
In thouſands pours the mountain peaſants forth,
Each with his batter'd arms and ruſty helm,
In ſportive diſcipline well train'd, and prompt
Againſt the day of peril—thus diſguiſed,
Already have I ſtirr'd their latent ſparks
Of ſlumbering virtue, apt as I could wiſh
To warm before the lighteſt breath of liberty.
ARN. How will they kindle, when confeſt to view
Once more their loved GUSTAVUS ſtands before them,
And pours his blaze of virtues on their ſouls.
ARV. It cannot fail.
AND. It has a glorious aſpect.
ARV. Now, Sweden! riſe and re-aſſert thy rights,
Or be for ever fallen.

And. Then be it ſo.

Arn. Lead on, thou arm of war,
To death or victory.

Gust. Let us embrace.—
Why thus, my friends, thus join'd in ſuch a cauſe,
Are we not equal to a hoſt of ſlaves!
You ſay the foe's at hand—why let him come;
Steep are our hills nor eaſy of acceſs,
And few the hours we aſk for his reception.
For I will take theſe ruſtic ſons of liberty
In the firſt warmth and hurry of their ſouls;
And ſhould the tyrant then attempt our heights,
He comes upon his fate—Ariſe, thou ſun!
Haſte, haſte to rouze thee to the call of liberty,
That ſhall once more ſalute thy morning beam,
And hail thee to thy ſetting.

Arn. O bleſs'd voice!
Prolong that note but one ſhort day thro' Sweden,
And tho' the ſun and life ſhould ſet together,
It matters not—we ſhall have lived that day.

Arv. Were it not worth the hazard of a life
To know if Cristiern leads his powers in perſon,
And what his ſcope intends? Be mine that taſk;
Even to the tyrant's tent I'll win my way,
And mingle with his councils.

Gust. Go, my friend—
Dear as thou art, whene'er our country calls,
Friends, ſons, and ſires, ſhould yield their treaſure up,
Nor own a ſenſe beyond the public ſafety.
But tell me, my Arvida, 'ere thou goeſt,
Tell me what hand has made thy friend its debtor,
And given thee up to freedom and Gustavus?

Arv.

ARV. Ha! let me think of that—'tis ſure ſhe loves him! [Aſide.
Away thou ſkance and jaundice eye of jealouſy,
That tempts my ſoul to ſicken at perfection;
Away! I will unfold it—To thyſelf
ARVIDA owes his freedom.

GUST. How, my friend?

ARV. Some months are paſt ſince in the Daniſh dungeon,
With care emaciate, and unwholeſome damps,
Sickening I lay, chained to my flinty bed,
And called on death to eaſe me—ſtraight a light
Shone round, as when the miniſtry of Heaven
Deſcends to kneeling ſaints. But O! the form
That poured upon my ſight—Ye angels, ſpeak!
For ye alone are like her, or preſent
Such viſions pictured to the nightly eye
Of fancy tranced in bliſs. She then approach'd,
The ſofteſt pattern of embodied meekneſs;
For pity had divinely touch'd her eye,
And harmonized her motions—" Ah," ſhe cried,
" Unhappy ſtranger! art not thou the man
" Whoſe virtues have endear'd thee to GUSTAVUS?"

GUST. GUSTAVUS, did ſhe ſay?

ARV. Yes, yes; her lips
Breathed forth that name with a peculiar ſweetneſs.
Loos'd from my bonds, I roſe at her command;
When, ſcarce recovering ſpeech, I would have kneel'd—
But, " Haſte thee, haſte thee for thy life!" ſhe cried;
" And O, if e'er thy envied eyes behold

" Thy

" Thy loved Gustavus—ſay, a gentle foe
" Has given thee to his friendſhip."

Gust. You have much amazed me!—Is her name a ſecret?

Arv. To me it is—but you, perhaps, may gueſs.

Gust. No, on my word.

Arv. You too had your deliverer.

Gust. A kind, but not a fair one—Well, my friends!

Our cauſe is ripe, and calls us forth to action.—
Tread ye not lighter? Swells not every breaſt
With ampler ſcope to take your country in,
And breathe the cauſe of virtue? Riſe, ye Swedes!
Riſe greatly equal to this hour's importance.
On us the eyes of future ages wait,
And this day's arm ſtrikes forth deciſive fate;
This day, that ſhall for ever ſink, or ſave;
And make each Swede, a monarch, or a ſlave.

END OF THE FIRST ACT.

ACT II.

SCENE The Camp.

Enter CRISTIERN, Attendants, &c. TROLLIO meets him.

TROLL. ALL hail, moſt mighty of the thrones of Europe!
The morn ſalutes thee with auſpicious brightneſs;
No vapour frowns prophetic on her brow,
But the clear ſun, who travels with thy arms,
Still ſmiles, attendant on thy growing greatneſs:
His evening eye ſhall ſee thee peaceful lord
Of all the North, of utmoſt Scandinavia;
Whence thou may'ſt pour thy conqueſts o'er the earth,
'Till fartheſt India glows beneath thy empire,
And Lybia knows no regal name but yours.

CRIST. Yes, TROLLIO, I confeſs the godlike thirſt,
Ambition, that would drink a ſea of glory.
But what from Dalecarlia?

TROLL. Late laſt night,
I ſent a truſty ſlave to PETERSON,
And hourly wait ſome tidings.

CRIST. Think you?—Sure,
The wretches will not dare ſuch quick perdition.

TROLL.

TROLL. I think they will not—Tho' of old I know them,
All born to broils, the very ſons of tumult:
Waſte is their wealth, and mutiny their birthright;
And this the yearly fever of their blood,
Their holiday of war; a day apart,
Torn out from peace, and ſacred to rebellion.
Oft has their battle hung upon the brow
Of yon wild ſteep, a living cloud of miſchiefs,
Pregnant with plagues, and emptied on the heads
Of many a monarch.

CRIST. Monarchs they were not;
Pageants of wax, the mouldings of the populace,
Tame paultry idols, ſcepter'd up for ſhew,
And garniſh'd into royalty!—No, TROLLIO;
Kings ſhould be felt, if they would find obedience.
The beaſt has ſenſe enough to know his rider:
When the knee trembles, and the hand grows ſlack,
He caſts for liberty; but bends and turns
For him, that leaps with boldneſs on his back,
And ſpurs him to the bit.

SCENE II.

Enter a GENTLEMAN USHER, and ſeveral PEASANTS, who kneel and bow at a diſtance.

CRIST. What ſlaves are thoſe?

GENT. My gracious liege, your ſubjects.

CRIST. Whence?

GENT. Of Sweden.
From Angermannia, from Helſingia ſome,
Some from Gemtian, and Nerician provinces.

CRIST.

CRIST. Their bufinefs.

GENT. They come to fpeak their griefs.

CRIST. Their griefs? their infolence!
Is not the camel mute beneath his burden?
Were they not born to bear? Away!—Hold! come,
What would thefe murmurers?

GENT. Moft royal CRISTIERN.
They fay they have but one—one gracious king,
And yet are bow'd beneath a hoft of tyrants,
Tafk-mafters, foldiers, gatherers of fubfidies,
All officers of rapine, rape, and murder;
Will-doing potentates, the lords of licence,
Who weigh their fweat and blood, and heavier fhame,
Even as a feather puff'd away in fport,
The paftime of a gale.

CRIST. I'll hear no more.—
I know ye, well I know ye, ye bafe fupplicants!
Fear is the only worfhip of your fouls;
And ever where ye hate, ye yield obeyfance.
Wretches! Shall I go poring on the earth,
Left my imperial foot fhould tread on emmets?
Is it for you I muft controul my foldier,
And coop my eagles from their carrion? No—
Are ye not commoners, vile things in nature,
Poor pricelefs peafants?—Slaves can know no property.
Out of my fight! [Exeunt Peafants.

SCENE

SCENE III.

Enter ARVIDA guarded, and a GENTLEMAN.

ARV. Now fate I am caught, and what remains
is obvious.
GENT. A priſoner, my dread lord.
CRIST. When taken?
GENT. Now, even here, before your tent.
I mark'd his careleſs action, but his eye
Of ſtudied obſervation—then his port
And baſe attire ill ſuiting—I enquired,
But found he was a ſtranger.
CRIST. Ha! obſerve
(Damn'd affectation) what a ſullen ſcorn
Knits up his brow, and frowns upon our preſence.
What—ay—thou wouldſt be thought a myſtery;
Some greatneſs in eclipſe!—Whence art thou,
ſlave?—
Silent! Nay, then—bring forth the torture there—
A ſmile! Damnation!—How the wretch aſſumes
The wreck of ſtate, the ſuffering ſoul of majeſty!
What have we no pre-eminence, no claim?
Doſt thou not know thy life is in our power?
ARV. 'Tis therefore I deſpiſe it.
CRIST. Matchleſs inſolence!
What art thou? Speak!
ARV. Be ſure no friend to thee;
For I am a foe to tyrants.
CRIST. Fiends and fire!——
A whirlwind tear thee, moſt audacious traitor!

ARV.

ARV. Do, rage and chafe; thy wrath's beneath me, CRISTIERN.
How poor thy power, how empty is thy happineſs,
When ſuch a wretch, as I appear to be,
Can ride thy temper, harrow up thy form,
And ſtretch thy ſoul upon the rack of paſſion!

CRIST. I'll know thee—I will know thee! Bear him hence!
Why, what are kings, if ſlaves can brave us thus?
Go, TROLLIO, hold him to the rack—tear, ſearch him,
Prove him thro' every poignance, ſting him deep.

[Exit TROLLIO with ARVIDA guarded.

SCENE IV.

Enter a MESSENGER in Haſte.

CRIST. What would'ſt thou, fellow?

MESS. O my ſovereign lord,
I am come faſt and far, from even 'till morn:
Five times I have croſt the ſhade of ſleepleſs night,
Impatient of thy preſence.

CRIST. Whence?

MESS. From Denmark;
Commended from the conſort of thy throne
To ſpeed and privacy.

CRIST. Your words would taſte of terror—Wretch ſpeak out,
Nor dare to tremble here—For didſt thou bear
Thy tidings from a thouſand leagues around,

Unmoved, I move the whole, the centering nave,
Where turns that mighty circle—Speak thy
message.

Mess. A secret malady, my gracious liege,
Some factious vapour, risen from off the skirts
Of southmost Norway, has diffused its bane,
And rages now within the heart of Denmark.

Crist. It must not, cannot, 'tis impossible!
What, my own Danes? Nay, then the world wants
weeding.
I will not bear it—Hell! I had rather see
This earth a desart, desolate and wild,
And like the lion stalk my lonely round,
Famish'd and roaring for my prey—Call Trollio—
I'll have men studied, deeply read in mischiefs.

SCENE V.

Enter a Servant, who kneels and delivers a Letter.

Crist. From whom?

Serv. From Peterson.

Crist. "To Trollio"——Right. [Reads.
How's this——Be gone——
Go all——without there——wait my pleasure.
O curse! How hell has timed its plagues!

SCENE

SCENE VI.

Enter TROLLIO.

CRIST. Come near, my TROLLIO.
We have heard ill news from Denmark—that's a trifle——
But here's to blaſt thy eyes!—Read——

TROLL. Ha! GUSTAVUS!
So near us, and in arms!

CRIST. What's to be done?—Now, TROLLIO, now's the time
To ſubtilize thy ſoul, ſound every depth,
And waken all the wondrous ſtateſman in thee.
For I muſt tell thee (ſpite of pride and royalty,
Of guarding armies, and of circling nations
That bend beneath my nod) this curs'd GUSTAVUS
Invades my ſhrinking ſpirits, awes my heart,
And ſits upon my ſlumbers—All in vain
Has he been daring, and have I been vigilant;
Spite of himſelf he ſtill evades the hunter,
And if there's power in heaven or hell it guards him.
When was I vanquiſh'd, but when he oppoſed me?
When have I conquer'd, but when he was abſent?
His name's a hoſt, a terror to my legions:
And by my tripled crown, I ſwear, GUSTAVUS,
I had rather meet all Europe for my foe,
Than ſee thy face in arms!

TROLL. Be calm, my liege,
And liſten to a ſecret big with conſequence;

That gives thee back the ſecond man on earth,
Whoſe valour could plant fears around thy throne:
Thy priſoner—

CRIST. What of him?

TROLL. Is the prince ARVIDA—

CRIST. How!

TROLL. The ſame.

CRIST. My royal fugitive?

TROLL. Moſt certain.

CRIST. Now then 'tis plain who ſent him hither.

TROLL. Yes.
Pray give me leave, my lord—a thought comes croſs me—
If ſo, he muſt be ours— [Pauſes.
Your pardon for a queſtion—Has ARVIDA
E'er ſeen your beauteous daughter, your CRISTINA?

CRIST. Never—yes—poſſibly he might that day,
When the proud pair, GUSTAVUS and ARVIDA,
Thro' Copenhagen drew a length of chain,
And graced my chariot wheels—But why the queſtion?

TROLL. I'll tell you—while even now he ſtood before us,
I mark'd his high demeanor; and my eye
Claim'd ſome remembrance of him, tho' in clouds
Doubtful and diſtant; but a nearer view
Renew'd the characters effaced by abſence.
Yet, leſt he might preſume upon a friendſhip
Of ancient league between us, I diſſembled,
Nor ſeem'd to know him—On he proudly ſtrode;
As who ſhould ſay, back Fortune, know thy diſtance!

Thus ſteadily he paſt, and mock'd his fate.
When, lo! the princeſs to her morning walk
Came forth attended—quick amazement ſeiz'd
ARVIDA at the ſight; his ſteps took root;
A tremor ſhook him; and his altering cheek
Now ſudden fluſh'd, then fled its wonted colour;
While with an eager and intemperate look
He bent his form, and hung upon her beauties.

CRIST. Ha! Did our daughter note him?

TROLL. No, my lord;
She paſt regardleſs—Straight his pride fell from him,
And at her name he ſtarted:
Then heaved a ſigh, and caſt a look to Heaven,
Of ſuch a mute, yet eloquent emotion,
As ſeem'd to ſay, now fate thou haſt prevail'd,
And found one way to triumph o'er ARVIDA!

CRIST. But whither would this lead?

TROLL. Liſt, liſt, my lord!
While thus his ſoul's unſeated, ſhook by paſſion,
Could we engage him to betray GUSTAVUS—

CRIST. O empty hope—impoſſible, my TROLLIO.
Do I not know him, and the curs'd GUSTAVUS?
Both fix'd in reſolution deep as hell,
And proud as high Olympus!

TROLL. Ah, my liege,
No mortal footing treads ſo firm in virtue,
As always to abide the ſlippery path,
Nor deviate with the bias—Some have few,
But each man has his failing, ſome defect
Wherein to ſlide temptation—Leave him to me.

Crist. I know thou haſt a ſerpentizing genius,
Can'ſt wind the ſubtleſt mazes of the ſoul,
And trace her wanderings to the ſource of action.
If thou canſt bend this proud one to our purpoſe,
And make the lion crouch, 'tis well—if not,
Away at once, and ſweep him from remembrance.

Troll. Then I muſt promiſe deep.

Crist. Ay, any thing; out-bid ambition.

Troll. Love?

Crist. Ha! Yes—our daughter too—if ſhe can bribe him:
But then to win him to betray his friend?

Troll. O doubt it not, my lord—for if he loves,
As ſure he greatly does, I have a ſtratagem
That holds the certainty of fate within it.
Love is a paſſion whoſe effects are various;
It ever brings ſome change upon the ſoul;
Some virtue, or ſome vice, 'till then unknown,
Degrades the hero, and makes cowards valiant.

Crist. True, when it pours upon a youthful temper,
Open and apt to take the torrent in;
It owns no limits, no reſtraint it knows,
But ſweeps all down tho' heaven and hell oppoſe;
Even virtue rears in vain her ſacred mound,
Razed in its rage, or in its ſwellings drown'd.

[Exeunt.

SCENE

SCENE VII.

Opens and diſcovers ARVIDA in chains, guards preparing inſtruments of death and torture. He advances in confuſion.

ARV. Off, off, vain cumbrance, ye conflicting thoughts!
Leave me to Heaven. O peace!—It will not be—
Juſt when I roſe above mortality,
To pour her wondrous weight of charms upon me—
At ſuch a time—it was, it was too much!—
To pluck the ſoaring pinion of my ſoul,
While eagle-eyed ſhe held her flight to Heaven,
O'er pain and death triumphant! Help ye ſaints,
Angelic miniſters deſcend, deſcend,
And lift me to myſelf! hold, bind my heart
Firm and unſhaken in the approaching ruin,
The wreck of earth-born frailty! And O Heaven!
For every pang theſe tortured limbs ſhall feel,
Deſcend in ten-fold bleſſings on GUSTAVUS!
Yes, bleſs him, bleſs him! Crown his hours with joy,
His head with glory, and his arms with conqueſt;
Set his firm foot upon the neck of tyrants,
And be his name the balm of every lip
That breathes thro' Sweden!—worthieſt to be ſtiled
Their friend, their chief, their father, and their king!

SCENE VIII.

Enter TROLLIO.

TROLL. Unbind your priſoner.
ARV. How?
TROLL. You have your liberty,
And may depart unqueſtion'd.
ARV. Do not mock me—
It is not to be thought, while power remains,
That CRISTIERN wants a reaſon to be cruel.
But let him know I would not be obliged:
He who accepts the favours of a tyrant,
Shares in his guilt; they leave a ſtain behind them.
TROLL. You wrong the native temper of his ſoul;
Cruel of force, but never of election.
Prudence compell'd him to a ſhew of tyranny:
Howe'er theſe politicks are now no more,
And mercy in her turn ſhall ſhine on Sweden.
ARV. Indeed!—It were a ſtrange, a bleſt reverſe,
Devoutly to be wiſh'd; but then the cauſe,
The cauſe, my lord, muſt ſurely be uncommon.
May I preſume?—
Perhaps a ſecret.
TROLL. No—or if it were,
The boldneſs of thy ſpirit claims reſpect,
And ſhould be anſwer'd. Know, the only man,
In whom our monarch ever knew repulſe,
Is now our friend; that terror of the field,
The invincible GUSTAVUS.

ARV.

ARV. Ha! Friend to CRISTIERN? Guard thyself my heart! [Aside.
Nor seem to take alarm—Why, good my lord,
What terror is there in a wretch proscribed,
Naked of means, and distant as GUSTAVUS?

TROLL. There you mistake—Nor knew we till this hour
The danger was so near—From yonder hill
He sends proposals, back'd with all the powers
Of Dalecarlia, those licentious resolutes,
Who, having nought to hazard in the wreck,
Are ever foremost to foment a storm.

ARV. I were too bold to question on the terms.

TROLL. No—trust me, valiant man, whoe'er thou art,
I would do much to win a worth like thine,
By any act of service, or of confidence.
The terms GUSTAVUS claims, indeed, are haughty;
The freedom of his mother and his sister;
His forfeit province, Gothland, and the isles,
Submitted to his scepter—But the league,
The bond of amity, and lasting friendship,
Is, that he claims CRISTINA for his bride.
You start, and seem surprized.

ARV. A sudden pain
Just struck athwart my breast—But say, my lord,
I thought you named CRISTINA.

TROLL. Yes.

ARV. O torture! [Aside.
What of her, my good lord?

TROLL. I said, GUSTAVUS claimed her for his bride.

ARV. His bride! his wife!
You did not mean his wife!—Do fiends feel this?— [Aside.
Down, heart, nor tell thy anguiſh!—Pray excuſe me;
Did you not ſay, the princeſs was his wife?
Whoſe wife, my lord?

TROLL. I did not ſay what was, but what muſt be.

ARV. Touching GUSTAVUS, was it not?

TROLL. The ſame.

ARV. His bride!

TROLL. I ſay his bride, his wife; his loved CRISTINA!—
CRISTINA, fancied in the very prime
And youthful ſmile of nature; form'd for joys
Unknown to mortals. You ſeem indiſpoſed.

ARV. The crime of conſtitution—O GUSTAVUS! [Aside.
This is too much!—And think you then, my lord—
What, will the royal CRISTIERN e'er conſent
To match his daughter with his deadlieſt foe?

TROLL. What ſhould he do? War elſe muſt be eternal.
Beſides, ſome rumours from his Daniſh realms
Make peace eſſential here.

ARV. Yes—peace has ſweets,
That Hybla never knew; it ſleeps on down,
Cull'd gently from beneath the cherub's wing—
No bed for mortals!—Man is warfare—all
A hurricane within; yet friendſhip ſtoops,

And

And gilds the gloom with falsehood—smiles and varnish!
For still the storm grows high; and then no shore,
No rock to split on! It were a kind perdition
To sink ten thousand fathom at a plunge,
And fasten on oblivion—there we hold,
And all is—— [Faints.

TROLL. Help, bear him up.—O potency of love!
That plucks this noble fabrick from his base.—
Bend, bend him forward—He revives—How fare you?

ARV. I know not—yet a dagger were most friendly.
Return me, TROLLIO, O return me back
To death, to racks!—Undone, undone ARVIDA!

TROLL. Is it possible?—my lord, the prince ARVIDA!
My friend! [Embraces him.

ARV. Confusion to the name! [Turns.

TROLL. Why this, good Heaven? And wherefore thus disguised?

ARV. Yes, that accomplish'd traitor, that GUSTAVUS,
While he sat planning private scenes of happiness—
O well dissembled!—he, he sent me hither;
My friendly, unsuspecting heart a sacrifice,
To make death sure, and rid him of a rival.

TROLL. A rival! Do you then love CRISTINA?

ARV. Name her not, TROLLIO—since she can't be mine.

GUSTAVUS!

GUSTAVUS! how, ah! how haft thou deceiv'd me!
Who could have look'd for falſehood from thy brow,
Whoſe heavenly arch was as the throne of virtue?
Thy eye appear'd a ſun to chear the world,
Thy boſom truth's fair palace, and thy arms,
Benevolent, the harbour for mankind!—

TROLL. What's to be done?—Believe me, valiant prince,
I know not which moſt ſways me to thy intereſts,
My love to thee, or hatred to GUSTAVUS.

ARV. Would you then ſave me? Think, contrive it quickly!
Lend me your troops—by all the powers of vengeance,
Myſelf will face this terror of the North,
This ſon of fame—this—O GUSTAVUS—What?
Where had I wander'd?—Stab my bleeding country!
Save, ſhield me from that thought.

TROLL. Retire, my lord;
For ſee, the princeſs comes.

ARV. Where, TROLLIO, where?—
Ha! Yes, ſhe comes indeed! her beauties drive
Time, place, and truth, and circumſtance before them!
Perdition pleaſes there—pull—tear me from her!
Yet muſt I gaze—but one—but one look more,
And I were loſt for ever. [Exeunt.

SCENE

SCENE IX.

Enter CRISTINA, MARIANA, and Attendants.

CRISTINA. Forbid it ſhame! Forbid it virgin modeſty!—
No, no, my friend, GUSTAVUS ne'er ſhall know it.
O I am over-paid with conſcious pleaſure;
The ſenſe but to have ſaved that wondrous man,
Is ſtill a ſmiling cherub in my breaſt,
And whiſpers peace within.

MAR. 'Tis ſtrange a man, of his high note and conſequence,
Should ſo evade the buſy ſearch of thouſands;
That ſix long months have ſhut him from enquiry,
And not an eye can trace him to his covert.

CRISTINA. Once 'twas not ſo; each infant liſp'd, GUSTAVUS!
It was the favourite name of every language.
His ſlighteſt motions fill'd the world with tidings:
Wak'd he, or ſlept, fame watch'd the important hour,
And nations told it round.

MAR. I have heard, my princeſs,
What time GUSTAVUS lay detain'd in Denmark,
Your royal father ſought the hero's friendſhip,
And offer'd ample terms of peace and amity.

CRISTINA. He did; he offer'd that, my MARIANA,
For which contending monarchs ſued in vain—
He offer'd me, his darling, his CRISTINA:

But

But I was ſlighted, ſlighted by a captive,
Tho' kingdoms ſwell'd my dower.

MAR. Amazement fix me,
Rejected by GUSTAVUS!

CRISTINA. Yes, MARIANA—but rejected nobly.
Not worlds could win him to betray his country!
Had he conſented, I had then deſpiſed him.
What's all the gaudy glitter of a crown?
What, but the glaring meteor of ambition,
That leads a wretch benighted in his errors,
Points to the gulph, and ſhines upon deſtruction.

MAR. You wrong your charms, whoſe power might reconcile
Things oppoſite in nature—Had he ſeen you!—

CRISTINA. He has, my MARIANA, he has ſeen me.
I'll tell thee—Yet while inexpert of years,
I heard of bloody ſpoils, the waſte of war,
And dire conflicting man, GUSTAVUS' name
Superior roſe, ſtill dreadful in the tale:
Then firſt he ſeiz'd my infancy of ſoul,
As ſomewhat fabled of gigantic fierceneſs,
Too huge for any form; he ſcared my ſleep,
And fill'd my young idea. Not the boaſt
Of all his virtues, graces only known
To him, and heavenly natures! could eraſe
The ſtrong impreſſion; 'till that wondrous day
In which he met my eyes But O, O Heaven!
O love, and all ye cordial powers of paſſion!
What then was my amazement? He was chain'd,
Was chain'd, my MARIANA! Like the robes
Of coronation, worn by youthful kings,

He

He drew his ſhackles. The Herculean nerve
Braced his young arm; and ſoften'd in his cheek,
Lived more than woman's ſweetneſs! Then his eye!
His mein! his native dignity!—He look'd,
As tho' he led captivity in chains,
And all were ſlaves around.

MAR. Did he obſerve you?

CRISTINA. He did: for as I trembled, look'd, and ſigh'd,
His eyes met mine; he fix'd their glories on me.
Confuſion thrill'd me then, and ſecret joy,
Faſt throbbing, ſtole its treaſures from my heart;
And mantling upward, turn'd my face to crimſon.
I wiſh'd—but did not dare to look—he gazed;
When ſudden, as by force, he turn'd away,
And would no more behold me.

SCENE X.

Enter LAERTES.

LAER. Ah, bright imperial maid! my royal miſtreſs!

CRISTINA. What wouldſt thou ſay? Thy looks ſpeak terror to me.

LAER. O you are ruin'd, ſacrificed, undone!
I heard it all; your cruel, cruel father
Has ſold you, given you up a ſpoil to treaſon,
The purchaſe of the nobleſt blood on earth—
GUSTAVUS!——

CRISTINA. Ah! what of him? Where, where is he?

LAER. In Dalecarlia, on ſome great deſign,
Doom'd in an hour to fall by faithleſs hands!
His friend, the brave, the falſe, deceived ARVIDA,
Even now prepares to lead a band of ruffians
Beneath the winding covert of the hill,
And ſeize GUSTAVUS, obvious to the ſnares
Of friendſhip's fair diſſemblance. And your father
Has vow'd your beauties to ARVIDA's arms,
The purchaſe of his falſehood.

CRISTINA. Shield me Heaven!
Firſt, duty, break thy filial bands in ſunder,
And blot the name of parent from the world!
Is there no lett, no means of quick prevention!

LAER. Behold my life ſtill chain'd to thy direction!
My will ſhall have a wing for every word,
That breathes thy mandate.

CRISTINA. Will you, good LAERTES?—
Alas, I fear to overtaſk thy friendſhip—
Say, will you ſave me then?—O go, haſte, fly!
Acquaint GUSTAVUS—If, if he muſt fall,
Let hoſts that hem this ſingle lion in,
Let nations hunt him down—let him fall nobly.

LEAR. I go, my princeſs—Heaven direct me to him! [Exit.

CRISTINA. I would pray too, to ſave me from pollution;
Deteſted ſtain, the touch of the Betrayer!
But mighty love the partial prayer arreſts,
And leaves me only anxious for GUSTAVUS.

For

For him cold fears my fainting bosom chill,
His cares distract me, and his dangers kill.
Ye powers! if deaf to all the vows I make,
Yet shield GUSTAVUS, for GUSTAVUS' sake:
Protect his virtues from a faithless foe;
And save your only image, left below.

END OF THE SECOND ACT.

ACT III.

SCENE, The Mountains of DALECARLIA.

Enter GUSTAVUS as a Peaſant—DALECARLIANS following.

GUST. YE men of Sweden, wherefore are ye come?
See ye not yonder, how the locuſts ſwarm,
To drink the fountains of your honour up,
And leave your hills a deſart!—Wretched men!
Why came ye forth? Is this a time for ſport?
Or are ye met, with ſong and jovial feaſt,
To welcome your new gueſts, your Daniſh viſitants?
To ſtretch your ſupple necks beneath their feet,
And fawning lick the duſt?—Go, go, my countrymen,
Each to your ſeveral manſions! trim them out,
Cull all the tedious earnings of your toil
To purchaſe bondage—Bid your blooming daughters,
And your chaſte wives, to ſpread their beds with ſoftneſs;
Then go ye forth, and with your proper hands
Conduct your maſters in; conduct the ſons

Of

Of luſt and violation—O Swedes, Swedes!
Heavens! are ye men, and will ye ſuffer this?

SCENE II.

Enter ARNOLDUS, and SIVARD.

ARNOLDUS talks apart with GUSTAVUS.

1ſt DALE. How my blood boils!
2d DALE. Who is this honeſt ſpokeſman?
3d DALE. What, know ye not Rodolphus of the mines?
A better labourer ne'er ſtruck ſteel to ſtone.
GUST. There was a time, my friends! a glorious time;
When, had a ſingle man of your forefathers
Upon the frontier met a hoſt in arms,
His courage ſcarce had turn'd; himſelf had ſtood,
Alone had ſtood the bulwark of his country.
Your ſires were known but by their manly fronts;
On their black brows, enthron'd, ſat liberty,
The awe of honour, and contempt of death.
1ſt DALE. We are not baſtards.
2d DALE. No.
3d DALE. We are Dalecarlians.
GUST. Come, come ye on, then!—Here I take my ſtand;
Here on the brink, the very verge of liberty.
Altho' contention riſe upon the clouds,
Mix Heaven with earth, and roll the ruin onward;
Here will I fix, and breaſt me to the ſhock,
'Till I, or Denmark fall.

SIV. And who art thou?
That thus wouldst swallow all the glory up
That should redeem the times? Behold this breast—
The sword has till'd it; and the stripes of slaves
Shall ne'er trace honour here, shall never blot
The fair inscription—Never shall the cords
Of Danish insolence bind down these arms,
That bore my royal master from the field.

GUST. Ha! Say you, brother? Were you there
—O grief!—
Where liberty and STENON fell together?

SIV. Yes, I was there—A bloody field it was,
Where conquest gasp'd, and wanted breath to tell
Its o'er-toil'd triumph. There, our bleeding king,
There STENON on this bosom made his bed;
And rolling back his dying eyes upon me,
Soldier, he cried, if e'er it be thy lot
To see my valiant cousin, great GUSTAVUS,
Tell him—for once—that I have fought like him,
And would like him have——
Conquer'd—he should have said—But there, O there,
Death stopt him short!

GUST. Come to my arms, and let me hide thy tears,
For I have caught their softness—O Danes, Danes!
You shall weep blood for this. Shall they not, brother?
Yes, we will deal our might with thrifty vengeance,
A life for every blow; and when we fall,
There shall be weight in't, like the tottering towers
That draw contiguous ruin.

SIV. Brave, brave man!
My ſoul admires thee—By my father's ſpirit,
I would not barter ſuch a death as this
For immortality! Nor we alone—
Here be the truſty gleanings of that field
Where laſt we fought for freedom; here's rich poverty,
Tho' wrapp'd in rags, my fifty brave companions;
Who, thro' the force of fifteen thouſand foes,
Bore off their king, and ſaved his great remains.

GUST. Give me your hands, thoſe valiant hands—Why, captain,
We could but die alone; with theſe we'll conquer.
My fellow labourers too—What ſay ye, friends?
Shall we not ſtrike for't?

ALL. Death; victory or death!
No bonds, no bonds!

ARN. Spoke like yourſelves—Ye men of Dalecarlia,
Brave men and bold! whom every future age,
Tongues, nations, languages, and rolls of fame,
Shall mark for wondrous deeds, atchievements won
From honour's dangerous ſummit, warriors all!
Say, might ye chuſe a chief for high exploits,
From the firſt annal, to the lateſt praiſe
That breathes a hero's name—Speak, name the man,
Who then ſhould meet your wiſh.

SIV. Forbear the theme.
Why wouldſt thou ſeek to ſink us with the weight
Of grievous recollection?—O GUSTAVUS!

Could the dead wake, thou wert that man of men,
First of the foremost.

GUST. Didst thou know GUSTAVUS?

SIV. Know him!—O Heaven! what else, who else was worth
The knowledge of a soldier?—That great day,
When CRISTIERN, in his third attempt on Sweden,
Had summ'd his powers and weigh'd the scale of fight;
On the bold brink, the very push of conquest,
GUSTAVUS rush'd, and bore the battle down,
In his full sway of prowess; like Leviathan,
That scoops his foaming progress on the main,
And drives the shoals along—Forward I sprung,
All emulous, and labouring to attend him:
Fear fled before, behind him rout grew loud;
And distant wonder gazed—At length he turn'd;
And having eyed me with a wondrous look
Of sweetness mix'd with glory—grace inestimable!—
He pluck'd this bracelet from his conquering arm,
And bound it here—My wrist seem'd trebly nerv'd;
My heart spoke to him; and I did such deeds
As best might thank him—But from that blest day
I never saw him more!—Yet, still to this,
I bow, as to the relicks of my saint:
Each morn I drop a tear on every bead;
Count all the glories of GUSTAVUS o'er,
And think I still behold him.

GUST. Rightly thought;
For so thou dost, my soldier!
Give me my arms—Off, off, ye dark disguises!

For

For I will be myſelf. Behold your general,
Gustavus! come once more to lead ye on
To laurel'd victory, to fame, to freedom!
1ſt Dale. Is it?
2d Dale. Yes.
3d Dale. No.
4th Dale. 'Tis he!
5th Dale. 'Tis he!
6th Dale. 'Tis he! [A ſhout.
Siv. Strike me, ye powers!—It is illuſion all!
It cannot——
Gust. What, no nearer?
Siv. It is, it is!— [Falls and embraces his knees.
Gust. O ſpeechleſs eloquence!
Riſe to my arms, my friend.
Siv. Friend! ſaid you, friend?
O my heart's lord! my conqueror! my!——
Gust. Approach, my fellow ſoldiers—your Gustavus
Claims no precedence here: friendſhip like mine
Throws all reſpects behind it—It is enough—
I read your joys, your tranſports in your eyes;
And would, O, would I had a life to ſpend,
For every ſoldier here! whoſe every life's
Far dearer than my own; dearer than aught,
Except your liberty, except your honour.
Periſh Gustavus, 'ere this ſacred ſun,
That lights the reſt of Sweden to their ſhame,
Should bluſh upon your chains—Why ſaid I, chains?
To ſouls like yours, I ſhould have talk'd of triumphs,

Empire, and fame, and hazards imminent,
Occasions wish'd, for glory—Haste, brave men!
Collect your friends to join us on the instant;
Summon our brethren to their share of conquest;
And let loud echo, from her circling hills,
Sound freedom, 'till the undulation shake
The bounds of utmost Sweden.

[Exeunt DALECARLIANS, crying GUSTAVUS, GUSTAVUS, Liberty.

SCENE III.

Enter ANDERSON.

AND. There was a glorious sound!

GUST. Yes, ANDERSON,
The long wish'd hour is come—the storm is up,
And wrecks will follow—Where they are to light,
Let Heaven determine—Well, my noble friend,
Has PETERSON set out?

AND. He has, this instant;
And bears your pacquet to the tyrant's camp.

GUST. What think you of his zeal?

AND. In truth, my lord,
It wears a gallant show.

GUST. 'Tis specious all;
Flash without fire, the lightning of a cloud
That carries darkness in the rear—For PETERSON,
To spread my letters through the camp of CRISTIERN,
And seek for succours in the jaws of death—

It ſhow'd too bold, too much the flaming patriot.
Beſide, I know him for the friend of Trollio.
And. Why would you then employ him?
Gust. There's the myſtery.
'Tis not his faith, but treachery I truſt to.
My letters are directed to the chiefs
Of thoſe inglorious mercenary Swedes,
Whom Cristíern has ſeduced to join his hoſt,
And turn the ſword of conqueſt on their country:
To each of theſe I have addreſt in terms
Of ſpecial correſpondence, meant to rouze
The jealouſy of Cristiern; as I think
My pacquet can't eſcape him—What enſues?
The tyrant hence concludes himſelf betray'd,
Sifts all his legions, thins the ranks of fight,
And leaves them open to our bold invaſion.
But grant that Peterson deceive my aim,
And hold the rank of virtue; then the Swedes
May waken to the glorious call of honour.
So, every way, it ſaves us from the guilt
Of Swedes encountering Swedes, and ſpares the blood
Of brethren, tho' revolted.
And. On my ſoul,
This is a ſtratagem that ſaps the miner;
Makes treaſon turn a traitor to itſelf,
And mock its own deſigns.
Gust. O noble friend, faſt winds the great machine
That ſtrikes the fate of Sweden!—Go, my Anderson,
Aſſemble all thy brave adherents round thee;

With warlike inſpiration warm their ſouls,
And haſte to join me here.
AND. I will, my lord. [Exit.

SCENE IV.

Enter LAERTES.

LAER. Thy preſence nobly ſpeaks the man I wiſh—

GUSTAVUS.

GUST. Yes. Thou haſt a hoſtile garb—
Ha! ſay—Art thou LAERTES? If I err not,
There is a friendly ſemblance in that face,
Which anſwers to a fond impreſſion here,
And tells me I am thy debtor—My deliverer!
LAER. No, valiant prince, you over-rate my ſervice.
There is a worthier object of your gratitude,
Whom yet you know not—O, I have to tell—
But then to gain your credit, muſt unfold
What haply ſhould be ſecret—Be it ſo;
You are all honour.
GUST. Let me to thy mind;
For thou haſt waked my ſoul into a thought,
That holds me all attention.
LAER. Mightieſt man!
To me alone you held yourſelf obliged
For life and liberty—Had it been ſo,
I were moſt bleſt, with retribution juſt
To pay thee for my own—For on the day
When by your arm the mighty Thraces fell,

Fate

Fate threw me to your ſword—You ſpared my youth,
And in the very whirl and rage of fight
Your eye was taught compaſſion—From that hour,
I vow'd my life the ſlave of your remembrance;
And often, as CRISTINA, heavenly maid!
The miſtreſs of my ſervice, queſtion'd me
Of wars and venturous deeds, my tidings came
Still freighted with thy name, until the day
In which yourſelf appear'd, to make praiſe ſpeechleſs.
CRISTINA ſaw you then, and on your fate
Dropt a kind tear—and when your noble ſcorn
Of proferr'd terms provoked her father's rage
To take the deadly forfeit; ſhe, ſhe only,
Whoſe virtues watch'd the precious hour of mercy,
All trembling, ſent my ſecret hand to ſave you;
Where, thro' a paſs unknown to all your keepers,
I led you forth, and gave you to your liberty.

GUST. O I am ſunk—o'erwhelm'd with wondrous goodneſs!
But were I rich and free as opening mines
That teem their golden wealth upon the world,
Still I were poor, unequal to her bounty.
Nor can I longer doubt whoſe generous arm,
In my ARVIDA, in my friend's deliverance,
Gave double life and freedom to GUSTAVUS.

LAER. A fatal preſent!—Ah, you know him not:
ARVIDA is miſled, undone by paſſion;
Falſe to your friendſhip, to your truſt unfaithful.

GUST. Ha! hold—

LAER.

LAER. I muſt unfold it.—

GUST. Yet forbear.—
This way—I hear ſome footing—Pray you, ſoft—
If thou haſt aught to urge againſt ARVIDA,
The man of virtue, tell it not the wind;
Leſt ſlander catch the ſound, and guilt ſhould triumph. [Exeunt.

SCENE V.

ARVIDA entering ſpeaks to a Soldier.

ARV. He's here!—Bear back my orders to your fellows,
That not a man, on peril of his life,
Advance in ſight 'till call'd.

SOLD. My lord, I will——

ARV. Have I not vow'd it, faithleſs as he is,
Have I not vow'd his fall? Yet, good Heaven!
Why ſtart theſe ſudden tears?—On, on I muſt,
For I am half way down the dizzy ſteep,
Where my brain turns—A draught of Lethe now!—
O that the world would ſleep—to wake no more!
Or that the name of friendſhip bore no charm
To make my nerve unſteady, and this ſteel
Flee backward from its taſk!—It ſhall be done,—
Empire! CRISTINA!—tho' the affrighted ſun
Start back with horror of the direful ſtroke,
It ſhall be done!—Calm, calm the hell within,
Thy looks may elſe turn traitors—Ha, he comes!
How ſteadily he looks, as Heaven's own book,

The

The leaf of truth, were open'd on his aſpect.
Up, up, dark miniſter—his fate call out
[Puts up the Dagger.
To nobler execution; for he comes
In oppoſition, ſingly, man to man,
As tho' he braved my wiſh.

SCENE VI.

Enter GUSTAVUS.

They look for ſome time on each other—ARVIDA lays his hand on his ſword, and withdraws it by turns—then advances irreſolutely.

GUST. Is it then ſo?
ARV. Defend thyſelf.
GUST. No—ſtrike——
I would unfold my boſom to thy ſword,
But that I know the wound you give this breaſt
Would doubly pierce thy own.
ARV. I know thee not——
It is the time's eclipſe; and what ſhould be
In nature, now is nameleſs.
GUST. Ah, my brother!
ARV. What wouldſt thou?
GUST. Is it thus we two ſhould meet?
ARV. Art thou not falſe?—Deep elſe, O deep, indeed,
Were my damnation!
GUST. Dear, unhappy man!
My heart bleeds for thee. Falſe I had ſurely been,
Had I like thee been tempted.

ARV.

ARV. Ha! Speak, ſpeak,—
Didſt thou not ſend to treat with CRISTIERN?
GUST. Never.—
I know thy error; but I know the arts,
The frauds, the wiles that practiſed on thy virtue;
Firm how you ſtood, and towered above mortality;
'Till in the fond unguarded hour of love,
The wily undermining TROLLIO came,
And won thee from thyſelf—a moment won thee—
For ſtill thou art ARVIDA; ſtill the man,
On whom thy country calls for her deliverance.
Already are her braveſt ſons in arms;
Mark how they ſhout, impatient of our preſence,
To lead them on to a new life of liberty,
To fame, to conqueſt—Ha! Heaven guard my brother—
Thy cheek turns pale, thy eye is wild upon me—
Wilt thou not anſwer me?
ARV. GUSTAVUS!
GUST. Speak.
ARV. Have I not dream'd?
GUST. No other I eſteem it.
Where lives the man whoſe reaſon ſlumbers not?
Still pure, ſtill blameleſs, if at wonted dawn
Again he wakes to virtue.
ARV. O, my dawn
Muſt ſoon be dark. Confuſion diſſipates,
To leave me worſe confounded.
GUST. Think no more on't.
Come to my arms, thou deareſt of mankind!
ARV. Stand off! Pollution dwells within my touch,

And

And horror hangs around me—Cruel man!
O, thou haſt doubly damn'd me with this goodneſs;
For reſolution held the deed as done;
That now muſt ſink me—Hark! I am ſummoned
hence—
My audit opens!—Poiſe me! for I ſtand
Upon a ſpire, againſt whoſe ſightleſs baſe
Hell breaks his wave beneath. Down, down I
dare not;
And up I cannot look, for juſtice fronts me.—
Thou ſhalt have vengeance; tho' my purpling
blood
Were nectar for Heaven's bowl, as warm and rich
As now 'tis baſe, it thus ſhould pour for pardon.

[GUSTAVUS catches his arm, and in the ſtruggle
the dagger falls.

GUST. Ha! Hold, ARVIDA—No, I will not
loſe thee——
Forbid it Heaven! thou ſhalt not rob me ſo—
No, I will ſtruggle with thee to the laſt,
And ſave thee from thyſelf. O, anſwer me!
Wilt thou forſake me?—Anſwer me, my brother,
My beſt ARVIDA.

ARV. I would ſpeak to thee—
But let it be by ſilence—O GUSTAVUS!

GUST. Say but you'll live.

ARV. O!—

GUST. For my ſake.

ARV. Yes, take me—
Expoſe me, cage me, brand me for the tool
Of crafty villains; for the verieſt ſlave,
On whom the bend of each contemptuous brow

Shall

Shall look with loathing. Ah, my turpitude
Shall be the vile comparative for knaves,
To boaſt and whiten by!

GUST. Not ſo, not ſo—
Who knows no fault, my friend, knows no perfection.
The rectitude that Heaven appoints to man
Leads on thro' error; and the kindly ſenſe
Of having ſtrayed, endears the road to bliſs;
It makes Heaven's way more pleaſing! O my brother,
'Tis hence a thouſand cordial charities
Derive their growth, their vigour, and their ſweetneſs.
This ſhort lapſe
Shall to thy future foot give cautious treading,
Erect and firm in virtue.

ARV. Give me leave. [Offers to paſs.

GUST. You ſhall not paſs.

ARV. I muſt.

GUST. Whither?

ARV. I know not—O GUSTAVUS!

GUST. Speak.

ARV. You can't forgive me.

GUST. Not forgive thee!

ARV. No.
Look there!— [Points to the dagger.
And yet when I reſolved to kill thee
I could have died—indeed I could—for thee,
I could have died, GUSTAVUS!

GUST. O I know it.
A generous mind, tho' ſwayed a-while by paſſion,

Is

Is like the steely vigour of the bow,
Still holds its native rectitude, and bends
But to recoil more forceful. Come, forget it.

SCENE VII.

Enter a DALECARLIAN.

DALE. My lord, as now I past the mountain's brow,
I spied some men, whose arms, and strange attire,
Give cause for circumspection.
GUST. Danes, perhaps;
Haste, intercept their passage to the camp. [Exit Dal.
ARV. Those are the Danes that witness to my shame.
GUST. Perish the opprobrious term! Not so, ARVIDA;
Myself will be the guardian of thy fame;
Trust me, I will—Our friends approach—O clear,
While I attend them, clear that cloud, my brother,
That sits upon the morning of thy youth;
It hangs too near the heart of thy GUSTAVUS. [Exit.
ARV. Of thy GUSTAVUS!—O wretch, wretch, cursed wretch!
What is this time and place, and toys of circumstance,
That wind our actions, so, as Heaven's own hand
What's done may not unravel?—Pardon may!—
There's the Lethean sweet, the snow of Heaven,
New blanching o'er the negro front of guilt,
That to the eye of mercy all appears

Fair

Fair as the unwritten page—Yet, ſelf-convict,
Tho' Heaven's free power ſhould pardon, where's
my peace?
Thus, thus to be driven out from my own breaſt!
To have no ſhade, no ſheltering nook at home
To take reflection in!—How looks the wretch,
Whoſe heart cries villain to itſelf? I'll not
Endure its battery—Somewhat muſt be done
Of high import 'ere night, that I may ſleep,
Or wake for ever.

SCENE VIII.

Enter GUSTAVUS followed by the Dalecarlians, ANDERSON, ARNOLDUS, SIVARD, Officers, &c.

1ſt DALE. Let us all ſee him!
2d DALE. Yes, and hear him too.
3d DALE. Let us be ſure 'tis he himſelf.
4th DALE. Our general.
5th DALE. And we will fight while weapons can be found.
6th DALE. Or hands to wield them.
7th DALE. Get on the bank, GUSTAVUS.
AND. Do, my lord.
GUST. My countrymen!—
1ſt DALE. Ho! hear him.
2d DALE. Peace!
3d DALE. Peace!
4th DALE. Peace!
GUST. Amazement I perceive hath fill'd your hearts,

And

And joy for that your lost GUSTAVUS, 'scaped
Thro' wounds, imprisonments, and chains, and deaths,
Thus sudden, thus unlook'd for, stands before ye.—
As one escaped from cruel hands I come,
From hearts that ne'er knew pity, dark and vengeful!
Who quaff the tears of orphans, bathe in blood,
And know no musick but the groans of Sweden.
Yet, not for that my sister's early innocence,
And mother's age, now grind beneath captivity;
Nor that one bloody, one remorseless hour,
Swept my great sire and kindred from my side;
For them GUSTAVUS weeps not—tho' my eyes
Were far less dear, for them I will not weep.
But, O great parent, when I think on thee!
Thy numberless, thy nameless, shameful infamies—
My widow'd country—Sweden!—when I think
Upon thy desolation—spite of rage
And vengeance that would choak them—tears will flow.

AND. O, they are villains, every Dane of them,
Practised to stab and smile; to stab the babe
That smiles upon them!

ARN. What accursed hours
Roll o'er those wretches, who, to fiends like these,
In their dear liberty have bartered more
Than worlds will rate for?

GUST. O liberty, Heaven's choice prerogative,
True bond of law, thou social soul of property,
Thou breath of reason, life of life itself—
For thee the valiant bleed! O sacred liberty!

Wing'd from the ſummer's ſnare, from flattering ruin,
Like the bold ſtork you ſeek the wintery ſhore;
Leave courts, and pomps, and palaces to ſlaves,
Cleave to the cold, and reſt upon the ſtorm.
Upborn by thee, my ſoul diſdain'd the terms
Of empire, offer'd at the hands of tyrants.
With thee, I ſought this favourite ſoil; with thee,
Theſe favourite ſons I ſought;—thy ſons, O liberty!
For even amid the wilds of life you lead them,
Lift their low rafted cottage to the clouds,
Smile o'er their heaths, and from their mountain tops
Beam glory to the nations!

ALL. Liberty! liberty!

GUST. Are ye not mark'd, ye men of Dalecarlia!
Are ye not mark'd by all the circling world,
As the great ſtake, the laſt effort for liberty?
Say, is it not your wealth, the thirſt, the food,
The ſcope and bright ambition of your ſouls?
Why elſe have you, and your renowned forefathers,
From the proud ſummit of their glittering thrones,
Caſt down the mightieſt of your lawful kings
That dared the bold infringement? What, but liberty,
Thro' the famed courſe of thirteen hundred years,
Aloof hath held invaſion from your hills,
And ſanctified their ſhade?—And will ye, will ye
Shrink from the hopes of the expecting world;
Bid your high honours ſtoop to foreign inſult,

And

And in one hour give up to infamy
The harveſt of a thouſand years of glory?

1ſt Dale. No.—

2d Dale. Never, never.

3d Dale. Periſh all firſt!

4th Dale. Die all!

Gust. Yes, die by piecemeal!
Leave not a limb o'er which a Dane may triumph!—
Now from my ſoul I joy, I joy, my friends,
To ſee ye fear'd; to ſee, that even your foes
Do juſtice to your valour!—There they be,
The powers of kingdoms, ſumm'd in yonder hoſt;
Yet kept aloof, yet trembling to aſſail ye.
And O, when I look round and ſee you here,
Of number ſhort, but prevalent in virtue,
My heart ſwells high and burns for the encounter.
True courage but from oppoſition grows;
And what are fifty, what a thouſand ſlaves,
Matched to the ſinew of a ſingle arm
That ſtrikes for liberty?—that ſtrikes to ſave
His fields from fire, his infants from the ſword,
His couch from luſt, his daughters from pollution,
And his large honours from eternal infamy?
What, doubt we then? Shall we, ſhall we ſtand here
'Till motives that might warm an ague's froſt,
And nerve the coward's arm, ſhall poorly ſerve
To wake us to reſiſtance?—Let us on!—
O, yes, I read your lovely fierce impatience;
You ſhall not be withheld; we will ruſh on them—
This is indeed to triumph, where we hold
Three kingdoms in our toil! Is it not glorious,—

Thus to appal the bold, meet force with fury,
And puſh yon torrent back, 'till every wave
Flee to its fountain?

3d DALE. On, lead us on, GUSTAVUS! one word more
Is but delay of conqueſt.

GUST. Take your wiſh.
He, who wants arms, may grapple with the foe
And ſo be furniſh'd. You, moſt noble ANDERSON,
Divide our powers, and with the famed Olaus
Take the left route—You, ERIC, great in arms!
With the renowned NEDERBI, hold the right,
And ſkirt the foreſt down; then wheel at once,
Confeſt to view, and cloſe upon the vale:
Myſelf, and my moſt valiant couſin here
The invincible ARVIDA, gallant SIVARD,
ARNOLDUS, and theſe hundred hardy veterans,
Will pour directly on, and lead the onſet.
Joy, joy, I ſee confeſt from every eye;
Your limbs tread vigorous, and your breaſts beat high!
Thin tho' our ranks, tho' ſcanty be our bands,
Bold are our hearts, and nervous are our hands.
With us, truth, juſtice, fame, and freedom cloſe,
Each, ſingly equal to an hoſt of foes.
I feel, I feel them fill me out for fight;
They lift my limbs as feather'd Hermes light!
Or like the bird of glory, towering high,
Thunder within his graſp, and lightning in his eye!

END OF THE THIRD ACT.

ACT

ACT IV.

SCENE before the CAMP.

Enter CRISTIERN, TROLLIO, and Attendants.

CRIST. YOUR obſervation's juſt; I ſee it, TROLLIO.
Men are machines, with all their boaſted freedom;
Their movements turn upon ſome favourite paſſion:
Let art but find the latent foible out,
We touch the ſpring, and wind them at our pleaſure.

TROLL. Let Heaven ſpy out for virtue, and then ſtarve it;
But vice and frailty are the ſtateſman's quarry,
The objects of our ſearch, and of our ſcience;
Mark'd by our ſmiles, and cheriſh'd by our bounty.
'Tis hence, you lord it o'er your ſervile ſenates:
How low the ſlaves will ſtoop to gorge their luſts,
When aptly baited! Even the tongues of patriots,
Thoſe ſons of clamour, oft relax the nerve
Within the warmth of favour.

CRIST. How elſe ſhould kings ſubſiſt? For what is power,
But the nice conduct of another's weakneſs?

That thing called virtue, is the bane of government;
A libel on the ſtate, that aſks ſuppreſſion:
It has a hateful and unbending quality;
It ſerves no end, ſtill reſtive to the rein,
And to the ſpur unſpeedy: they who boaſt it
Are traitors, rivals of their king, my TROLLIO;
And, wanting other ſubjects, greatly dare
To lord it o'er themſelves. Such is GUSTAVUS,
If yet he be——
And ſuch ARVIDA was; tho' now, I truſt,
He is too far advanced in our deſigns
To think of a retreat.

TROLL. Impoſſible!
Already has he leap'd the guilty mound
That might appal his virtue; for the world
He dare not now look back, where ſhame purſues,
And cuts off all retreat.

SCENE II.

Enter GENTLEMAN USHER and PETERSON, who kneels.

GENT. My liege, lord PETERSON.

CRIST. Riſe to our truſt, moſt worthy PETERSON;
Riſe to our friendſhip. By my head, I ſwear,
Bar but our TROLLIO here, there's not a Swede,
Who holds thy valued level in our heart!
For thou art unſhaken, tho' thy nation ſwerve;
Faithful among the faithleſs!

PETER.

PETER. What I am,
Let this inform your majeſty. [Gives a Pacquet.

TROLL. A pacquet!
Whence had you that, my friend?

PETER. Even from the hands
Of the once great GUSTAVUS.

CRIST. Then you have ſeen him. Tell me, tell me PETERSON,
What ſaid he? Eh! How look'd the mighty rebel?
His means, his ſcope, the pride of his preſumption—
Give me the whole!

PETER. Laſt night, my gracious lord,
While yet I held your meſſenger in conference;
Arrived, who brought a letter from GUSTAVUS,
Wherein, digeſting many flagrant terms
Of mutinous import againſt the ſtate
Of your high dignity, by morning light
He prayed me to attend him; boaſting much
Of plenteous hopes, and means of boldeſt enterprize.
Of this I gave you notice; and 'ere dawn
Set out for freſh intelligence—I came;
I ſaw him ſhrunk, that glory of the north,
Soil'd with the vileneſs of a ſlave's attire;
Where in the depth and darkneſs of the mines,
For ſix long months he hath not ſeen the ſun;
Colleagued with circling horrors, hourly toil
Hath been his watch, and penury his earning:
But like the lion, newly broke from bonds,
The mingling paſſions from his eyes dart glory;

Pride lifts his ſtature, and his opening front
Still looks dominion.

CRIST. Who were his adherents?

PETER. The traitor ANDERSON, and a few friends;
To whom, 'ere I ſet out, he ſtood revealed.
And when I ſeemed to queſtion on his powers
Of rivalſhip, the props whereon he meant
To lift contention to the princely front
Of ſuch high oppoſition; he replied,
His powers were near your perſon.

CRIST. How! what's here? [Looks on the Pacquet.
To Laurens, Aland, Haquin, and Roderic!—
Confuſion! Treaſon's in our camp! Who's there?

GENT. My liege!

CRIST. Bear this to Norbi—Bid him ſeize [Gives a Signet.
The Swediſh captains.

TROLL. Might I but preſume——

CRIST. I will not be controuled—bid him ſeize all,
Soldiers and chiefs!—By hell, there's not a Swede,
But lurks an inſtrument to prompt rebellion,
And plots upon my life! Look there, 'tis evident: [Gives TROLLIO a Letter.
They are all leagued, confederate with GUSTAVUS,
The abettors of his treaſon.

TROLL. It ſhould ſeem ſo:
And yet it ſhould not—Tell me, PETERSON,
Art thou aſſured thy credit with GUSTAVUS
Will anſwer to a truſt like this?—Ha! Say.

PETER.

PETER. Yes, well assured: my zeal appeared too warm
To give the least cold colour for suspicion.
TROLL. I fear, my friend, I fear he has o'er-reach'd you.
"Divide and conquer," is the sum of politics.
Beyond the dreaded circle of his sword,
GUSTAVUS triumphs in an ample genius;
He walks at large, sees clear and wide around him,
Calm in the storm and turbulence of action;
He ponders on the last event of things,
And makes each cause subservient to the consequence.
CRIST. You over-rate his craft—they are false, my TROLLIO,
False every Swede of them; I read their souls.

SCENE III.

Enter CRISTINA and MARIANA.

CRISTINA. I heard it was your royal pleasure, sir,
I should attend your highness.
CRIST. Yes, CRISTINA,
But business interferes.

SCENE IV.

Enter an OFFICER.

OFF. My sovereign liege!
Wide o'er the western shelving of yon hill,

We

We think, tho' indiſtinctly, we can ſpy,
Like men in motion muſtering on the heath;
And there is one who ſaith he can diſcern
A few of martial geſture, and bright arms,
Who this way bend their action.
CRIST. Friends, perhaps;
For foes it were too daring—Haſte thee, TROLLIO,
Detach a thouſand of our Daniſh horſe
To rule their motions—We will out ourſelf,
And hold our powers in readineſs—Lead on.
[Exeunt.

SCENE V.

CRISTINA and MARIANA.

MAR. Ha! did you mark, my princeſs, did you mark?
Should ſome reverſe, ſome wondrous whirl of fate
Once more return GUSTAVUS to the battle,
New nerve his arm, and wreathe his brow with conqueſt;
Say, would you not repent that e'er you ſaved
This dreadful man, the foe of your great race;
Who pours impetuous in his country's cauſe
To ſpoil you of a kingdom?
CRISTINA. No, my friend.—
Had I to death, or bondage, ſold my ſire;
Or had GUSTAVUS on our native realms
Made hoſtile inroad—then, my MARIANA!
Had I then ſaved him from the ſtroke of juſtice,
I ſhould not ceaſe my ſuit to Heaven for pardon.

But

But if, tho' in a foe, to reverence virtue,
Withſtand oppreſſion, reſcue injured innocence,
Step boldly in betwixt my ſire and guilt,
And ſave my king, my father, from diſhonour;
If this be ſin—I have ſhook hands with penitence.
Firſt, periſh crowns, dominion, all the ſhine
And tranſience of this world, 'ere guilt ſhall ſerve
To buy the vain incumbrance!

MAR. Do not think
I meant, my princeſs, to arraign your virtues,
Howe'er I ſeemed to queſtion on the conſequence.

CRISTINA. The conſequence of virtue muſt be good:
It muſt.—Tho' it ſhould prove my father's lot,
In being reſcued from one act of guilt,
To loſe the whole of all his wide dominions,
He were a gainer—Blaſted be that royalty,
Which murder muſt make ſure, and crimes inglorious!
The bulk of kingdoms, nay, the world is light,
When guilt weighs oppoſite—O would to Heaven,
The loſs of empire could reſtore his innocence,
Reſtore the fortunes, and the precious lives
Of thouſands fallen, the victims of ambition!

SCENE VI.

Enter LAERTES.

Ha! LAERTES! moſt welcome! well—and have you?—Say, LAERTES.

LAER. O royal maid!——

CRISTINA.

CRISTINA. Thy looks are doubtful—Speak,—
Why art thou silent?—Does he live?

LAER. He does:
But death, 'ere night, must fill a long account!
The camp, the country's in confusion: war,
And changes, ride upon the hour that hastes
To intercept my tongue—I else could tell
Of virtues hitherto beyond my ken;
Courage, to which the lion stoops his crest,
Yet grafted upon qualities as soft
As a rocked infant's meekness; such as tempts
Against my faith, my country, and allegiance,
To wish thee speed, GUSTAVUS!

CRISTINA. Then you found him.

LAER. I did: and warned him, but in vain; for death
To him appeared more grateful than to find
His friend's dishonour.

CRISTINA. Give me the manner—quick—soft, good LAERTES! [They retire.

SCENE VII.

Enter CRISTIERN, TROLLIO, PETERSON, DANES, &c.

CRIST. Damn'd! double traitor! O cursed, false ARVIDA!
Guard well the Swedish prisoners, bind them hard—
Stand to your arms—Bring forth the captives there!

SCENE

SCENE VIII.

Enter AUGUSTA and GUSTAVA guarded.

TROLL. My liege——

CRIST. Away! I'll hear no more of politics.—
Fortune! we will not truſt the changeling more;
But wear her girt upon our armed loins,
Or pointed in our graſp.

SCENE IX.

Enter an OFFICER.

OFF. The foe's at hand:
With gallant ſhew your thouſand Danes rode forth,
But ſhall return no more!—I marked the action:
A band of deſperate reſolutes ruſh'd on them,
Scarce numbering to a tenth, and in mid way
They cloſed; the ſhock was dreadful, nor your Danes
Could bear the madding charge: a while they ſtood,
Then ſhrunk, and broke, and turned—When, lo, behind,
Faſt wheeling from the right and left there pour'd,
Who intercepted their return, and caught
Within the toil they periſhed.

CRIST. It is GUSTAVUS!
No mortal elſe, not Ammon's boaſted ſon,
Not Cæſar would have dared it. Tell me, ſay,
What numbers in the whole may they amount to?

OFF.

OFF. About five thousand.

CRIST. And no more.

OFF. No more,
That yet appear.

CRIST. We count six times their sum.——
Haste, soldier, take a trumpet; tell GUSTAVUS
We have of terms to offer, and would treat
Touching his mother's ransom; say, her death,
Suspended by our grace, but waits his answer.

[Exit OFFICER.

Madam, it should well suit with your authority,

[To AUGUSTA.

To check this frenzy in your son—Look to it;
Or by the saints this hour's your last of life!

AUGUST. Come, my GUSTAVA, come, my little captive,
We shall be free; our tyrant is grown kind!
And for these chains that bind thy pretty arms,
The golden cherubim shall lend thee wings,
And thou shalt mount amid the smiling choir
Of little heavenly songsters, like thyself,
All robed in innocence.

GUSTAVA. Will you go, mother?

AUGUST. So help me, mercy!—Yes, I'll go, my child;
And I will give thee to thy father's fondness,
And to the arms of all thy royal race
In Heaven; who sit on thrones, with loves, and joys,
And pleasures, smiling round.

CRIST. Is this my answer?
Come forth, ye ministers of death, come forth.

SCENE

SCENE IX.

Enter RUFFIANS, who ſeize AUGUSTA and GUSTAVA.

Pluck them aſunder! We ſhall prove you, lady!
'Tis my damn'd lot, thus ever to be croſſed
With rank blown pride, and inſolence eternal.

GUSTAVA. O mother, take me, take me from theſe men;
They fright me with their looks.

AUGUSTA. Alas, my child, I cannot take thee from them.

GUSTAVA. O, they will hurt me: can't you take me, mother?

AUGUSTA. They cannot, cannot hurt you, my GUSTAVA!
Fear not, my little one; your name ſhould be
A charm o'er cowardice, for you are called
After your valiant brother; he'll diſown you,
He will not love you, if you fear, GUSTAVA.

CRISTINA. Ah! I can hold no longer.—Royal ſir,
Thus on my knees, and lower, lower ſtill——

CRIST. My child! what mean you?

CRISTINA. O my gracious father!
Kill, kill me rather—let me periſh firſt;
But do not ſtain the ſanctity of kings
With the ſweet blood of helpleſs innocence—
Do not, my father! ſpare the little orphans,
And let the lambs go free!

Augusta. Ha! who art thou?
That look'ſt ſo like the inhabitants of Heaven—
Like mercy ſent upon the morning's bluſh,
To glad the heart, and cheer a gloomy world
With light 'till now unknown?

Crist. Away, they come.
I'll hear no more of your ill-timed petitions.

Cristina. O yet for pity!

Crist. I will none on't—leave me.
Pity! it is the infant fool of nature—
Tear off her hold, and bear her to her tent.

[Exeunt Cristina, Mariana, Laertes, and Attendants.

SCENE X.

Enter an Officer.

Off. My liege, Gustavus, tho' with much reluctance,
Conſents to one hour's truce. His ſoldiers reſt
Upon their arms; and, followed by a few,
He comes to know your terms.

Crist. I ſee; fall back——
Stand firm—Be ready ſlaves, and on the word
Plunge deep your daggers in their boſoms.

[Points to Augusta.

SCENE

SCENE XI.

Enter GUSTAVUS, ARVIDA, ANDERSON, ARNOLDUS, SIVARD, &c.

Hold!

GUST. Ha!—it is, it is my mother!

CRIST. Tell me, GUSTAVUS, tell me, why is this?
That, as a ſtream diverted from the banks
Of ſmooth obedience, thou haſt drawn thoſe men
Upon a dry unchannel'd enterprize,
To turn their inundation?—Are the lives
Of my miſguided people held ſo light,
That thus thou'dſt puſh them on the keen rebuke
Of guarded majeſty; where juſtice waits,
All awful, and reſiſtleſs, to aſſert
The impervious rights, the ſanctitude of kings,
And blaſt rebellion?

GUST. Juſtice!—ſanctitude!—
And rights!—O patience! rights!—what rights, thou tyrant?
Yes, if perdition be the rule of power,
If wrongs give right; O then, ſupreme in miſchief!
Thou wert the lord, the monarch of the world,
Too narrow for thy claim! But if thou think'ſt
That crowns are vilely propertied, like coin,
To be the means, the ſpecialty of luſt,
And ſenſual attribution—if thou think'ſt
That empire is of titled birth, or blood;
That nature, in the proud behalf of one,

Shall disenfranchise all her lordly race,
And bow her general issue to the yoke
Of private domination—then, thou proud one,
Here know me for thy king!—Howe'er be told,
Not claim hereditary, not the trust
Of frank election,
Not even the high anointing hand of Heaven,
Can authorize oppression; give a law
For lawless power; wed faith to violation;
On reason build misrule, or justly bind
Allegiance to injustice—Tyranny
Absolves all faith; and who invades our rights,
Howe'er his own commence, can never be
But an usurper—But for thee, for thee
There is no name!—thou hast abjured mankind;
Dash'd safety from thy bleak unsocial side,
And waged wild war with universal nature!

CRIST. Licentious traitor! thou canst talk it largely—
Who made thee umpire of the rights of kings,
And power, prime attribute—as on thy tongue
The poise of battle lay, and arms, of force,
To throw defiance in the front of duty?
Look round, unruly boy, thy battle comes
Like raw, disjointed mustering; feeble wrath!
A war of waters borne against the rock
Of our firm continent, to fume, and chafe,
And shiver in the toil.

GUST. Mistaken man!
I come impower'd, and strengthen'd in thy weakness.
For tho' the structure of a tyrant's throne

Rise

Riſe on the necks of half the ſuffering world,
Fear trembles in the cement; prayers and tears,
And ſecret curſes, ſap its mouldering baſe,
And ſteal the pillars of allegiance from it:
Then, let a ſingle arm but dare the ſway,
Headlong it turns, and drives upon deſtruction.

Troll. Profane, and alien to the love of Heaven!
Art thou ſtill hardened to the wrath divine,
That hangs o'er thy rebellion?—Know'ſt thou not,
Thou art at enmity with grace? caſt out,
Made an anathema, a curſe enrolled
Among the faithful, thou and thy adherents
Shorn from our holy church, and offered up
As ſacred to damnation?

Gust. Yes, I know,
When ſuch as thou, with ſacrilegious hand,
Seize on the apoſtolic key of Heaven,
It then becomes a tool for crafty knaves
To ſhut out virtue; and unfold thoſe gates,
That Heaven itſelf had barr'd againſt the luſts
Of avarice and ambition—Soft, and ſweet,
As looks of charity, or voice of lambs
That bleat upon the morning, are the words
Of Chriſtian Meekneſs! miſſion all divine!
The Law of Love ſole mandate—But your gall,
Ye Swediſh prelacy! your gall hath turn'd
The words of ſweet, but indigeſted peace,
To wrath and bitterneſs—Ye hallowed men!
In whom vice ſanctifies; whoſe precepts teach
Zeal without truth, religion without virtue;
Who ne'er preach Heaven, but with a downward eye

That turns your ſouls to droſs; who ſhouting looſe
The dogs of hell upon us!—thefts, and rapes,
Sack'd towns, and midnight howlings thro' the
realm,
Receive your ſanction—O it is glorious miſchief,
When vice turns holy, puts religion on,
Aſſumes the robe pontifical, the eye
Of ſaintly elevation, bleſſeth ſin,
And makes the ſeal of ſweet offended Heaven
A ſign of blood, a label for decrees
That hell would ſhrink to own.—

CRIST. No more of this.
GUSTAVUS, would'ſt thou yet return to grace,
And hold thy motions in the ſphere of duty,
Acceptance might be found.

GUST. Imperial ſpoiler!
Give me my father, give me back my kindred;
Give me the fathers of ten thouſand orphans;
Give me the ſons in whom thy ruthleſs ſword
Has left our widows childleſs: mine they were—
Both mine, and every Swede's, whoſe patriot breaſt
Bleeds in his country's woundings! O thou can'ſt
not;
Thou haſt out-ſinn'd all reckoning! Give me then
My all that's left—my gentle mother there;
And ſpare yon little trembler!

CRIST. Yes, on terms
Of compact, and ſubmiſſion.

GUST. Ha! with thee?
Compact with thee!—and mean'ſt thou for my
country?
For Sweden? No—ſo hold my heart but firm,

Altho'

Altho' it wring for it; tho' blood drop for tears,
And at the ſight my ſtraining eyes ſtart forth—
They both ſhall periſh firſt.

CRIST. Slaves, do your office.

GUST. Hold yet,—Thou can'ſt not be ſo damn'd.—My mother!
I dare not aſk thy bleſſing—Where's ARVIDA?
Where art thou? Come, my friend, thou haſt known temptation—
And therefore beſt can'ſt pity, or ſupport me.

ARV. Alas! I ſhall but ſerve to weigh thee downward;
To pull thee from the dazzling, ſightleſs height,
At which thy virtue ſoars. For, O GUSTAVUS,
My ſoul is dark, diſconſolate and dark:
Sick to the world, and hateful to myſelf,
I have no country now; I have nought but thee,
And ſhould yield up the intereſt of mankind,
Where thine's in queſtion.

AUGUSTA. See, my ſon relents;
Behold, O king!—yet ſpare us but a moment:
His little ſiſter ſhall embrace his knees;
And theſe fond arms, around his duteous neck,
Shall join to bend him to us.

CRIST. Could I truſt ye——

ARV. I'll be your hoſtage.

CRIST. Granted.

GUST. Hold, my friend.

[ARVIDA breaks from GUSTAVUS, and paſſes to CRISTIERN's party, while AUGUSTA and GUSTAVA go over to GUSTAVUS.

Augusta. Is it then given, yet given me, 'ere
I die,
To see thy face, Gustavus?—thus to gaze,
To touch, to fold thee thus?—My son, my son!
And have I lived to this? It is enough,
All arm'd, and in thy country's precious cause
Terribly beauteous, to behold thee thus!
Why, 'twas my only, hourly suit to Heaven,
And now 'tis granted. O my glorious child,
Blest were the throes I felt for thee, Gustavus!
For from the breast, from out your swathing bands,
You stepp'd the child of honour.

Gust. O my mother!—

Augusta. Why stands that water trembling in
thy eye?
Why heaves thy bosom? Turn not thus away—
'Tis the last time that we must meet, my child,
And I will have thee whole. Why, why, Gus-
tavus,
Why is this form of heaviness? For me
I trust it is not meant; you cannot think
So poorly of me: I grow old, my son;
And to the utmost period of mortality,
I ne'er should find a death's hour like to this,
Whereby to do thee honour.

Gust. Roman patriots!
Ye Decii, self-devoted to your country!
You gave no mothers up!—Will annals yield
No precedent for this, no elder boast
Whereby to match my trial?

Augusta. No, Gustavus;
For Heaven still squares our trial to our strength,

And

And thine is of the foremoſt—Noble youth!
Even I, thy parent, with a conſcious pride,
Have often bowed to thy ſuperior virtues.
O, there is but one bitterneſs in death,
One only ſting——

GUST. Speak, ſpeak!

AUGUSTA. 'Tis felt for thee.
Too well I know thy gentleneſs of ſoul,
Melting as babes; even now the preſſure's on thee,
And bends thy lovelineſs to earth—O, child!
The dear but ſad foretaſte of thy affliction
Already kills thy mother—But behold,
Behold thy valiant followers, who to thee,
And to the faith of thy protecting arm,
Have given ten thouſand mothers; daughters too,
Who in thy virtue yet may learn to bear
Millions of free-born ſons to bleſs thy name,
And pray for their deliverer—O farewell!
This, and but this—the very laſt adieu!
Heaven ſit victorious on thy arm, my ſon!
And give thee to thy merits!

CRIST. Ah, thou traitoreſs!

GUSTAVA. O brother, ar'n't you ſtronger than that man?
Don't let him take my mother.

AUGUSTA. See, GUSTAVUS,
My little captive waits for one embrace.

GUST. Come to my arms, thou lamb-like ſacrifice!
O that they were of force to fold thee ever,
To let thee to my heart! there lock thee cloſe,
And circle thee with life!—But 'twill not be!

GUSTAVA. I'll ſtay with you, my brother.

GUST. Killing innocence!—
That I was born to ſee this hour!
The pains of hell are on me!—Take her, mother!

GUSTAVA. I will not part with you, indeed, I will not!

GUST. Take her—Diſtraction! Haſte, my deareſt mother:
O—elſe I ſhall run mad—quite mad, and ſave ye.

ARV. Hold, madam!—Hear me, thou moſt dear GUSTAVUS!—
Thus low I bend my prayer—reject me not:—
If once, if ever thou didſt love ARVIDA,
O leave me here to anſwer to the wrath
Of this fell tyrant. Save thy honour'd mother,
And that ſweet lamb from ſlaughter!

GUST. Cruel friendſhip!

CRIST. And by my life I'd take thee at thy word,
Thou doubly damn'd! but that I know 'twould pleaſe thee.

AUGUSTA. No, generous prince, thy blood ſhall never be
The price of our diſhonour. Come, my child!—
Weep not, ſweet babe, there ſhall no harm come nigh thee.

CRIST. 'Tis well, proud dame; you are return'd I ſee——
Each to his charge—Here break we off, GUSTAVUS;
For to the very teeth of thy rebellion
We daſh defiance back.

GUST,

Gust. Alas, my mother!
Grief choaks up utterance, elſe I have to ſay
What never tongue unfolded—Yet return,
Come back, and I will give up all to ſave thee;
For on the covering of thy ſacred head
My heart drops blood. Thou fountain of my life!
Dearer than mercy is to kneeling penitence,
My early bleſſing, firſt and lateſt joy—
Return, return, and ſave thy loſt Gustavus!

Crist. No more, thou trifler!

Augusta. O farewel for ever!

[Exeunt Cristiern and his Party. Gustavus and his Party remain.

Gust. Then ſhe is gone—Arvida! Anderson!
For ever gone!—Arnoldus, friends, where are ye?
Help here, heave, heave this mountain from me —O—
Heaven keep my ſenſes!—So—We will to battle;
But let no banners wave—Be ſtill thou trump,
And every martial ſound that gives the war
To pomp or levity! for vengeance now
Is clad with heavy arms, ſedately ſtern;
Reſolv'd, but ſilent as the ſlaughter'd heaps
O'er which my ſoul is brooding.

Arn. O Gustavus!
Is there a Swede of us, whoſe ſword and ſoul
Grapples not to thee, as to all they hold
Of earthly eſtimation? Said I more,
It were but half my thought.

And. On thee we gaze,
As one unknown 'till this important hour;
Pre-eminent of men!

Siv.

SIV. Accurs'd be he,
Who, in thy leading, will not fight, and ſtrive,
And bleed, and gaſp with pleaſure!
AND. We are thine;
All, all, both we and ours, whom thou this day
Haſt dearly purchaſed.
ARN. Tho', to yield us up,
Had ſcarce been leſs than virtue.
GUST. O my friends!
I ſee, 'tis not for man to boaſt his ſtrength
Before the trial comes—This very hour,
Had I a thouſand parents, all ſeem'd light
When weigh'd againſt my country; and but now,
One mother ſeem'd of weight to poize the world,
Tho' conſcious truth and reaſon were againſt her.
For, O, howe'er the partial paſſions ſway,
High Heaven aſſigns but one unbiaſs'd way;
Direct thro' every oppoſition leads,
Where ſhelves decline, and many a ſteep impedes.
Here hold we on, tho' thwarting fiends alarm;
Here hold we on, tho' devious Syrens charm!
In Heaven's diſpoſing power events unite;
Nor aught can happen wrong, to him who acts aright.

END OF THE FOURTH ACT.

ACT V.

SCENE the ROYAL TENT.

Enter CRISTINA and MARIANA.

CRISTINA. HARK! MARIANA, lift!—No—
All is filent——
It was not fancy fure—didft thou hear aught?
MAR. Too plain; the voice of terror feiz'd my ear,
And my heart finks within me.
CRISTINA. O, I fear
The war is now at work—As winds, methought,
Long borne thro' hollow vaults, the found approach'd;
One found, yet laden with a thoufand notes
Of fearful variation! Then it fwell'd
To diftant fhouts, now coming on the gale;
Again borne backward with a parting groan,
All funk to horrid ftillnefs.
MAR. Look, my princefs—
Ah, no! withold thy eyes!—the place grows dark;
A fudden cloud of forrow ftains the day,
And throws its gloom around.

SCENE

SCENE II.

Enter four Slaves bearing the bodies of AUGUSTA and GUSTAVA on a bier covered—four women in chains follow weeping.

CRISTINA. Whence are ye, ſay, you daughters of affliction?
Their ſpeech is in their tears—Avert, ye ſaints!
Avert that thought!—Soft! hold ye! I have a tear
For every mourner—Ah! [Looks under the Covering.

MAR. What mean you, madam?

CRISTINA. Reflection come not there! See it not eyes!—
How art thou ſpilt, thou blood of royalty!—
Cloſe at the paleneſs of its parent breaſt
The babe lies ſlaughter'd!—Tell me, who did this?—
No, hold ye! Say not that my father did it;
For duty then turns rebel—Cruel father!
O, that ſome villager, whoſe early toil
Lifts the penurious morſel to his mouth,
Had claim'd my birth! ambition had not then
Thus ſtepp'd 'twixt me and Heaven.

MAR. Go, bear it hence——
Turn, turn, my royal miſtreſs!

CRISTINA. Ah, AUGUSTA!
Among thy foes thou art fallen, thou art fallen in virtue!—
Exalt thyſelf, O guilt! For here the good
Have none who may lament them. Sit we down;

For

For I grow weary of the world. Let death
Within his vaulty durance, dark and ſtill,
Receive me too; and where the afflicted reſt,
There fold me in for ever. ——

SCENE III.

Enter LAERTES.

LAER. Ariſe, CRISTINA! fly, thou royal virgin!
This morn beheld thee miſtreſs of the north,
Bright heir of Scandinavia; and this hour
Has left thee not, throughout thy wide dominions,
Whereon to reſt thy foot.

CRISTINA. Now, praiſe to Heaven!
Say but my father lives.

LAER. At your command
I went; and, from a neighbouring ſummit, view'd
Where either hoſt ſtood adverſe, ſternly wedg'd;
Reflecting on each other's gloomy front,
Fell hate and fix'd defiance—When at once
The foe moved on, attendant to the ſteps
Of their GUSTAVUS—He, with mournful pace,
Came ſlow and ſilent; 'till two hapleſs Danes
Prick'd forth, and on his helm diſcharg'd their fury:
Then rouz'd the lion! To my wondring ſight
His ſtature grew twofold; before his eye
All force ſeem'd wither'd, and his horrid plume
Shook wild diſmay around: as Heaven's dread bolt,
He ſhot, he pierc'd our legions; in his ſtrength

His

His ſhouting ſquadron gloried, ruſhing on
Where e'er he led their battle—Full five times,
Hem'd by our mightier hoſt, the foe ſeem'd loſt,
And ſwallow'd from my ſight; five times again
Like flame they iſſued to the light—And thrice,
Theſe eyes beheld him, they beheld GUSTAVUS
Unhors'd, and by a hoſt girt ſingly in;
And thrice he broke thro' all.

CRISTINA. My blood runs chill.

LAER. With ſuch a ſtrenuous, ſuch a labour'd conflict,
Sure never field was fought—until GUSTAVUS
Aloud cried, Victory! and on his ſpear
High rear'd the imperial diadem of Denmark.
Then ſlack'd the battle; then recoil'd our hoſt;
His, echoed, Victory! and now would know
No bounds; rout follow'd, and the face of fight—
—She heeds me not.

CRISTINA. O, ill ſtarr'd royalty!
My father! Cruel, dear, unhappy father!
Summon'd ſo ſudden! fearful, fearful thought!—
Step in, ſweet mercy! For thy time was—Ha!

SCENE IV.

Enter CRISTIERN *flying without his helmet, in diſorder, his ſword broke, and his garments bloody; he throws away his ſword, and ſpeaks.*

CRIST. Give us new arms of proof—freſh horſes —quick!
A watch without there—Set a ſtandard up

To guide our ſcattered powers! Haſte, my friends, haſte!
We muſt be gone— O for ſome cooling ſtream
To ſlake a monarch's thirſt!

LAER. A poſt, my liege,
A ſecond poſt from Denmark ſays——

CRIST. All's loſt.—
Is it not ſo? Be gone! Perdition choak thee—
Give me a moment's ſolitude—Thought, thought,
Where wouldſt thou lead?

CRISTINA. He ſees me not—Alas, alas, my father!
O, what a war there lives within his eye,
Where greatneſs ſtruggles to ſurvive itſelf!
I tremble to approach him; yet I fain
Would bring peace to him—Don't you know me, ſir?
My father, look upon me, look, my father!
Why ſtrains your lip, and why that doubtful eye
Thro' fury melting o'er me? Turn, ah, turn!
I cannot bear its ſoftneſs—How? nay, then,
There is a falling dagger in that tear,
To kill thy child, to murder thy CRISTINA.

CRIST. Then thou art CRISTINA?

CRISTINA. Yes.

CRIST. My child?

CRISTINA. I am.

CRIST. Curſe me, then, curſe me!—Join with heaven and earth
And hell to curſe!

CRISTINA. Alas! on me, my father,
Thy curſes be on me; but on thy head

Fall

Fall bleſſings from that Heaven which has this day
Preſerv'd thy life in battle!

CRIST. What have I
To do with Heaven? Damnation! What am I?
All frail and tranſient as my laps'd dominions!
Even now the ſolid earth prepares to ſlide
From underneath me. Nature's power cries out,
Leave him thou univerſe!—No—Hold me Heaven!
Hold me thou Heaven, whom I have forſaken!—hold
Thy creature, tho' accurs'd!

CRISTINA. Patience and peace
Poſſeſs thy mind! Not all thy pride of empire
E'er gave ſuch bleſt ſenſation, as one hour
Of penitence, tho' painful—Let us hence—
Far from the blood and buſtle of ambition.
Be it my taſk to watch thy riſing wiſh,
To ſmooth thy brow, find comfort for thy cares,
And for thy will obedience; ſtill to cheer
The day with ſmiles, and lay the nightly down
Beneath thy ſlumbers.

CRIST. O thou all that's left me!—
Even in the riot, in the rage of fight,
Thy guardian virtues watch'd around my head,
When elſe no arm could aid—for thro' my ranks,
My circling troops, the fell GUSTAVUS ruſh'd:
Vengeance! he cried; and with one eager hand
Griped faſt my diadem—his other arm,
High rear'd the deathful ſteel—ſuſpended yet;
For in his eye, and thro' his varying face,
Conflicting paſſions fought—He look'd—he ſtood
In wrath reluctant—then, with gentler voice,

"CRISTINA thou haſt conquered!—Go," he cried,
"I yield thee to her virtues."

SCENE V.

Enter TROLLIO, and Guards with Swords drawn.

TROLL. Haſte, O king!—
The foe has hem'd us round—O haſte to ſave
Thyſelf and us!

CRIST. Thy ſword. [Takes a ſword from one of the guards.

TROLL. What means my——

CRIST. Villain!
Well thought, by hell!—Ha! Yes,—thou art our miniſter,
The reverend monitor of vice—the ſoil,
Baneful and rank with every principle,
Whence grow the crimes of kings! Firſt periſh thou— [Stabs him.
Who taught the throne of power to ſix on fear,
And raiſe its ſafety from the public ruin!
Fall thou into the gulph thyſelf haſt fixt
Between the prince and people; cutting off
Communion from the ear of royalty,
And mercy from complaint—Away, away!
Thy death, old man, be on thy monarch's head—
On thine, the blood of all thy countrymen,
Who fell beneath thy counſels! [Exeunt.

TROLLIO attempts to riſe, and then ſpeaks.

TROLL. Thou bloody tyrant!—Late, too late I find,

Nor faith, nor gratitude, nor friendly trust,
No force of obligations, can subsist
Between the guilty—O, let none aspire
To be a king's convenience! Has he virtues,
Those are his own; his vices are his minister's.
Who dares to step 'twixt envy and the throne,
Alike to feel the caprice of his prince,
As public detestation.—Ha! I am going—
But whither?—No one near! to feel! to catch!
The world but for an instant! for one ray
To guide my soul!—Her way grows wondrous dark,
And down, down, down! [Dies.

SCENE VI.

Enter GUSTAVUS, ANDERSON, ARNOLDUS, SIVARD, &c. in Triumph.

GUSTAVUS advances, and the rest range themselves on each side of the Stage.

GUST. That we have conquer'd, first we bend to Heaven!
AND. And next to thee!
ALL. To thee, to thee, GUSTAVUS!
GUST. No, matchless men! my brothers of the war!
Be it my greatest glory to have mixt
My arms with yours, and to have fought for once
Like to a Dalecarlian; like to you,
The sires of honour, of a new-born fame,
To be transmitted, from your great memorial,
To climes unknown, to age succeeding age,
Till time shall verge upon eternity,
And patriots be no more—

ARN.

Arn. Behold, my lord,
The Danish prisoners, and the traitor Peterson,
Attend their fate.

Gust. Send home the Danes with honour;
And let them better learn, from our example,
To treat whom next they conquer, with humanity.

And. But then for Peterson!

Gust. His crimes are great.
A single death were a reward for treason:
Let him still languish—let him be exiled;
No more to see the land of liberty,
The hills of Sweden, nor the native fields
Of known, endear'd idea.

And. Royal sir,
This is to pardon, to encourage villains;
And hourly to expose that sacred life,
Where all our safety centers.

Gust. Fear them not.
The fence of virtue is a chief's best caution;
And the firm surety of my people's hearts
Is all the guard that e'er shall wait Gustavus.
I am a soldier from my youth; yet Anderson,
These wars, where man must wound himself in man,
Have somewhat shocking in them: trust me, friend,
Except in such a cause as this day's quarrel,
I would not shed a single wretch's blood
For the world's empire!

Arn. O exalted Sweden!
Blest people!—Heaven! wherein have we deserv'd
A man like this to rule us?

SCENE VII.

Enter ARVIDA leading in CRISTINA. He runs to GUSTAVUS.

GUST. My ARVIDA!

ARV. My king! O hail! Thus let me pay my homage. [Kneels.

GUST. Rise, rise, nor shame our friendship.

ARV. See, GUSTAVUS! Behold, nor longer wonder at my frailty.

GUST. Be faithful eyes! Ha! Yes, it must be so.
'Tis she—For Heaven would chuse no other form
Wherein to treasure every mental virtue.

CRISTINA. Renown'd GUSTAVUS! mightiest among men!
If such a wretch, the captive of thy arms,
Trembling and awed in thy superior presence,
May find the grace that every other finds—
For thou art said to be of wondrous goodness!—
Then hear—and O excuse a foe's presumption!—
While low, thus low you see a suppliant child,
Now pleading for a father, for a dear,
Much loved; if cruel, yet unhappy father.
O, let him 'scape who ne'er can wrong thee more!
If he with circling nations could not stand
Against thee singly; singly, what can he,
When thou art fenced with nations?

GUST. Ha! that posture!
O rise—surprised, my eye perceiv'd it not.
CRISTINA! thou all form'd for excellence!

I have

I have much to ſay, but that my tongue, my thoughts
Are troubled, warr'd on by unuſual paſſions.
'Twas hence thou had'ſt it in thy power to aſk,
'Ere I could offer—Come, my friend, aſſiſt,
Inſtruct me to be grateful. O CRISTINA!
I fought for freedom, not for crowns, thou fair one!
They ſhall ſit brighter on that beauteous head,
Whoſe eye might awe the monarchs of the earth,
And light the world to virtue—My ARVIDA!

ARV. O great and good, and glorious to the laſt!
I read thy ſoul, I ſee the generous conflict,
And come to fix, not trouble thy repoſe.
Could you but know with what an eager haſte
I ſprung to execute thy late commands;
To ſhield this lovely object of thy cares,
And give her thus, all beauteous to thy eyes!
For I have no bliſs but thine, have loſt the form
Of every wiſh that's foreign to thy happineſs.
But, O, my king! my conqueror! my GUSTAVUS!
It grieves me much that thou muſt ſhortly mourn,
Even on the day in which thy country's freed,
That crowns thy arms with conqueſt and CRISTINA.

GUST. Alas! your cheek is pale—You bleed, my brother!

ARV. I do indeed—to death.

GUST. You have undone me:
Raſh, headſtrong man! O was this well, ARVIDA?
[Turns from him.

ARV. Pardon, GUSTAVUS! mine's the common lot,

 The

The fate of thousands fallen this day in battle.
I had resolv'd on life, to see you blest;
To see my king and his CRISTINA happy.
Turn, thou belov'd, thou honour'd next to Heaven!
And to thy arms receive a penitent,
Who never more shall wrong thee.

GUST. O ARVIDA!—
Friend! friend! [Turns and embraces him.

ARV. Thy heart beats comfort to me!—In this breast,
Let thy ARVIDA, let thy friend survive.
O, strip his once lov'd image of its frailties;
And strip it too of every fonder thought,
That may give thee affliction—Do, GUSTAVUS—
It is my last request—for Heaven and thou
Are all the care and business—of ARVIDA. [Dies.

GUST. Friend! Brother! speak—He's gone—and here is all
That's left of him who was my life's best treasure.
How art thou fallen, thou greatly valiant man!
In ruin graceful, like the warrior spear
Tho' shiver'd in the dust—so fall GUSTAVUS!—
But thou art sped, hast reach'd the goal before me;
And one light lapse throughout thy course in virtue,
Shews only thou wer't man, ordain'd to strive,
But not attain perfection.—
Dost thou too weep? transcendent, loveliest maid?—
Pardon a heart o'ercharg'd with swelling grief,
That in thy presence will not be exiled,
Tho' every joy dwells round thee.

CRISTINA. O GUSTAVUS!
A bosom pure like thine must soon regain

The heart-felt happineſs that dwells with virtue;
And Heaven on all exterior circumſtance
Shall pour the balm of peace, ſhall pay thee back
The bliſs of nations; breathing on thy head
The ſweets that live within the prayers of foes
Subdued unto thy merits—O farewell!

GUST. Thou ſhalt not part, CRISTINA.

CRISTINA. O—I muſt—

GUST. No, thou art all that's left to ſweeten life,
And reconcile the wearied to the world.

CRISTINA. It will not be—I dare not hear—

GUST. You muſt.
I am thy ſuppliant in my turn—but O
My ſuit is more, much more than life or empire,
Than man can merit, or worlds give without thee.

CRISTINA. Now aid me, aid me all ye chaſter powers
That guard a woman's weakneſs!—It is reſolv'd—
Thy own example charms thy ſuit to ſilence.
Nor think alone to bear the palm of virtue,
Thou, who haſt taught the world, when duty calls,
To throw the bar of every wiſh behind them!
Exalted in that thought, like thee I riſe,
While every leſſening paſſion ſinks beneath me.
Adieu, adieu, moſt honoured, firſt of men!
I go, I part, I fly, but to deſerve thee.

GUST. Yet ſtay—a moment—till my uttering heart
Pour forth in love, in wonder pour before thee.
Thou cruel excellence—would'ſt thou too leave me?

Not if the heart, the arms of thy GUSTAVUS
Have force to hold thee.
CRISTINA. O delightful notes!—
That I do love thee, yes, 'tis true, my lord:
The bond of virtue, friendſhip's ſacred tie,
The lover's pains, and all the ſiſter's fondneſs,
Mine has the flame of every love within it.
But I have a father—guilty if he be,
Yet is he old; if cruel, yet a father.
Abandon'd now by every ſupple wretch
That fed his years with flattery, I am all
That's left to calm, to ſooth his troubled ſoul,
To penitence, to virtue; and perhaps
Reſtore the better empire o'er his mind,
True ſeat of all dominion—Yet, GUSTAVUS,
Yet there are mightier reaſons—O farewell!
Had I ne'er lov'd, I might have ſtaid with honour.
[Exit.

GUSTAVUS looks after CRISTINA, then turns and looks on ARVIDA—ANDERSON, ARNOLDUS, &c. advance.

AND. Behold my lord, behold the ſons of war,
Of triumph, turn'd to tears! while from that eye
All Sweden takes her fate; and ſmiles around,
Or weeps with her GUSTAVUS.
ARN. Wilt thou not cheer them, ſay thou great deliverer?
SIV. O general!
1ſt DALE. King!
2d DALE. Brother!
3d DALE. Father!
ALL. Friend!

GUST.

GUST. Come, come, my brothers all! Yes, I will ſtrive
To be the ſum of every title to ye;
And you ſhall be my ſire, my friend revived,
My ſiſter, mother, all that's kind and dear,
For ſo GUSTAVUS holds ye—O I will
Of private paſſions all my ſoul diveſt,
And take my dearer country to my breaſt;
To public good transfer each fond deſire,
And claſp my Sweden with a lover's fire:
Well pleas'd, the weight of all her burdens bear;
Diſpenſe all pleaſure, but engroſs all care:
Still quick to find, to feel my people's woes;
And wake, that millions may enjoy repoſe.

A TRAGI-COMIC

EPILOGUE,

BY WAY OF ENTERTAINMENT.

By Mr. OGLE.

Intended for Mr. WRIGHT, Mrs. GIFFARD, and Mrs. CLIVE.

Mr. WRIGHT.

WELL, ladies, to the court your plea submit,
Box, upper-region, gallery, and pit.
Our poet trembling for his first essay,
Fear'd to dismiss you, tho' you saved his play.
Cried NELL (in pity for the bashful rogue)
" Give them a joke—a joke was once in vogue!
" Thus authors used, in less judicious times,
" When merry epilogues were thought no crimes.
" That (said CRISTINA) would his ruin crown;
" Nothing, but virtue, takes this virtuous town.
" No! let his epilogue be clean and chaste:
" This, is the sense, of every man of taste!"—
High rose the conflict in our room of state,
Where tragic kings and queens maintain debate.
When, lo! we heard " your powers begin to rise,"

Whose

Whose horrid cat-call is our worst excise!
Our inmost palace felt the loud dissention;
Where each new tragedy's a new convention.
Whence we determined without further pother,
To give you, of the one, and of the other.

Mrs. GIFFARD.

Our author, on the brave, and chaste, relies;
He thinks, the virtuous are the only wise.
And, if his muse, with voice exalted, sings,
Of camps, and courts; of ministers, and kings;
Yet, be not, to the great, his rules confined!
His moral is, a lesson to mankind.
If virtue beauteous, vice deformed he draws;
You, that applaud him, sound your own applause.
Where vice distaste, where virtue gives delight,
Alike, who judge, or paint, are just and right.
Virtue, like vice, escapes the public eye,
In humble life; yet, blazes in the high.
Hence, tragedy, that owns no vulgar flight,
Shines, with the king, in a mild sphere of light;
Or vagrant, with the tyrant, strains to run,
A burning comet! not a cheering sun!
That worth is worth, be by GUSTAVUS known;
More glorious in a mine, than on a throne!
And, for CRISTINA, might I hope a smile,
Less great was she, in empire, than exile!
Some worth, it shows, to aim at worthy praise.—
Then, wither not the plant, that you may raise!
Crush not his youth. No!—give him age to spread!
For, we have heard you rumbling o'er his head.
Fell a few flashes, with portentous blaze,

To blaſt the ambitious branches of his bays?
Yet, if ſoft ſorrows ſtream'd from virtuous eyes,
If roſe from generous breaſts regaling ſighs:
Refreſhed by the attack, the laurel ſtands,
And dares the loudeſt thunder—of your hands.

Mrs. Clive.

Great, the deſign! I grant—the moral, good!
But, ('tis my weakneſs) I am fleſh, and blood.
What virgin, here, ſo tender, and ſo kind,
Would not, her love, with her own hands, unbind?
Preliminaries ſettle in the dark?
And, tho' ſhe loſt her father, fix her ſpark?
Or, when ſhe bade the attendant, "Save him! fly!"
Would ſhe not ſend, a billet, by-the-by?
Not article?—'Tis nonſenſe to ſay, Not!
Had ſhe no feel, no gueſs, of what-is-what?
At her expence, the great Gustavus ſhines;
My lover, he!—I'd ſend him to his mines.—
Arvida falls!—Gustavus wails his end!
And many a ſpouſe careſſes ſuch a friend.
Well, let him wail his death; then, riſe to life;
Claſp the fond maid, too ſtrict to be his wife!
He held her, in his camp; might hold, alone:
Compulſion ſome humanity had ſhown.
Thy countrymen—will damn thee—thy third day—
This, is not, ſure, the true Hibernian way?
But, I forgive him—he's a young beginner!
Not quite a proſtitute! and yet, a ſinner!
Forward, to pleaſe! yet aukward, to delight!
He wants a kindly hand to guide him right!

A novice

A novice yet—inſtruct him—he will mend—
Full many a widow wiſhes ſuch a friend!
Even married dames, may think, a greater curſe
The ſlow performer, that grows worſe-and-worſe!
This, with a bluſh, I ſay, behind my fan—
Cheriſh the boy, you'll raiſe him to a man!

Mr. Wright.

The cauſe is heard.—Ye gentle, and ye brave,
'Tis yours to damn him—But, you join to ſave—
Then, hail Gustavus, who his country freed!
Ye ſons of Britain, praiſe the glorious Swede!
Who, bravely raiſed, and generouſly releas'd,
From blood-ſtain'd tyrant, and perfidious prieſt,
The ſtate and church, expiring at a breath!
Who held a life of ſlavery, worſe than death!
Reform'd religion! re-eſtabliſh'd law!
—And, that you dare to praiſe him, hail Nassau!*—

* The Deliverer of our Country.

THE

EARL of ESSEX;

A

TRAGEDY:

AS IT WAS ACTED AT THE

THEATRE-ROYAL IN DRURY-LANE.

PROLOGUE.

Spoken by Mr. SHERIDAN.

WHENE'ER the brave, the generous, and the juſt,
Whene'er the patriot ſinks to ſilent duſt,
The tragic muſe attends the mournful hearſe,
And pays her tribute of immortal verſe.
Inſpired by noble deeds, ſhe ſeeks the plain,
In honour's cauſe where mighty chiefs are ſlain;
And bathes with tears the ſod that wraps the dead,
And bids the turf lie lightly on his head.

Nor thus content, ſhe opens death's cold womb,
And burſts the cearments of the awful tomb
To caſt him up again—to bid him live,
And to the ſcene his form and preſſure give.

Thus once famed Eſſex at her voice appears,
Emerging from the ſacred duſt of years.

Nor deem it much, that we retrace to night,
A tale to which you have liſtened with delight.
How oft of yore, to learned Athens' eyes,
Did new Electras and new Phædras riſe?
In France, how many Theban monarchs groan
For Laius' blood, and inceſt not their own?
When there new Iphigenias heave the ſigh,
Freſh drops of pity guſh from every eye:

On the ſame theme tho' rival wits appear,
The heart ſtill finds the ſympathetic tear.

If there ſoft pity pours her plenteous ſtore,
For fabled kings and empires now no more;
Much more ſhould you—from freedom's glorious plan,
Who ſtill inherit all the rights of man—
Much more ſhould you with kindred ſorrows glow
For your own chiefs, your own domeſtic woe;
Much more a Britiſh ſtory ſhould impart
The warmeſt feelings to each Britiſh heart.

R 2

Dramatis Perſonæ.

Essex,	Mr. SHERIDAN.
Southampton,	Mr. HOLLAND.
Cecil,	Mr. DAVIES.
Raleigh,	Mr. PACKER.
Lieutenant of the Tower,	Mr. ACKMAN.
Queen Elizabeth,	Mrs. PRITCHARD.
Counteſs of Rutland,	Miſs MOWAT.
Counteſs of Nottingham,	Mrs. KENNEDY.

Guards, Attendants, &c.

THE

EARL of ESSEX.

ACT I. SCENE I.

NOTTINGHAM enters, CECIL following.

NOTT. LEAVE me—Away!—
CECIL. I cannot; no—thoſe ſtarts,
Thoſe deep fetch'd ſighs, theſe changes of complexion,
Muſt have a cauſe.
NOTT. How dared you to intrude?
'Twas poor, 'twas little in you, thus to lurk,
To watch and ſteal upon my hour of weakneſs.
CECIL. But as the kind phyſician, who attends
To learn the malady of ſome loved patient,
'Ere he adventures to preſcribe the cure,
And bring the healing draught, the balm of friendſhip.
NOTT. Friendſhip from man?—Perdition on the ſex!
Fathers, and brothers, huſbands, lovers, all,
Serve but to double or repeat our chains,
And give a long variety of tyrants.

May every evil, every pang they bring
To the fond hearts of weak defenceless woman,
Return in tenfold mischiefs on their heads!

CECIL. Are none exempt? Can charity involve
The harmless with the guilty, undistinguished?
Shall he, who longs to do and suffer greatly,
To save the dear loved object from affliction,
Be as the cruel wretch who caused her pain?

NOTT. O CECIL!—if, indeed, you ever loved;
If you have felt the stings of slighted passion,
Of heart-torn hope, and raging disappointment;
You then will cast a kindred eye of pity
On the most lost, the most undone of women.
ESSEX!——

CECIL. Ha! what of ESSEX?—

NOTT. Read that letter——

CECIL. From him?

NOTT. The traitor!—Read, and then revenge!
Yet stay—the scroll that would reveal my shame,
And his unworthy triumph—thus I tear,
Thus rend and scatter in ten thousand pieces.

CECIL. And could the brave, the gentle, gallant ESSEX,
ESSEX, whose name was fondly tied to praise,
For whom the female eye look'd out, who taught
Their tongues inquiry, and their ears attention—
Could he be this barbarian?

NOTT. I could tell you,
Did shame not shut up utterance—But, in vain,
I send my eyes around, to find a friend;
Some arm of kind support, whereon to rest
The weight of sorrow, and the lapse of weakness.

CECIL. And can you be to ſeek, while CECIL ſtands
With offer'd powers, all open to receive you?
CECIL, whoſe ſtrong and ſelf-ſupported flame,
Hath braved the laſting froſt of cold indifference?
Who loves a length beyond the rate of man,
Since never woman, like his NOTTINGHAM,
Was fair, or found deſerving?

NOTT. O, my friend!—
If I have ſeem'd or diſtant, or averſe
To your great merit and your kind regard,
Think of the cauſe—he claims your full reſentment—
The cruel!—the ungrateful!—he, alone,
Engroſs'd me from the world. I had no ſenſe,
Thought, ſight, or ſoul, but for the barbarous ESSEX.
Nor did he then appear quite blind to charms
Like mine, however mean—his tongue was needleſs;
Each action ſpoke; and, as his eyes met mine,
Or mine were fondly prone to be deceiv'd,
Or love was all their language.—Soon to Ireland
His high commiſſion bore him—Torn, diſtracted,
Rack'd by a conflict of oppoſing paſſions,
Strong love at length prevail'd—Hear it not, CECIL,
What thought would hide—where memory recoils,
And ſcarce believes itſelf—I ſent this man—
O, death to modeſty!—this frozen ESSEX—
Pity and pardon, CECIL—I did ſend him

My vows, myſelf, my ſoul, a willing ſlave,
In a fond letter.
  CECIL. That, indeed, did merit
A fair return, at leaſt.
  NOTT. A fair return?—
The proud, inhuman, the inſulting villain!—
O for a breath that would at diſtance blaſt him!—
Fair anſwer, ſaidſt thou? No—by all the powers
Of ſhame and rage, that work in ſlighted woman,
——a rude repulſe!
  CECIL. And ſhall bright NOTTINGHAM,
Who leads the ſtarry train of Britain's beauties,
And finds no peer; ſhall ſhe have lived to this—
To ſue and be refuſed?
  NOTT. Confuſion, tortures!—
Be quick, my vengeance! Rage will ſtrangle, elſe,
The birth of its own purpoſe.
  CECIL. Then, mayhap,
You love him leſs.
  NOTT. Love, CECIL!—ſaidſt thou, love?
Hate, hate—within it labours, fell and deadly!
O, all the milk, the kindly flow of love,
Runs with envenomed poiſon through my veins;
And, like the baſiliſk, my baleful eyes
Could ſhoot immediate death, and kill with gazing.
  CECIL. Know, then, the guardians of your injured beauties,
Whiſper'd, ere this, to my prophetic ſoul,
The vengeance due; and high as ESSEX ſits,
The love and glory of admiring England,

He

He waits but for your voice to doom his fall,
Then ſinks to quick perdition.

NOTT. Down with him,
From his proud zenith to the unbottom'd deep,
Although the gorge of his wide opening gulph
Should ſwallow me and all!—If CECIL bids,
Fate ſigns the mandate; CECIL's breath alone,
Informs our councils, and arrays our armies,
Fills out the wide expanſe of Britain's ſails,
And ſteers her veſſels proudly through the world.

CECIL. Praiſe from that mouth, is high reward!
—What more?
What may he hope, who vindicates your charms,
And ſlakes your thirſting ſoul with glorious vengeance.

NOTT. That ſoul and body too.

CECIL. A bargain ſeal'd.
The QUEEN prepares for council; wait her preſence,
And you ſhall hear of miſchief, ſuch as minds
That ſoar uncommon flights, alone can reliſh.

NOTT. I go, I fly—O be the moments ſhort
Till vengeance come to eaſe my tortured ſoul!
[Exit NOTT.

SCENE II.

CECIL alone.

CECIL. The fate of ESSEX leaves my road high paved
To love, as to ambition—What, although
Both objects be enforced: Reluctance gives
Impatient

Impatient bliſs, and heightens each enjoyment.
SOUTHAMPTON here!—the ſecond man on earth
Who ſtirs my fear; and, therefore, claims my hatred.
A ſtately branch he is, ingrafted firm
On the proud ſtem of our aſpiring ESSEX—
But hew the hoſtile trunk, and every bough
Partakes the kindred ruin.

SCENE III.

Enters SOUTHAMPTON.

Fair morning wait upon the brave SOUTHAMPTON!
SOUTH. Not ſo, my lord; there hangs a cloud upon it,
Pregnant with poiſonous vapours, as they ſay,
Exhaled from CECIL's breath, to blaſt the land,
And nip her brighteſt bloſſoms.
CECIL. Good, my lord,
Is myſtery the mode? What means your lordſhip?
SOUTH. No myſtery to CECIL's conſcious ſpirit.
'Tis rumour'd, that ſome dark malignant faction
Has leagued with hell, in plotting an impeachment
Of the moſt loyal heart that England holds,
Our great, our glorious ESSEX.
CECIL. I have heard
Of this ſome whiſpers; but, for me, my lord,
I hold his nature to be noble, valiant,
And rich in all the fair demands of honour—
SOUTH. And, therefore, with an eye of wan regard,
Look envious up, and ſicken at the glory.

CECIL.

CECIL. I grieve not at the merits of your friend,
Nor wiſh to ſhare his guilt.
SOUTH. Guilt!—ſaid you, guilt?
Come, ſhew this monſter of your own creation—
The phantom that ſtate wizards conjure up,
Amid the depth of their nocturnal councils,
To make their power look dreadful o'er the land,
And ſcare our Britons from the ſide of virtue.
CECIL. My lord, your zeal for this unhappy man,
Has cloſed your eyes to what a nation ſees
With clear unſway'd diſcernment—his ambition;
His late cabal with rebels; and the ſtorm,
Brew'd and concerted with his Iriſh colleagues,
To wreck the veſſel of his country's peace.
SOUTH. Rather concerted in the cabinet
Where ſpurious treaſons are begot, and taught
To call ſome pre-appointed victim father,
As ſtateſman pleaſe to bid, whene'er they find
Talents to croſs, or virtue to offend them.
CECIL. Be witneſs for me, that I urge you not
To this raſh mood; but rather warn SOUTHAMPTON,
To bear himſelf aloof, ſedate and ſeparate,
Leſt he be held a partner in that guilt
His advocation warrants.
SOUTH. Patience, Heaven!
Shall inſolence, unpuniſh'd, thus preſume
To ſtain the viſage of untainted loyalty?
We had a CECIL once—O, thou degenerate
From thy fair ſire! quite alien, ſoul and body!
Dare you proclaim a hunting through the land,
And point out worth and honour for the quarry?
Baſe politician!—By the ſacred name

That

That warms a Briton's breaſt, by liberty!
There's not a peaſant in the train of Essex,
But holds a fund of golden honeſty,
Beyond what Cecil and his cloſe cabal
With all their worth can weigh—thoſe bearded dons,
Who ſit, like midnight hags, within their conclave,
Muttering dire bans, to wither all the land,
And blaſt the bloom of every envied virtue.

Cecil. Thanks, gentle lord.—O, you oppreſs my modeſty
With this exceſs of praiſe!—from any other,
'Twould look like adulation. Fare you well—
And if you are a friend to bold Southampton,
Bid him not croſs the way that Cecil walks,
Or look to fall with Essex.

SCENE IV.

Southampton alone.

South. Fall with Essex!
Stateſman, 'tis falſe, he ſits above your ſoaring!—
But ſee, ſhe comes, the guardian of his honours;
The virgin ſtar, that lights up liberty,
And beams out true religion to the world!
She comes, the glory of each newborn day;
And the dark foes of virtue and her Essex,
Retire like miſts before her.

SCENE

SCENE V.

Enter QUEEN, NOTTINGHAM, RUTLAND, CECIL, LORDS, and ATTENDANTS.

The QUEEN aſcends a Chair of State.

QUEEN. From Spain, my lords, have ye had tidings lately,
By any private letters, that import
Their new deſigns?

CECIL. Not any, royal madam.

QUEEN. 'Twas rumour'd, ſome time ſince, that they intended
A ſecond viſit, with a new Armada;
But the laſt pacquet from our agent there,
Speaks no ſuch purpoſe.

CECIL. No, my glorious miſtreſs,
They're ſick—war-ſurfeited: they yet do pant
From the ſore memory of their laſt encounter.
Sooner the bulk of the retreating bear,
Scarce ſcaped the fangs of the imperial lion,
Again would riſque his mangled corps in fight,
And take his lordly conqueror by the beard,
Than Spain return on Britain.

SOUTH. While time ſhall travel down, from age to age,
Leading white handed Faith and Liberty
To nations yet unborn; oft ſhall they turn,
And, through paſt worlds, roll back their grateful eye
On your diſtinguiſh'd day—wherein the powers

Of

Of darkneſs were confederate, when Rome
Roſe up, with all her champions, to impoſe
Chains on the limbs, and night upon the mind.
Then had the worlds of freedom and of truth,
Return'd to chaos, if ELIZABETH,
Heaven's miniſter, had not ſent forth the ſons
Of light and order—her immortal DRAKE,
Her laurell'd ESSEX, with the all-conquering hoſt
Of free born Britons: Heaven that day avow'd
His virgin champion, and confirm'd the gift,
The eternal gift of liberty to man.

QUEEN. Yes, my all-dear, my ſtill unconquer'd people,
Ye have derived a glory on your QUEEN,
That lifts her ſex above the warring chiefs
Of Ægypt and of Macedon: they fought,
Impoſing ſlavery; we, conferring freedom.
And, O, believe me, when I ſwear I love ye,
As never monarch loved!—Now, on my ſoul,
There's not the pooreſt peaſant born in Britain,
But my fond eye beholds him as it would
A ſon or brother.

CECIL. O, you are too gracious,
Too good for this bad world! Heaven make us equal
To the leaſt part of all your wondrous bounties;
So ſhould TYRONE, and wild rebellion, ſoon
Sink in the force of Britain's loyalty,
And your firm hoſt ſtill find a faithful leader.

QUEEN. Why, CECIL, have you freſh accounts from Ireland?

CECIL.

CECIL. Nothing, my royal miſtreſs, more than uſual;
Old ills repeated.

SOUTH. Now, the ſnake begins
To wind his venom'd train. [Aſide.

QUEEN. What ills, good CECIL?

CECIL. Amazing grace!—How willingly your majeſty
Forgets the faults committed by a ſubject!

QUEEN. That ESSEX you would ſay, ſo verſed in conqueſt,
For once became remiſs, and loſt a ſeaſon—
Is not that all?

CECIL. And holds cloſe amity,
With the moſt deadly foe of queen and country,
The fierce TYRONE; confers in ſecret with him;
Parleys with traitors, and cabals with rebels,
No friend to Britain preſent; whence enſue
Scandalous truces, ſhameful to——

QUEEN. Hold, CECIL;
You grow inveterate—it is his firſt offence.
None here can boaſt perfection: ESSEX too,
Like us, good ſtateſman, may not want his failings.
I would not be extreme to condemnation.
Nor clear in his excuſe. I have, therefore, ſent him
Commands of purpoſed chiding, that enjoin
Quick reparation; and no more to bend
His brow, unlaurell'd, to the coaſt of Britain.

SCENE

SCENE VI.

Enter Sir Walter Raleigh, attended by other Members of the House of Commons.

Cecil. May it please your Majesty, your faithful Raleigh,
With others, in commission from your Commons,
Attend with their address; and some few bills,
Humbly presented for your people's safety.

Queen. Ay, that's a theme, to which my charmed ear
Could list for ever—Welcome to your queen,
To your true servant welcome! Give me to know
How I may best attain the glorious end
For which alone I wish to live; to feast
Upon that royal luxury of soul,
The peace, the weal, the bliss of my kind people.

Raleigh. Bright star of christendom! the virgin light
Which guides our steps to truth, our arms to honour!
Queen of true-hearted Britons! who do wish
The sun should be extinguish'd in his orb,
Ere you, their better glory, should decline,
And leave your realms in more lamented darkness!
Your parliament, in care of these your kingdoms,
(Who live but in your life) present three bills
With humblest suit to pass them into acts
For the dear safety of your throne and person.

Queen. Let Cecil see what they contain.

Cecil.

CECIL. The firſt
Is for eſtabliſhing a train'd militia
Thro' every ſhire; and for a further levy
Of certain horſe and foot, as a ſtrong guard
Of ſafety to our QUEEN's moſt ſacred perſon.
The ſecond, that two hundred thouſand pounds
Be rais'd in part for payment of thoſe troops,
Further to be diſpoſed of as our ſovereign
In her dear pleaſure ſhall appoint.

QUEEN. How poor
Were thanks to ſuch a people! But be ſure
For you I'll prove a thrifty uſurer;
And every talent truſted to your QUEEN,
Shall be return'd with fivefold intereſt
Of love, and due beneficence—Proceed.

CECIL. The third conſiſts of ſeveral articles
Expreſſive of your ſubjects juſt abhorrence
Of plots, and treaſonous practices—concluding
With a ſubmiſſive prayer, moſt humbly offer'd,
For the impeaching ROBERT earl of ESSEX.

QUEEN. Great power, who art the majeſty of thrones,
Support me, now! [Starts from the Throne and pauſes.
Wake me, SOUTHAMPTON! Was this thunder clap
From the dread arm that rules in earth and Heaven,
Or merely mortal daring?—Who—what am I?

CECIL. All that is bleſt, and great, and good, on earth.

RALEIGH. Our QUEEN, our royal miſtreſs.

QUEEN. It is falſe——
A waxen pageant, only ſet aloft

For mockery and moulding!—What a dream
Have I been in!—And are we thought unworthy
To be apprized, consulted?—Come, what further,
Would your despotic wills?—I'm all submission.
'Tis yours to dictate, my imperial lords—
At your command, I'll drench my innocence
In the most brave and loyal blood of England;
Tread out offensive virtue; pluck fidelity
Even from the heart of Britain!—You, my masters,
Shall rule unrivall'd then; and your ambition
Be propt by pillars, like unto yourselves—
Fools for your senate, knaves for every office,
And cowards for commanders!—O, my heart!—

SOUTH. Most horrid combination!—What shall guard
The throne or kingdom, when their fences thus
Are sapt in secret, or confessedly
Assail'd in open day? When even our ESSEX,
Who stood the bulwark of his QUEEN and country,
By whose atchievments, by whose dauntless courage,
The cowards, who impeach him, live in safety;
When he must fall, to make a public breach,
Where mask'd ambition may encroach on majesty,
And treasons gain free entrance?

QUEEN. That I have loved thee, Britain—O, how fondly!—
Too much of that—Down foolish throbbing—Had I,
Had I the spirit of my father Harry,
I had array'd my majesty in terrors,
And thence derived respect; held the rein hard,

And

And the lash active—then, ye had known your ruler!

CECIL. First, and best of monarchs!
Vex not your royal heart: not all our lives
Are worth the least emotion, that may give
Your sovereign mind disturbance.

QUEEN. O, 'tis plain,
I have reign'd too long! their hunger is variety;
They have ta'en a Jewish surfeit of their sweets,
And thence have turn'd to loathing.—It is enough—
Their pleasures be accomplish'd!—Lie thou there,

[Takes off her crown and lays it on the chair.

Thou thorny circle!—What a bustling croud
Of thankless cares, that lived in that small ring,
Are now divested!—And thou pageant scepter,
Thou banisher of truth, who dost invite
The knee of flattery, and the smile of falsehood,
Thus do I hurl thee to thy worshippers,

[Throws away the scepter, and descends.

And am myself alone.

RALEIGH. O QUEEN beloved, revered to adoration!
Lo! to the dust, beneath your dread rebuke,
All awed and humbled, your repentant subjects
Fall prostrate for forgiveness.

[RALEIGH returns the scepter.

QUEEN. Look not, then,
To take me to tame leading. I am a Briton—
Born free as well as you, and know my privilege.
Henceforward, ye shall feel that I am your QUEEN,
The guardian and protectress of my people,

And not your instrument to oppress them;
No passive engine, for cabals to ply,
Or faction to appropriate. In my name
Ye shall not lord it. I will see and hear,
Not by state organs, ear'd and spectacled
To your presentments; but with face to face,
Sovereign and subject. I will have no more
Of state worn manacles, and royal bondage;
But walk, with truth and honour, unconfined,
And found my empire in the free born mind.

[Exeunt.

END OF THE FIRST ACT.

ACT II.

SCENE I.

Countess of Rutland.

Rut. SURE love is witchcraft; and the wondrous ground,
Where lovers tread, like that of Fairy land,
Enchanted, and unknown to vulgar feet!
Love has a world, where none but lovers dwell—
New objects all; and for those objects too,
New organs well provided—hopes, and fears,
And thrillings, numberless; but, ah! its joys
Are rare, and thinly stated to the account
Of sufferance multiplied—O my loved Essex!
Short were our sweets, and stealthy; like the feast
Of midnight hunger, where the ear and eye
Are trembling centinels—Sure, never time,
Like that, was fleeting; yet, endear'd to memory,
'Tis the whole sum, that I, poor creditor,
E'er got from bliss; for, at the morning's dawn,
Ambition came, ambition, like the sun,
That goes its round, and wakes the world to war,
And snatch'd him from me, as a dream of Heaven—
Ere I could say, or sigh the thousandth part
Of all the rapturous, tender, nameless things,
With which my breast still labours.

SCENE II.

SOUTHAMPTON enters.

SOUTH. Ah, thou dear consort of my dearest friend,
Forgive my barbarous tongue its fatal tidings—
ESSEX is near, the most undone of men!
RUT. Now, by the sudden transport of my heart,
That bounds and kindles, spite of thy foreboding,
What can thy fears portend?—And does he come?
Does my lord come, indeed?
SOUTH. Too sure, too sure.
But, O, that gulphs, far sunk beneath all fathom,
And wide as ocean flows, were now betwixt you!
RUT. Be quick, and say, what ill hath chanced, what change,
Since late the QUEEN, like circling Providence,
Planted her heavenly guardianship around him?
SOUTH. His rashness has undone us—His return,
Against the appointment of his high commission,
And in the palpable and daring breach
Of the QUEEN's absolute commands, hath forfeited
All his proud titles, honours, offices—
Perhaps his precious life!
RUT. Ah—hold thee there.
Help, save, support me—'tis a gulph, my eye
Can never dare, though distant—Thought would onward
Rush headlong, and anticipate perdition.

SOUTH

SOUTH. There's yet Omnipotence in Heaven to
save him,
And mercy in the QUEEN—let hope ſtill live,
To put our means in action.

RUT. O, dear friend,
Haſte, intercept, conjure him to embark
Again for Ireland, e'er the blabbing wind
Can whiſper his arrival—Though the world,
For one loved look were ſhort and poor of purchaſe,
What's world, or looks, or I, or all, to ESSEX?

SOUTH. Alas, 'tis now too late—malicious fame
Has publiſhed his approach; within this hour,
He enters London. As I haſted hither,
I met the haughty CECIL, envious RALEIGH,
And treacherous NOTTINGHAM, in cloſe cabal:
From ear to ear death murmur'd; and, aſkance
They caſt a ſmile of ſcorn, and with their eye
Bid me defiance as I paſt.

RUT. Ah, friend!
I ſink beneath my fears, my heart dies in me.
I'll to the QUEEN this moment—fall proſtrate,
Cling to her royal feet, declare our marriage;
Weep, pray, conjure her—yet, if not for ESSEX,
Not for her RUTLAND's ſake, to ſpare him—yet,
Even for the little trembling pledge I bear him,
For whoſe moſt precious ſafety ſhe ſtands charg'd
To her whole people.

SOUTH. Stop—beware of that!
There's not another ſtep 'twixt that and ruin.
Time—prudence checks my tongue—Let it ſuffice,
All other treaſons would appear as loyalty

To that dread ſecret—that alone is wanting
To ſeal the doom of Essex—Soft—the Queen!—
Severe and ſlow ſhe comes; upon her brow,
In mute, but diſcontented characters,
I read her inward tumult.—You had beſt retire.
[Exit Rutland.

SCENE III.

Enter Queen, Cecil, Countess of Nottingham Raleigh, Attendants, and Guards.

Queen. Is Essex then return'd?
Cecil. He is.
Queen. What hither?
It is impoſſible.
Cecil. Juſt now arrived.
Queen. Arrived againſt our perſonal injunctions!
'Tis treaſon but to think it.
Cecil. Will your majeſty
Be pleaſed to ſee him?
Queen. No.
Cecil. Shall I then publiſh
Your royal will forbidding him the court?
Queen. Neither.—Know yourſelf, Cecil—
You are, ſir, but a creature call'd to council,
Not to controul or dictate:
Your time to know my pleaſure, ſubtle ſtateſman,
Is, when I ſpeak it.
South. Firſt, beſt, and brighteſt!
Regent of hearts, whoſe voluntary throne
Riſes ſupreme amid the bliſsful tracts

Of

Of liberty and reaſon! at your feet
A faithful ſubject falls.—O, royal miſtreſs!
I tremble to excuſe my valiant friend.
He may be raſh, erroneous, of a temper
Not tuned to each occaſion; for the earl
Has artful foes, who ſtudiouſly provoke
The faults for which they ambuſh: but that he
Is firm and loyal, as the pillar'd earth
Is to its baſe; that his great heart o'erflows
With fulneſs of his QUEEN, with truth and faith,
And wondrous gratitude—I would ſtake down
The worth of my eternal ſoul to warrant.

QUEEN. Still this bad world, I ſee, contains a friend; [Aſide.
And ſuch SOUTHAMPTON is,—at leaſt to ESSEX.—

CECIL. May it pleaſe your majeſty, the earl is come,
And waits your royal pleaſure.

QUEEN. ——Tell the rebel——
Yet hold—I have better thought—Yes, I will ſee him—
But it ſhall be to ſting his haughty ſoul:
Anger would give him conſequence—Contempt
Is what he leaſt can bear. Give him admittance.

SCENE

SCENE IV.

Enter Essex, with Attendants.

Essex kneels—The Queen turns from him to the Counteſs of Nottingham.

Essex. Health to the virgin majeſty of England!
Your ſervant, your true ſoldier, Queen of monarchs!
For the firſt time now trembles to approach you,
As being here in conſcious diſobedience
Of your dread orders. Yet, when I have ſhewn
That 'twas the laſt neceſſity compell'd me
(Thanks to the artful malice of my foes)
To this now ſeemingly unduteous act;
When I have ſhewn that no alternative
Was left me, but to ſeem or diſobedient,
Or bear a traitor's name; I ſhall rely
Upon your majeſty's accuſtom'd grace,
Weighing the jealous honour of the ſoldier,
To palliate, if not clear, the ſubject's fault.
—I am charg'd with guilt, with being falſe, diſloyal,
Falſe to my Queen, to England falſe—could Essex
Bear ſuch a charge, and live? No—ſwift as thought,
And bold as innocence, fearleſs of danger,
Of death—or what is worſe, his Queen's diſpleaſure—
He comes to front his foes; even to the teeth

Of

Of malice comes he, to aſſert his honour,
And claim due reparation of his wrongs.

QUEEN. CECIL, are thoſe petitions anſwer'd yet,
Which late I gave in charge?

CECIL. They are, an't pleaſe you.

ESSEX. What not a word, a look?—not one bleſt look
Of wonted influence, whoſe kindly warmth
Might chaſe theſe envious and malignant clouds,
With which your ſervant is begirt? Nay then—
My night comes on apace—I ſee—I ſee
The birds of dark and evil omen round me;
CECILS, and RALEIGHS: how they ſcent their feaſt—
Sagacious ravens, how they ſnuff from far
The promis'd carcaſs—Be it ſo—for ESSEX
Is but the creature of imperial favour,
By his QUEEN's voice exalted into greatneſs,
And by her breath reduced again to nothing.

QUEEN. Ha! that's mournful——
I muſt not liſten to that well known voice;
I feel the woman riſing in my breaſt.
—But rouſe thee, Queen of Britain, be thyſelf! [Aſide.
What, does the traitor ſtill abide our preſence?
All who have truth, or fealty to their QUEEN,
Forſake that faithleſs wretch, and follow me.

[Exeunt all but ESSEX.

SCENE

SCENE V.

ESSEX alone.

ESSEX. Ha! Is it come to this?—Not heard—
 ſcarce ſeen—
Inſulted, ſpurn'd—damnation!—O how ſoon
May fall the mightieſt!—What a ſteepy length
Ambition has to ſcale!—the toilſome way
With difficulties barr'd, beſet with dangers!
Till the proud ſummit painfully attain'd,
A fearful height we ſtand; and one ſhort ſtep
Precipitates to nothing—O, accurs'd
Is that deluded architect, who builds
Upon imperial favour! 'tis a quick-ſand
Whoſe ſudden falſehood ſhall ingulph himſelf,
With all his ſubſtance.

SCENE VI.

SOUTHAMPTON enters.

One friend yet left!
Then ESSEX ſtill is rich. [They embrace.
 SOUTH. My ſoul's elect!
Be firm, be all yourſelf—the weight impends
With inſtant preſſure. From the angry throne,
Lo CECIL comes, commiſſion'd to diſcharge
Its thunder at thy head!
 ESSEX. I ſee, my brother——
Never did that Leviathan appear,
But as the prophet of ſome coming wreck,
Foretaſting

Foretasting ill, and writhing in his nostrils
The promise of a tempest.

SCENE VII.

Enter CECIL and RALEIGH.

CECIL. Hear ye, sir,
What the unquestion'd Majesty of England,
With gentlest mercy tempering awful justice,
By us pronounces—ROBERT Earl of ESSEX,
She here divests you of your trusts, and offices;
Your dignities of governor of Ireland,
Earl marshal, master of the horse, prime general
Of all her forces both by land and sea,
And lord lieutenant of the several counties
Of Essex, Hereford, and Westmoreland.

ESSEX. Then I'm divested—Well—what more? for these
Are but the lightness of a summer's robe,
The gauds and outward trappings of her ESSEX.
What further?

CECIL. ——That you instantly depart
The court, and stir no further than your house,
Without an order from the QUEEN and council.
And lastly, 'tis her pleasure, that you send
Your staff by us.

ESSEX. Ha! that indeed requires
Some pause——

CECIL. What say you? What may we return
In answer to her Majesty?

ESSEX.

ESSEX. But wilt thou—
Wilt thou be ſure expreſsly to deliver
What ESSEX gives in charge?

CECIL. I will, moſt truly.

ESSEX. Then tell her, treaſon never harbour'd yet
In bold blunt truths, or openeſs of action:
It ſeeks cloſe covert in the ſmiles of courts,
Fleers in the cringe, and ſkulks behind the vizard.
Tell her—my honeſt CECIL!—tell thy miſtreſs,
That treaſon is a ſtateſman, near her throne,
Who holds his QUEEN beſieged, and calls it guardianſhip;
Who ſeals the imperial ſenſe; cuts the dear ties
'Twixt ſovereign and ſubject; fills her church
With proſelytes to vice; and ſets corruption
Aloft, even on the ſeats of injured juſtice:
For guilt ſeeks fellowſhip and league with guilt,
And vice ſupports his kindred.

CECIL. All this I ſhall remember.

SOUTH. ——Tell her too,
That while ſhe ſlumber'd, that arch felon, CECIL,
Scaled her high ſeat, and ſeiz'd the reins of empire;
Thence bids the dews deſcend, and thunders roll,
To his direction; ſheds her bounties down
Where his vile minions for vile ends may proſper;
But ever plants the bolt, and deadly blaſt,
Where worth or wiſdom flouriſh—Wretched Britons!
Is there a patriot, is there yet a man,
Whoſe blood, whoſe toils, whoſe virtues have acquired
Aught to his country's ſervice—'tis a crime

Set down for capital; a barbed mote,
Fretting the eye of envy, and of CECIL.
But O! the brave, the valiant never ſcape him,
For cowards ſtill are cruel.

CECIL. Well obſerv'd—
This I ſhall tell, and that SOUTHAMPTON ſaid it.

RALEIGH. My lords, in ſpeaking thus, you tax her Majeſty
Of weakneſs, and injuſtice both.

ESSEX. I care not——
Suggeſt whate'er your malice may deviſe,
'Tis equal all to ESSEX.

CECIL. May we then
Preſume your anſwer ſumm'd in this?

ESSEX. You may.

CECIL. You'll not return your ſtaff by us.

ESSEX. I will not.
From my QUEEN's hand did I receive that ſtaff,
Nor will I yield it back to any other.

CECIL. Fare ye well, lords——

[Exeunt CECIL and RALEIGH.

SCENE VIII.

ESSEX and SOUTHAMPTON.

ESSEX. O, my SOUTHAMPTON, thou, who to thy ESSEX,
Art now the world's whole wealth, his laſt of merchandize,
Dearer than all that's loſt—fly to the QUEEN,
Entreat, implore, but for a moment's audience,
For one bleſt ſight—'tis all her ſervant ſues for.
Tell her, this ſtar, theſe glories, wherewithal

She

She once adorn'd the bridegroom of her favour;
This ſword, with which ſhe graced her ſoldier's hand,
And wiſh'd him Cæſar's fortune; this proud ſtaff,
That triumph'd in a hundred victories;
All her bright virgin honours, yet untainted,
I will reſign, with humble adoration,
As pilgrims lay their reliques at the ſhrines
Of ſaints they went a thouſand leagues to worſhip.

SOUTH. I fly, my lord, and doubt not yet to gain
An interview—O! may its end be proſperous.
[Exit.

SCENE IX.

ESSEX alone.

ESSEX. Where now is ESSEX? Where the late rebuke
Of nations hoſtile to the peace of Britain,
Who ſpread their lands with rout, their ſeas with terror?——
Diminiſh'd—ſhrunk—as tho' he had never triumph'd;
As tho' he ne'er had conquer'd for his country!
O hard earn'd glory! long wrought pile of greatneſs!
Are your enchanted works no more than ſo,
A word, and vaniſh?—Now, where are they now,
The ruſhing mob, the ſhouting multitude,
The ſweeping levee, and the bending circle?
All fled, all mute, and loneſome now around me!

As

As tho' I walk'd o'er graves and charnel ground;
As tho' I carried famine in one hand,
And pestilence in t'other.

SCENE X.

Enter RUTLAND.

RUT. My ESSEX!
ESSEX. RUTLAND! O, my better angel!
How has thy presence fill'd this solitude;
And like a beam from heaven dispers'd the gloom
That overspread my soul!
RUT. I could not bear
To think you were so near me, and not rush
To snatch one look—But I must haste—
ESSEX. Fear nothing.
RUT. We shall be seen.
ESSEX. No eye is bent this way,
No footstep turn'd; for a discarded favourite,
Shun'd like the plague, makes every place a desert.
RUT. May I then look? indulge my longing eyes?—
I cannot speak to thee, my heart's too full.
ESSEX! you turn away.
ESSEX. Alas, my love,
What object now is ESSEX for thy eyes?
Stripp'd of his honours, all his glories wither'd,
A bare and sightless trunk!
RUT. O ESSEX, ESSEX!
Can'st thou then think so meanly of thy RUTLAND,
As to believe the gaudy pageantry,

The trappings of ambition, ever made thee
More lovely in her ſight? No, ESSEX, no,
I loved thee for thyſelf. Thy pompous titles,
Thy ſplendid dignities, commands in war,
I look'd upon as my worſt enemies,
Which interpoſed, and held me from my lord.
Are they remov'd? then there's no obſtacle
Between his RUTLAND, and her ſoul's elect;
And thus ſhe claims him, thus ſhe folds him in,
From war, and from ambition, cruel rivals!
For all ſhe wedded, all ſhe ever wiſh'd,
Her wealth, her every want, her world is here,
And ſcorns addition.

ESSEX. Heaven make me worthy
Of ſo much tenderneſs!—Yes, I have run
Where e'er ambition led; but 'twas in hopes
To raiſe my love as high above her ſex
In dignity, as ſhe tranſcends in merit:
Elſe I had never barter'd one bleſt hour
Of thy ſociety for what the world,
Thro' a proud life of conqueſt and dominion,
Could yield in abſence.

RUT. And will you then
No longer liſten to deluſive fame?
No more be guided by the witching fires
Of wandering glory? Homeward wilt thou turn,
Where love, and RUTLAND, have prepared the ſeat
Of humble rapture, and of inward peace;
A little empire of ſerene delights,
Of guardian virtues, and obſervant ſmiles,
All ready, waiting for their lord's arrival?

ESSEX. O, my fantaſtick folly, that could liſten
To the enchantments of that ſyren fame!
But now the ſpell is ended—never more
Shall vain ambition tempt me to forego
My ſoul's ſubſtantial bliſs. Adieu falſe ſplendours!
My reſt is fix'd even here—We'll find ſome ſpot
Secluded from the world, like that fair garden,
Where firſt the princely parent of mankind,
Bleſt in his conſort's ſweet ſociety,
Wiſh'd for no other pleaſure: there we'll live,
Far from the haunts of men, from vice, and folly;
Reign in each other's hearts with mutual ſway,
The nobleſt royalty! Be love our treaſure,
We ſhall be wondrous rich!—love our ambition,
And who exalted like us?

RUT. O my ESSEX!
What a new paradiſe were there! to know
No pangs of parting; ſee thee every day,
And ſometimes all the day—Sweet holiday!
Peace round my pillow; and my morning ſun
Cheer'd by thy preſence; and thine eyes to ſpeak
Love's language; and thy ſmiles to interfuſe
The ſwell of cordial joy—O, my loved ESSEX,
That life indeed were bleſt!—Ha! who comes here?

ESSEX. Be not alarm'd my love, it is my friend.

SCENE XI.

Enter SOUTHAMPTON.

Well, my SOUTHAMPTON——
SOUTH. Heavens, what madneſs this!
Should any eye behold you—And the QUEEN
Has juſt enquired for you—Fly with ſpeed.
RUT. Alas! from what a happy dream of heaven,
Haſt thou awaked me!—What is human bliſs?
A moment's meeting, a long age of abſence!
One rich and precious drop of cordial joy,
Drench'd in a current of inſipid time,
Or deep affliction.
ESSEX. Light, and life of ESSEX,
From thee be evil far!—We ſoon ſhall meet,
To part no more.
RUT. Farewel—Remember, RUTLAND
Knows not one happy hour, when thou art from her.
[Exit RUTLAND.
SOUTH. The QUEEN to my importunate request
Has granted you a hearing; be prepared:
You muſt command your temper; for believe me
'Tis on the warmth of that, the generous warmth,
(Which ſtill accompanies the nobleſt natures)
Your foes rely, to fire the ſubtle train,
Which they have laid to blaſt your hopes for ever.
ESSEX. Well, I will try—altho' 'tis wondrous hard
Calmly to bear th' envenom'd ſhafts of malice,
And poiſonous tooth of foul mouth'd calumny!
Yet

Yet I will try—Be truth my only weapon,
Patience my ſhield! But no diſſimulation
Shall, with its baſe alloy, bring down the ore,
The pure rich ore, of which the noble mind
By nature's hand is form'd, below truth's ſtandard.
No, let me periſh, e're one grain of falſehood
Infect and leaven that integrity
Of ſoul, in which man's dignity conſiſts.
Had I the choice to make, I ſwear by heaven,
I ſhould eſteem it far more eligible,
To fall with honour, than to riſe by baſeneſs.

[Exeunt.

END OF THE SECOND ACT.

ACT III.

SCENE I.

Enter CECIL and NOTTINGHAM.

CECIL. NO more, bright NOTTINGHAM!—we ſtrive in vain—
ESSEX can only be ſubdued by ESSEX;
He ſtands impregnable to all beſide:
And if his native pride, and proper paſſions,
Serve not to pull his own deſtruction on him,
He bids for perpetuity in favour.

NOTT. The QUEEN, I fear, has motives for her favour,
Which queens may feel, but not avow. Unmark'd
Within this hour I ſtole upon her privacy:
Her brow was ſunk from royalty; and ſad
And deſolate her aſpect, as of one
Betroth'd to lonelineſs; in whom the pride
Of power, and beauty, was no more remember'd.
I liſten'd—But her broken accents ſpoke
A voice ſuppreſt by grief; while down her cheek
Stole the pale tear, which ever as ſhe wiped,
A piteous heir ſucceeded.

CECIL.

CECIL. I perceive
She is much moved of late, and prone to ſtarts
Of ſudden paſſion, even beyond her temper.

NOTT. How did ſhe brook the haughty earl's reply
To her laſt meſſage?

CECIL. Never did I ſee her
So ſtung, ſo thoroughly enkindled—Straight
She iſſued haſty orders for impeachment;
When in the very ſtroke of inſtant fate,
SOUTHAMPTON came, and with a ſubtle tale
Calm'd all her rage. And now is ESSEX ſent for,
To plead to what SOUTHAMPTON boldly ſtiles
The gall of falſe accuſers.

NOTT. Curs'd be his tongue!
For then the ground we have gain'd will all be loſt.

CECIL. I ſee the QUEEN but ſeeks ſome thin pretext
To cover inclination; ſome ſmooth terms
Of ſoft ſubmiſſion, or acknowledg'd error,
To reinſtate this minion of her fancy
In wonted height of arrogance.—But ſee
Her cloſet opens—Let us not appear
To pry on her retirement.

NOTT. You withdraw;
I'll wait within her call. [Exit CECIL.

SCENE II.

Enter QUEEN.

QUEEN. The proud, inſenſible, ungrateful wretch!
Falſe to his loving QUEEN, his friend, his patron!

Falſe to his—Hold thee there, for I will tear him
From my fond boſom, tho' the vital drops
Of my ſad heart ſhould follow.—Queen of Britain
To what art thou reduced? with not one friend;
Forlorn, and deſolate, amidſt a people,
Whom as a parent bird, with hovering wings
Thy daily love has gathered in from danger,
And foſter'd with thy life—Ha! Nottingham!
I thought I had been alone.—
  Nott. Pardon a duty
Perhaps too forward—Ah, my royal miſtreſs!
All is not well—Upon my knees I beg—
Somewhat hangs heavy on your mind, or haply
Your precious health's in danger.
  Queen. Riſe, my Nottingham—
I am in health, and thank thy tenderneſs;
Only a little troubled that my people
Grow weary of my love—I have reign'd long.
Such is the nature of inconſtant man,
The pureſt ore of happineſs below,
Without variety, will loſe its value;
Whilſt novelty can give the vileſt droſs
Both ſtamp and currency. Prithee, my friend,
What ſay the people to this haughty man,
And his late conduct?
  Nott. Pleaſe your Majeſty,
They ſeem to blame him highly.
  Queen. Blame him, ſay'ſt thou?
  Nott. Indeed it was not well.
  Queen. Not well—The traitor!
And is that all? Come, come, ſpeak plainly to me.
Is it thus tamely that my ſubjects ſee

This

This daring insult to my crown? Or warm'd
With duteous zeal, and loyal indignation,
Vent freely their reproaches?
NOTT. Thus commanded,
I shall without disguise speak what I have heard
Of this imperious soldier.
QUEEN. Aye, pray do—
Be plain—What says the world of me, and ESSEX?
NOTT. Of you they never speak, but in a prayer
Of due thanksgiving, and of wishes breathed
As incense up to Heaven, for length of life,
And days of happy omen.
QUEEN. Well, proceed—
Of ESSEX then?—
NOTT. Of him they utter terms
Of due reproach, and plenteous imprecation;
His popularity, they give to pride,
That cringes to be courted; his beneficence,
To niggard bribes for flattery; his high courage,
To bear-like brutal rashness; his atchievements,
To a mean fondness for th' applause of fame:
And all his acts stiled patriot, all his labours,
His risques, his wounds, his conquests for his country;
To close and treacherous plottings on her rights,
And sacred liberties.—For he's ambitious,
Dark, dreadful, and aspiring, as the fiend
Who first raised war in heaven, and tumbling thence
Unpeopled Paradise; and so they wish
The fall of ESSEX may be quick, and——
QUEEN. Hold——
The curse of everlasting silence on thee!—

In

In thee 'tis base, 'tis barbarous insolence,
To echo thus the vileness of the rabble.
Unhappy Essex! truly hast thou serv'd
A false base world, and now hast none to friend,
Save her thou hast offended.

Nott. Please your Majesty
Your own express command—

Queen. Away, away——
Thou see'st thy Queen, misfortune, and the world,
All bent against one man; and yet can'st find,
Within that ruthless and obdurate breast,
No room for pity.

Nott. Madam, I hope—

Queen. Well, well, no more of it—
'Tis past, and I forgive—Send Rutland hither.

[Exit Nottingham.

What has my passion done?—Perhaps unfolded
The very secret it attempts to cover;
What I would hide from thought.—Why stands my soul
Upon the watch to listen and enquire
Tidings, which most it dreads to learn, the faults
And errors of my Essex? Why, my heart,
Why art thou prone to utter terms of blame
Against the cruel troubler of thy quiet?
Yet can'st not bear the slightest censure drop'd
From any other tongue; as tho' all crimes
Against myself were light, and what is spoke
Against my Essex, stood alone for treason.

SCENE

SCENE III.

Enter RUTLAND.

My RUTLAND, I did ſend for thee my girl.
I have obſerv'd that thou art ſad of late:
Why are thy lovely eyes depreſs'd with ſorrow?
Can I do aught that may diſpel the cloud,
That envious cloud, which hangs upon thy beauties,
And robs me of my friend?

RUT. Ah, QUEEN of grace,
And heavenly goodneſs! you oppreſs your ſervant,
With this exceſs of condeſcenſion.

QUEEN. Why——
I love thee well, my RUTLAND, well, and warmly;
Truſt me I do.—Injurious NOTTINGHAM
Hath held diſpleaſing di ſputation with me,
Touching my lord of ESSEX; inſomuch
That I did ſend her from my ſight in anger.

RUT. Ha! that dear name ſtarts every pulſe within me! [Aſide.

QUEEN. Thou bluſheſt, RUTLAND.

RUT. At the wondrous grace,
The wondrous goodneſs of my QUEEN.

QUEEN. Indeed
Thou'rt of a grateful nature, ever ſweet,
And kindly temper'd. Come then to my boſom,
And ſhare its warmeſt love.—Tell me, my RUTland,
Is it not pity that ſo brave a man,
So form'd for gallant acts, and upright honour,
That ESSEX ſhould be falſe, ſhould prove a traitor?

And

And goaded by ambition, ſhould attempt
The ſceptre of his QUEEN; to whom he owes
A countleſs debt of favours; by whom raiſed
Beyond a ſubject's ſtate, he proudly now
Would graſp the crown, which ſeems within his reach.

RUT. It cannot be, it is impoſſible;
The ſoul of ESSEX is above ſuch baſeneſs,
Such black ingratitude. Ah! royal miſtreſs!
Had you but heard him, on the breath of praiſe
Lift up the exalted name of England's QUEEN,
As I have often heard him!—

QUEEN. Say'ſt thou, RUTLAND—
Haſt thou heard ESSEX talk of me?

RUT. Of you?
He owns no other theme. In courts, I grant,
He is no minion, but a ſoldier bold,
And jealous of his honour: but, when his ſpeech
Is free to ears of honeſty and friendſhip,
'Tis then he vents his ſwell of gratitude,
And tunes his voice to loyalty and love.
Your acts, your laws, your virtues, and your beauties,
Your every excellence of mind and perſon,
Vary his numbers thro' a ceaſeleſs round
Of untired praiſe; and all is of his miſtreſs,
And all of England's virgin majeſty,
And all is full of you.

QUEEN. Indeed, my RUTLAND,
I would fain hope that ESSEX ſtill is honeſt:
But then he's ſo ungovern'd, raſh, and headſtrong,
Nor law, nor duty hold him. I do fear,

I greatly

I greatly fear, with ſafety to my fame,
I may no more protect him.

RUT. Not protect him!—
By the bright ſtar of mercy in your ſoul,
That ſhines on the diſtreſt—O ſay you not
That he is honeſt?—Yes, he ſtill is loyal,
Faithful, and firm: the virgin light of heaven
E're yet it mingles with our groſſer elements,
Is not more pure. O will you not remember
His worth, his truth, his toils, and his atchievements?
A wondrous ſtory all! high deeds of fame
That gird the crown of England's QUEEN with glory.
His valour too! his valour, royal madam!
It foils the heroes of romance: a name
So formidable to the foes of Britain,
It ſpares our Engliſh hoſt, and of itſelf
Diſcomfits armies.

QUEEN. ——Ha! this heat is more
Than friendſhip's warmth; 'tis from a ſtronger fire—
She loves him—Aye, 'tis ſo—And is herſelf
Too lovely!—Wretched chance!—What have I done?
Juſt conjured up a ſecond ſtorm to wreck me.
Leave me.— [Exit RUTLAND.

SCENE

SCENE IV.

Enter CECIL, RALEIGH, NOTTINGHAM, &c.

CECIL. May it pleaſe your Majeſty, my lord of ESSEX,
Return'd by your command, entreats admittance.

QUEEN. Let him appear.
Now QUEEN of Britain, now ſupport thy ſtate!
Now guard thy treacherous heart, but for this once,
Againſt its dear, its inſolent controuler,
And fear no future foe—Come hither, NOTTINGHAM.

SCENE V.

Enter ESSEX, and SOUTHAMPTON.

ESSEX. Before I plead my cauſe, permit me thus,
Moſt gracious miſtreſs, thus, in due proſtration,
To pay my grateful thanks, for this laſt favour
In granting me a hearing; that once ended,
To my QUEEN's juſtice I ſubmit my life,
And what is dearer to me far, my honour:
Implicitly to your tribunal bow,
Humbly prepared, and equally reſigned
To either ſentence.

QUEEN. My lords, what ſuppliant's this?—Can this be he,
Our late imperious ſubject? He, who holds
A ſtaff of independence, and a ſtate

That

That ſcorns to yield to our ſupremacy?
O, theſe are gallant acts; and well become
The boaſted name of our all conquering ESSEX!
Who bravely turns his courage on his QUEEN;
But where his duty calls him to the combat,
Can coolly condeſcend to terms of peace,
And gentle treaty.
ESSEX. Is it come to this?
To be a term of ridicule, and mockery,
Where moſt I would be prized? caſt by my QUEEN
To public ſcorn, and mean contempt?—Then ESSEX,
Then art thou fallen indeed!—Why this, my miſtreſs?
Are there not chains, and dungeons; blocks, and axes?
Theſe had been fitter inſtruments of royalty,
And done a nobler juſtice on your ſoldier—
I think your Majeſty was pleas'd to ſpeak
Touching ſome treaty, as a charge againſt me
Of ſomething criminal—
QUEEN. Yes, with Tyrone,
Your parley, and your truce—Diſcharge thoſe ſtains,
Your covert articles with England's rebels.
ESSEX. Alas, how ſoon pretences may be found
To make the envy'd fall—Of treaty?—Yes—
I do avow it. Am not I your general,
Impower'd for war, for peace, to treat, to fight,
Levy, diſband, to puniſh, and to pardon?

QUEEN.

QUEEN. And ſhould the mighty ESSEX have confined
Theſe powers to peace alone, even when rebellion
Led forth his hoſts, and dared him to the combat?
Whilſt he——

ESSEX. Shrunk like a coward—Is't not ſo?—Ha! madam?
ESSEX, and cowardice!—let thoſe ſtand forth
Who dared to match them—Aſk your miniſters,
Why they witheld my army from the north,
By keeping back my due recruits and ſubſidies.

QUEEN. You grow too bold—You are call'd here to plead,
Not to impeach—Your army was ſufficient.

ESSEX. No, royal madam, it was not ſufficient
To war with Heaven, to fight againſt Omnipotence!
It was conſumed with fevers, and diſeaſes;
For ESSEX could have fear'd no other foe.
There's not a caſuiſt in Rome's artful ſchool,
Or CECIL's darker council, who can mark
The ſlighteſt lapſe of duty in your ſervant;
And ſhall he not retaliate? ſhall he not
Unwind the ſubtle clue, which leads his QUEEN
To cruel ſarcaſm, and unjuſt reſentment?

QUEEN. Unjuſt, and cruel! hold—no more, I charge you!

ESSEX. Not ſpeak, not ſpeak!—Madam, I am your ſubject;
The world contains not one more duteous; yet
Here I muſt not be ſilent—Thoughts to ſlaves,
But ſpeech to Britons!—Yes I will aſſert it,

The freedom of my native land, tho' death
Did croſs me to the teeth—A criminal debar'd
His privilege to plead! 'tis evident
My life's conſpired, my glories all traduced;
Theſe boſom'd ſnakes, and ear-informing ſycophants
Gape for my plenteous heirſhip; even my QUEEN
Foredooms her ſubject, and gives up her ſoldier
A ſacrifice to faction.

QUEEN. O, he'll be loſt!—undo himſelf, and me!— [Aſide.
What, I conſpire, traduce, foredoom thy ſentence?
Know, thou proud wretch, thou haſt no other friend:
Thou who art ſo obſervant! who didſt ſpurn
My orders, letters, meſſages!—But, ſoft;
Beware how thou doſt ſhake my wrongs too much,
Leſt they fall thick and heavy on thy head,
Raſh fool, and undiſcerning!—Yet thus far
I do forgive thee; pardon thee that life,
I did conſpire—But for thy offices——

ESSEX. I throw them at your feet—and proud indeed
To be acquitted of all debt to majeſty!
Now give them up to cowards, courtiers, paraſites;
And dub them champions, in whoſe doughty guardianſhip
Your ESSEX can't be miſs'd; whilſt he is baniſh'd,
And bears no mark of royal gratitude,
But wounds for toils, for dangers ignominy,
And ſufferings for allegiance; haply ſent
To deſerts, or to herd with ſavages—
There he may find more equity and honour,
Than in the faith of princes.

South. My lord, my lord!
Recall your temper.

Queen. The audacious traitor!

Essex. Ha, traitor!—Yes, becauſe I fenced your throne,
This breaſt its bulwark againſt all invaders;
For covering England with my ſpreading laurels,
Whilſt your ſafe ſubjects ſlept beneath the ſhade;
For humbling Spain, your proud, and dreaded rival,
And wafting all their India to your Thames;
For building up the fame of England's Queen
So high, it flames a beacon to the world.
Said I, your fame? Your life—your life—kind miſtreſs!
For ſaving that, and cutting bold Northumberland,
And hoſtile Westmoreland, ſhort by the head:
This did the faithleſs, and degraded Essex—
But I'll remove the traitor from your ſight.

Queen. Hold, ſir,—Go not without reward— [Strikes him.

Essex. Furies!—From whom? [Half draws his ſword.
My Queen!—Arreſt my arm, kind Heaven!

Queen. What, would the wretch attempt my life?

Essex. —Raſh woman!
Were you a man, you durſt not—your hot father,
Bold Harry, durſt not riſque it.—What talk I
Of Harries? not young Ammon, at whoſe nod
The ſervile earth fell proſtrate, had ſurvived.
To boaſt this deſperate deed.

Queen.

QUEEN. May the mark ſtick like Cain's, for thy rebellion!
Thou madding wretch, untamed, and dangerous ever,
I give thee up—I will no more, againſt
Thy own outrageous folly, ſtrive to ſave thee.
Like thy laſt hopes, I leave thee to the ſtings
Of guilt and deſperation—now caſt forth,
Unpitied and unbleſt of earth, and heaven,
And thy too partial QUEEN! [Exeunt.

SCENE VI.

ESSEX and SOUTHAMPTON.

SOUTH. What have you done? ruin'd yourſelf and friends
By your high carriage.—Fly, my lord, yet fly,
Follow the QUEEN, intreat, implore her pardon.

ESSEX. Away—The ſpot of infamy is on me!—
The blow has fired my ſoul; and all within,
Is deafening uproar—Never 'till this hour
Was ESSEX fit for treaſons, cruel joys,
And glutting horrors!—Get thee hence, SOUTHAMPTON,
For I'm the tumbling of a thouſand towers,
Ruins that threaten far, involving all
Who ſap, or prop, within the like perdition.

SOUTH. I fear no ruin, when my friend's in danger.
If thou muſt fall, thou ſhalt not fall alone:
SOUTHAMPTON never will forſake his ESSEX,

But ſhare his adverſe, as his proſperous fortune.
Away then, let us fly this dangerous place.

ESSEX. Aye, there thou ſay'ſt, my friend—avoid all courts,
The bane of native dignity and greatneſs!
But ſhall it be?—ſhall drones and waſps alone
Devour the treaſured ſweets of all the land,
And drive the bees from their long-labour'd manſion?
No—let us purge, or overturn the hive—
There yet is feeling, yet is fire in England!—
I'll to the ſtreets, the city, wake, alarm,
And kindle every ſpark of ſlumbering virtue:
Rouze every Briton to his country's call,
And in her freedom ſtand, or periſh in her fall.

[Exeunt.

END OF THE THIRD ACT.

ACT IV.

SCENE I.

Enter ſeverally CECIL and NOTTINGHAM.

NOTT. HA! CECIL—well—and is he, is he taken?

CECIL. Joy! joy! my NOTTINGHAM—he's ſunk for ever,
Caught in the very act of broad rebellion:
ESSEX is fallen, no more to riſe. No more
Shall politicians ſet the gins of ſtate,
Or nets of circumvention; for the lion,
In his blind rage, has ruſh'd upon the toil,
Where he may roar, and tear, and gnaſh in vain,
But never ſhall get free,

NOTT. O, it o'erjoys me,
Feeds the keen hunger of my vengeful ſoul,
To ſee this pride, this inſolence of manhood,
This ſcorner, hurl'd from his once dazzling height!
To ſee him drop with all his train of glory,
And vaniſh in the duſt!—Ha! CECIL.

CECIL. Hold!
The QUEEN,—if poſſible reſtrain your tranſport.

SCENE II.

Enter QUEEN and Attendants.

QUEEN. What is he crush'd? this trampler on authority!
The lofty one!—And is he fall'n?

CECIL. He is——
Thanks to the sacred power who guards your majesty!

QUEEN. Then he is humbled at the last—This proud one!
The manner of it Cecil?

CECIL. When the earl
Withdrew from court, all mad, and chafed with passion,
He hurried to his house; and severally
Summon'd the friends in whom he most confided.
A numerous band they were of lawless spirits,
Whose joy is riot, and whose hopes take fire
From the wild spark of dazzling novelty,
And gainful revolution. In their council
It was resolved, SOUTHAMPTON should attend
To form the numbers who were yet expected;
While the arch rebel march'd, as he did boast,
To raise the city.

QUEEN. What, my faithful citizens!
Could he hope that?

CECIL. He did; and as he past,
The vulgar, ever eager of events,
Pour'd in from every side, and swell'd the concourse,

To

To right, to left, he bended; and as one
Train'd to the Areopagus of old,
Or Rome's prevailing roſtrum, with ſmooth act
Of mute emotion, thro' the diſtant eye,
He ſought to reach the heart. To all around,
His voice now ſunk, now rais'd to exclamation,
Appealing to the wiſdom of the mob,
Againſt ſtate policy. Much did he talk
Of crowns begirt with evil counſellors;
Of truſt miſplaced—good monarchs, but miſled
By wicked miniſters—Stale topics all!
Yet theſe will gloſs and colour every cauſe,
While man ſhall kick at government—He then
Deſcended to himſelf; ſpoke piteouſly
Of ſuffering virtue; number'd o'er his wrongs,
And counted every ſcar; the time, the place,
The peril too of each; all borne, he ſaid,
For them, and for their children: then he wept;
And they wept too, ſoft ſouls! as tho' each gaſh
Had bled anew.

QUEEN. Alas! I wonder not—
That ſight had melted even his QUEEN to pity.
[Aſide.
Proceed——

CECIL. The earl perceiving in their eye
The work of paſſion, ſtraight he cry'd—Arm, arm,
For truth, for liberty! Arm ye, my friends!
Off with your galling riders! down oppreſſion!
If not for ESSEX—for yourſelves, your ſons,
Your lateſt iſſue! What are you to feel,
If me they ſpare not? what muſt 'fall the fold,
When their great guardian's murder'd?—Here he paus'd:

But none replied; for tho' his mournful ſtory
Had fill'd their hearts with ſorrow, yet the cloſe
Bore ſuch a frightful face of dangerous treaſon,
That terror ſoon ſucceeded—One ſlunk off,
Another follow'd; 'till, all ſoft and ſilent,
Like ſnow they melted from his ſide.

QUEEN. How then?
How look'd the rebel left alone?

CECIL. At once
Fear, guilt, and diſappointment, ruſh'd upon him,
Amazed he haſten'd where his barge attended,
And reach'd his houſe by water, at the time
When your brave troops had forced the outward gate,
And made SOUTHAMPTON and his faction priſoners.
Then might you ſee the indignant rebel caſt
A look of deſperation at high heaven,
As one renouncing hope: forth flew his ſword
As he would ruſh on death; but ſore begirt,
At length he yielded to ignoble hands,
And cloſed the tale of ESSEX.

QUEEN. I once hoped
His morning ſun, that brightned as he roſe,
Might alſo ſet with equal rays of honour.
Where is the earl?

CECIL. Under a ſufficient guard,
In order for his ſending to the Tower.

QUEEN. Ha! order'd to the Tower—whoſe orders, ſir?

CECIL. Madam, the earls are yet without.

QUEEN. 'Tis well——
To priſon with SOUTHAMPTON—But for ESSEX,

I'll

I'll ſee him e'er he goes. Let all withdraw,
And leave the priſoner here with me,
Unguarded. [Exeunt all but the QUEEN.
Heavens! what a ſcene is this?
How ſhall I bear it? Be compoſed, my heart!—
Can that be ESSEX?—the diſtreſt, the fallen,
The forlorn ESSEX!—What a ſtate he bears!
Still undiminiſh'd, ſtill himſelf—Away
With pomp, and borrow'd luſtre then; true greatneſs
Can build a ſeat of lovelier majeſty,
With ESSEX and misfortune.

SCENE III.

Enter ESSEX.

ESSEX, it is not thus we ſhould have met—
You ought to know it is not—I did hope—
But 'tis no matter—You may ſpeak, my lord,
If you have aught to offer.

ESSEX. Nothing, madam.

QUEEN. 'Tis well—And yet, perhaps, 'twere better, ſir,
You'd think again—Our meetings mayn't be frequent.

ESSEX. It might have been your Majeſty's good pleaſure,
To ſpare even this—I ſought it not.

QUEEN. I know it,
Ungrateful man! I know it—But I hold
No longer parley with thee—It is finiſh'd—

Thou

Thou everlasting troubler of my quiet,
Soon, soon we shall be both at peace.

Essex. Enough——
I have my death, and you your wish—

Queen. I, Essex!
I wish thy death? You know—But let me calmly
Demand of thee, what was it that could tempt thee,
To court, invite, and pull down on thine head
A ruin so reluctant? To o'erbear
All law, all order?

Essex. Is that yet to learn?
Tho' every packet brought me fresh advices
Of the malicious plottings of my foes;
Yet I could o'erlook that—secure in innocence,
Could wait my time—but when I found my Queen
Had listen'd to their tales, under her hand
Confirm'd; and felt that doubts and jealousies
Were deeply rooted—I no longer paused—
Law, order, even your own injunctions then
Were but as chaff before the wind. I flew
To see with my own eyes if it were true,
That I had lost your favour—That once gone,
The animating soul of all my hopes,
The end of all my thoughts, and all my actions;
The world had nothing in it worth my care,
And life or death were equally indifferent.

Queen. Was that the motive? Why was not I inform'd?

Essex. Inform'd!—which way? Was I once heard, regarded?—
When prostrate I implored my Queen to hear me,
Was she not cold as thawless ice, and deaf

As

As ears of adamant?—Rejected, ſpurn'd,
Caſt to the ravening jaws of my purſuers,
Like the lone pard, I was at length compell'd
To turn upon my hunters. But had Essex,
Had Essex been the traitor he is deem'd,
He had not ſingly faced a hoſt of foes,
But led up troops, inured to victory
Beneath his banner, to a man prepared
To fight, or fall for Essex.

Queen. There is ſome weight
In that; and I would fain believe your motive
Was ſuch as you declare—Yet, Essex, Essex!—
O thy raſh pride!—if thou had'ſt condeſcended
But to the light appearance of reproof
From thy kind Queen———

Essex. Appearance, madam?

Queen. Yes———.
And when I would have colour'd to the world
Subſtantial favour with a ſhew of chiding—

Essex. A ſhow of chiding!—O my gracious miſtreſs,
Did you not hate me? Did you not, indeed,
Abhor, deteſt your ſoldier?

Queen. No—too well,
Too well I loved thee, proud, unbending man!—
Could I have hated thee, I had been happy.

Essex. Ha! Lightning blaſt me firſt! my Queen in tears!

Queen. Away, thou hot, thou undiſcerning Essex!
Could'ſt thou not truſt a friendſhip, that had ſtood
Firm as the irrevocable doom of fate,

Againſt

Againſt thy enemies? their daily murmurs,
All their loud plaints, petitions, and impeachments,
Daſh'd back with indignation on the front
Of thy accuſers—might not ſuch a friend
Expect ſome ſmall conceſſion? Did'ſt thou grant it?
Did'ſt thou not ſtand in haughty oppoſition;
Fly to the city, levy cruel war
Againſt thy QUEEN, againſt thy kind protector?
Who could almoſt have pray'd for thy ſucceſs,
Altho' her crown, altho' her life, perhaps,
Had been the barbarous forfeit.

ESSEX. O my miſtreſs!
You have undone me—Your o'erpowering goodneſs
Has cruſh'd my heart—I ſee my folly now,
My crime broad ſtaring in my face—O wretch,
Blind wretch!—Yet let me not be charged
Beyond my proper guilt—the weight of that
Alone will overwhelm me. It was pride,
Unparallel'd preſumption, arrogance
Beyond example—But your crown!—your life!
To attempt thoſe—O no—in all the wilds
Of frenzy, ſuch a thought could never enter
This loyal boſom.

QUEEN. Fain would I believe——

ESSEX. Believe!—Ah, royal madam, can you doubt it?
By the dread ſecrets of that unknown world,
To which your ſervant haſtens, no—his thoughts
Ne'er aim'd at ſuch damnation—Then—even then,
When I did think your hatred of your ESSEX
Roſe to a hoſtile loathing—I had then

Laid

Laid down my life, to purchase to my QUEEN
Access of days and honour.

QUEEN. O! no more,
No more, my soldier—I have been to blame.
We both have err'd, mistaking each the other.
Fatal mistake! how can it be repair'd?
What's to be done?—

ESSEX. Nothing for me—my frenzy
Has borne me far beyond the bounds, beyond
The reach of mercy: I must die——
Your fame, your peace, your future welfare, all
Demand this sacrifice, and I will go
A willing victim; 'tis the only way
To expiate my crime. Yet ere I fall
Thus on my knee let me implore—

QUEEN. Rise Essex,
I cannot see you thus.

ESSEX. Permit me, madam!—
The hour's at hand, when all you see of ESSEX,
Shall be restored to dust—say, my blest mistress,
Say, if my blood may wash my stains away?
Will you then drop your heavenly pardon down
Upon the guilt and folly of your ESSEX?
And, when forgot by others, may he hope
To find some place within his QUEEN's remembrance?

QUEEN. I cannot speak to this—down swelling heart!—
May Heaven bestow, on both, a pardon free
And full, as that which now I grant to thee.
Can ESSEX too forgive his QUEEN the blow,
Her rashness gave him?

ESSEX.

Essex. 'Tis too much!—too much,
This condeſcenſion!—'tis a cruel goodneſs,
It pierces to my ſoul.

Queen. Our time is ſhort——
Soon will the lords, your judges, be aſſembled
For life, or death—You ſtand upon the brink!
I fear—and would do much—'Tis true my fame
Is dear—the pleaſure of my people too,
'Tis peril unto both—Yet Essex—yet—
I cannot ſee thee loſt—Here is my gage—
Take it; and with it take my royal word,
That whenſoever you return this ring,
Whate'er be your requeſt, it ſhall be granted,
To my crown's value.

Essex. On my knee I take it——
A radiant token, like the ſhowery bow,
When firſt the patriarch hail'd it in the heavens;
Bleſt envoy of divinity appeaſed,
And grace to wayward man!

Queen. Farewell!—Who waits?

SCENE IV.

Enter Lieutenant of the Tower.

There take your priſoner hence, and guard him ſafe,
Until his hour of trial.

[Exeunt Essex and Lieutenant.

Now I feel
My heart more eaſy—all may yet be well.

SCENE V.

Enter RUTLAND and Ladies.

RUT. Where is my QUEEN?—Where is my royal miſtreſs?
Yet hold—recall your ſentence—At your feet
I throw myſelf for mercy, mercy!

QUEEN. Ha!—What do'ſt thou mean?

RUT. O! never will I riſe,
But here take root, the very plant of ſorrow,
'Till you will hear, and grant; 'till I've implored,
Obtain'd my full petition.

QUEEN. This is frenzy!
Thou do'ſt amaze me RUTLAND—Riſe.

RUT. No, no.
Thus will I kneel, and weep, and hold for ever;
Cling to your feet, incumber all your ſteps,
For pity—'till you do relent—for pardon!
Pity, and pardon!—

QUEEN. Quick, declare your meaning.

RUT. I fear—and yet I muſt—The worſt is ſilence—
Will you then promiſe?—will you then prepare?—
It is a ſtory that may ſtart your patience.
My lord—your ſervant—your ill fated ſoldier—
Your ESSEX—ſave him—ſave him!

QUEEN. Ha! what ſaid'ſt thou?—
O my prophetic ſoul!—Is't thy concern?
How? Wherefore?

RUT.

RUT. Save him!
Save my lost lord—your ESSEX—save his life,
And save the life of RUTLAND—O! he is—
He is—my husband——

QUEEN. ——Heavens! thy husband?

RUT. Yes——
A dear, a fatal truth it is—I see it,
By the dread spark that quickens in your eye—
We were in secret married, a short while
Before my hapless lord set out for Ireland,
On his last expedition.

QUEEN. Serpents! vipers!
My curse it is to bosom such alone!
And all my fosterings, all my nourishments,
Are paid me back in poison—Married!-married!—
Then thou art wedded to thy death.

RUT. My death!
Alas! that's nothing; would my death appease
you—
His life is all I ask—O royal madam!
You cannot know—you never had a husband—
You cannot feel how dreadful are the terrors,
The agonizing pangs of a fond wife,
Who fears to lose the husband of her heart,
Her first, her only love!

QUEEN. O! I am rack'd!—
Off, off, I say, with those detested hands!

RUT. I will not, cannot—Ere you cast me from
you,
Think, feel, how I am torn—My throbbing heart,
My frantic pulses, how they start, and beat,

To break their limits—My affrighted infant
Who knows no guilt, yet trembles at your fury,
And ſtarts, as conſcious of his father's danger.

QUEEN. Quick, tear her from me—Drag her from my ſight—

RUT. O if you are woman, born of woman—firſt
Say but that he ſhall live—Shall he not live?
My love, my ESSEX, my life's lord.

QUEEN. Why am not I obey'd?—Hence—Tear her hence—

RUT. O, theſe inhuman creatures!—I am too weak,—
My laſt of ſtrength forſakes me, and I ſink
Into deſpair's deep gulph.

QUEEN. Be that thy portion!
May comfort never find thee! May thy offspring,
If it ſhould ſee the light, prove a freſh ſource
Of torment to thee!—May we never meet!
Be our appointments wide as pole from pole,
Nor let that hated aſpect ſhock me more!

[Exit QUEEN.

RUT. Yet ſtay, O ſtay, and RUTLAND ſhall aſſiſt
To frame new curſes on herſelf—She's gone—
His doom is ſeal'd—He dies—Then welcome all,
The blackeſt plagues, that ever clung to miſery!
May woes on woes be heap'd, 'till the full meaſure
O'erwhelm my ſoul, and cruſh me into reſt. [Exit.

END OF THE FOURTH ACT.

ACT V.

SCENE, The Tower.

CECIL, and LIEUTENANT of the TOWER.

CECIL. IF you regard your present place, or hope
For any future favour, to a moment you will
Observe my orders.

LIEUT. Most religiously.

SCENE II.

Enter NOTTINGHAM.

NOTT. Sir, by her Majesty's command, I bring
A message to my lord of ESSEX.

LIEUT. Madam,
I shall acquaint my lord.

CECIL. How's this, my NOTTINGHAM?—
To ESSEX from the QUEEN, and you the messenger?—
Is she not yet resolved?

NOTT. Not fix'd a moment.
First when she heard the traitor was condemn'd,
She started, and her colour turn'd to milk:

Then

Then blushing, scarlet deep, she strove to hide
Her inward tumult; thank'd the lords his judges,
And bade that execution should be speedy.
But, pausing said, upon a further thought,
She'd wait to hear if yet the criminal
Had aught to offer—Then retired, and past
An hour in private—Sent in haste for me;
Bid me draw near, look'd wistfully upon me,
And will'd me to convey her last of messages,
To ruin'd Essex—Let him know, said she,
I can no longer bar the pressing claims
Of justice on him—Yet if he has reasons
That are of weight to stay his execution,
Let him deliver them by you—Then blush'd;
Breathed a short sigh, and pressing close my hand,
Enjoin'd me to be secret, and return,
With speed and privacy, whatever Essex
Should give in answer.

Cecil. Ha! this covert message,
I like it not—Would heaven the deed were done!
Aye then—but now 'tis doubtful working all,
And curs'd suspension.

Nott. Cecil, do not fear,
But I shall render a well-pleasing issue
Of this same interview with my beloved!

Cecil. There rests my hope: state policy already
Hath spent its shafts, and waits the master stroke
From your superior genius. I will hence
With Raleigh to the Queen, and strive to fix
Her wavering mind. [Exit Cecil.

NOTT. Come now revenge, sole good
Of slighted woman!—come, and steel my breast
Against all sense of pity, or remorse!

SCENE III.

Enter ESSEX.

ESSEX. Fair visitant, to whom may ESSEX stand
Indebted for this grace?
NOTT. Chiefly, my lord,
To the QUEEN's majesty; and some small matter
To one, who, loving well, tho' most unhappily,
Has not yet learn'd entirely to erase
The fond impression.
ESSEX. Your reproof is gentle—
Were RUTLAND to be born, I must admit
All hearts had then been NOTTINGHAM's.
NOTT. Your pardon——
No more of hearts, I pray—but for your friendship,
I will dispute it even with her who claims
Possession of your love—The QUEEN, my lord,
Commends the value of her pity to you;
And kindly asks if you have aught to offer
In mitigation of your sentence?
ESSEX. Nothing.
NOTT. Some light exception, touching law, or form—
Apparent malice in the prosecution—
Error of judgment—but the slightest hinge,
Whereon to hang her mercy.

ESSEX. Not the ſlighteſt—
Tell her, moſt fair and charitable meſſenger,
My courſe of trial has been free and equal;
I ſtand ſelf-cenſured in my guiltineſs:
And mercy—what in mercy may enſue—
Is all her own, unpleaded.

NOTT. How, my lord,
No more than ſo? this cannot, muſt not be.
The appointed time is on you; this ſhort hour
May ſeal your doom—O let me beg, implore you,
As if for my own life, to uſe the means
Are left you to preſerve yourſelf, your friend—
Say, have you not a further plea?—You heſitate—
A further cauſe for hope?—You have, I know it—
Intruſt me with it; by yon heaven I ſwear,
I will not leave the QUEEN 'till ſhe has granted
My utmoſt wiſh.

ESSEX. I have not merited
This kind concern; but yet your generous warmth
Demands my confidence. Behold this ſignet!
It is a taliſman, and bears a charm,
By royal breath infuſed, of power to ſave
Even from the jaws of death.

NOTT. O let me catch it,
That I may fly——

ESSEX. Hold, generous fair one! firſt
Hear my requeſt—Preſent this to the QUEEN
From dying ESSEX—Say, her dying ESSEX
Adjures her by the virtue of this ring,
To ſave his friend, to ſpare SOUTHAMPTON's life,
And he ſhall fall content.

NOTT. O ſtint not thus
The royal bounty—do not circumſcribe
The bounds of mercy—By the ſame requeſt,
By the ſame breath, a life more precious far
May be preſerv'd—it muſt—it ſhall.

ESSEX I dare not
Urge ſuch a ſuit—Yet if my gracious miſtreſs
Still thinks me worth preſerving, I am not
So weary of the world, but I would take
The boon with grateful heart, and live to thank her.
But O, be ſure you urge my other ſuit;
Save my SOUTHAMPTON'S life, let him not fall
A victim to my crimes—alas! he knows
No guilt, but friendſhip. So may conſcious peace
Sweeten your days, and brighten your laſt moments.

[Exit ESSEX.

NOTT. Now he is mine—at leaſt in death my own,
For ever ſeal'd—tho' not for love's light rapture,
For hatred, full as joyous—deeper far,
And more enduring! Now to take him ſudden,
When the full tide, returning fraught with hope,
Lifts him elate—to plunge him down at once,
To the eternal bottom!—This, aye this
Alone can ſatiate—'tis the luxury
Of eager-eyed revenge. The QUEEN—no matter—
I am prepared—Be but my vengeance ſafe,
And for the reſt, events are equal all.

SCENE

SCENE IV.

Enter the QUEEN.

QUEEN. Well, my dear NOTTINGHAM, haſt ſeen the earl?

NOTT. Madam, I have.

QUEEN. I could not be at peace within my palace,
For crowds that urged petitions in his favour.
Well, and what paſt?

NOTT. Madam——

QUEEN. Say——

NOTT. I wiſh——

QUEEN. Madam—I wiſh—What mean'ſt thou?

NOTT. I wiſh your majeſty had ſpared your ſervant
This ſingle office.

QUEEN. Why?——

NOTT. I had not been
The unwelcome bearer of ungrateful tidings.

QUEEN. Inform me quick—ungrateful tidings ſay'ſt thou?

NOTT. O, on my knees I beg, my royal miſtreſs,
You will enquire no further.

QUEEN. Thou doſt amaze me!

NOTT. You lately held me for an enemy
To this brave man, and ſtill may think me apt
To miſinterpret——

QUEEN. No, I will believe thee.

NOTT. He's here at hand—Your majeſty in perſon
May now inform yourſelf——

QUEEN. No more, I charge you——
Be full, and ſpeedy—Give me up the whole
Of what has paſt.

NOTT. I muſt obey you then——
And yet I fear—When firſt the earl appear'd,
He wore a kind of haughty diſcontent,
That ſeem'd to mock misfortune; ſcarce he deign'd
To note that I was preſent.

QUEEN. What, ſo high?

NOTT. Yet not ungraceful. Greatly I deplored
The precipice to which miſdeeming error,
Or accident had led him—bid him yet
Not to deſpond—for much was in the power
Of royal pity—Then I minded him
Of your paſt favours—all his honours, offices,
Your late ſupport againſt his powerful foes,
And this laſt act of your divine compaſſion,
That would not let him finally be loſt,
But ſent your ſpecial ſervant to ſuggeſt
The means of ſafety to him.

QUEEN. Then he did melt.

NOTT. Let me ſtop here—for ſure ſuch height of pride,
In one of leſs exalted qualities,
Were not to be endured—Still as I ſpoke,
He look'd, and moved, and turn'd, and changed impatient.
Favours! he cry'd, what favours? poſts of danger,
And

And empty titles for eſſential ſervice!
Yes—ſhe has well avow'd her grace to Essex,
In all her public ſcoffs, and open inſults,
Laid as a ſubtle train to fire my temper
To acts obnoxious to the law; and then
Her jury of pack'd peers, and this ſmooth meſſage
To lull me to the laſt.

Queen. Hold, Nottingham——
O, he's the moſt accurs'd for deep ingratitude,
That e'er proved falſe to friendſhip—Tell me Nottingham—
I can no longer wait the tedious preface—
Say, did he claim no mercy at our hands?

Nott. Not any, madam.

Queen. Spoke he of no pledge?
No obligation that I had to ſave him?

Nott. No, on my honour.

Queen. By thy hopes of mercy,
Anſwer as at the laſt tremendous bar—
No pledge, no token?—ſent he not a ring?
Look at me, and reply—did he not ſend
A ring in anſwer?

Nott. You amaze me, madam!
I am quite to ſeek in this—What ring? what token!—
Had you but told me, had your majeſty
Once hinted ſuch a thing, I had required it.

Queen. O, I am choak'd! he pulls his own deſtruction
In his blind fury on himſelf.

Nott. Alas,

Tokens

Tokens of mercy! he disclaim'd the offer:
He said, he would no more of royal mercy—
Such as was shewn to RUTLAND, to his wife;
As tho' the British breed of noble bloods
Were slaves for pride to spurn!

QUEEN. No more, no more——
I am all on fire—This fever of the blood,
It thirsts to death!—Who waits?

SCENE V.

Enter CECIL and RALEIGH.

My lords,
See speedy execution done on ESSEX—
I have determined not to quit the Tower,
While he is master of his head—Lord CECIL,
Do you and RALEIGH see it done.

[Exeunt QUEEN and NOTTINGHAM.

RALEIGH. Think you, my lord, how long a woman's will,
Altho' the first, and firmest of her sex,
May hold its purpose?

CECIL. If a favourite point,
Mayhap, an hour or so; therefore the half
Shall now suffice us, RALEIGH—Who attends?

SCENE

SCENE VI.

Enter an OFFICER.

Bid the lieutenant have his prisoners ready.

[Exit OFFICER.

Now we may hope for sunny days in England,
When this all-covering cloud is overpast;
Whose greatness did imbibe the beams of majesty,
Nor suffer'd aught to pass but by transmission
Thro' its own radiant skirts.

SCENE VII.

Enter LIEUTENANT of the TOWER, with ESSEX and SOUTHAMPTON guarded.

CECIL. My lord of ESSEX,
We bring an order for your execution.
I have a christian's hope you stand prepared;
For even a portion of the present hour
Must be your last of life.

ESSEX. Ha! short indeed,
For infinite intendments!—'Tis thy will
O Heaven! collect me to it: give me strength
To face this king of terrors—fill my breast
With hope, and purest faith, that on the block
I may lie down, as on the plaintless bed
Of sleeping infancy.—Thanks, gracious Heaven!
I feel my granted prayer; and a new vigour
Springs in my breast!—I now can smile at death.

But

But O, my friend!—no pardon yet arrived!—
Can the QUEEN falsify her word?
  SOUTH. Come, ESSEX——
Let us now leave a lesson to our foes,
How men should die.
  ESSEX. Were I alone to suffer,
I think I should not give them cause to scorn me.
But O! 'tis here——
A weight of lead on my aspiring spirit,
That I have rent the virtues of SOUTHAMPTON
Untimely from the world.
  SOUTH. Be witness, Heaven!
The dearest wish SOUTHAMPTON's soul could form,
Would be to live for ever with his ESSEX;
The next, thus join'd, to lie in death together.

SCENE VIII.

Enter LIEUTENANT of the TOWER.

  LIEUT. My lord SOUTHAMPTON,
I have a message for your private ear.
  SOUTH. Speak out, nor fear to wound me with the tidings:
The worst is death, and that is past already.
  LIEUT. My lord, I must entreat you will withdraw—
Something of moment from her majesty.
[Exeunt SOUTHAMPTON and LIEUTENANT.
  ESSEX. CECIL, when you approach an hour like this,
You then may learn how low ambition is;

How

How groundleſs is the quarrel, which contends
For this vain world—'Till then—'till then and
ever,
The foes of Essex have free pardon. Ha!

SCENE IX.

Enter Southampton and Lieutenant.

What new diſtreſs? what can this mean? In tears!
Nay then the ſtroke muſt be ſevere indeed,
That ſhocks the manly firmneſs of thy ſoul.
O that the bitter cup were all my own!
What is it, ſay?

South. It is—it is—O miſery!
'Tis torture—'tis the death contrived by tyrants;
It is the ſpinning of life's lingering thread
To agony unſpeakable; it is
The death of friendſhip, the attempt to rend
The eternal bonds of ſoul and ſoul aſunder!
The Queen hath ſent me——

Essex. Warrant of death.

South. No, worſe——

Essex. Can there be worſe?

South. Yes—pardon!

Essex. Catch the ſound,
Ye choiring angels! and with hovering wings
Of ever wakeful 'tendance guard my Queen,
Whoſe mercy at an hour like this has ſpared
The guilt, the life of Essex, in his friend.

South. No, no, my brother,
We will not part—Southampton does diſclaim

Her

Her barbarous mercy—What a joyleſs wild
This world would be without thee! Where, alas,
Where ſhould I find the boſom to partake
And double every joy? Where ſhould I find
The tender ſympathizing heart, to feel
And lighten every woe? No more the tongue
Of friendſhip, ſweeteſt muſic to the ear!
Shall greet my deſert ſenſe: no more my hours
In ſocial raptures ſteal away unmark'd;
Thoſe bleſſed hours when ſoul with ſoul converſes,
Tranſparent, pure, as from their bodies freed.
O Essex, think upon the early ties
That in our tender years join'd our fond hearts;
Think how they grew, how they were twined together;
And ſhall they now be parted?—No, my Essex,
In life we have been one, and in our deaths
We will not be divided.

Essex. There is a cauſe, a precious cauſe, my brother—
Thou ſtill muſt live, to love, to ſerve, to ſave him,
All that ſhall ſuddenly be left of Essex;
Where yet he lives, much more than to himſelf,
Thro' every pulſe, and trembling chord infuſed
With quick and dear ſenſation—Lend thy boſom
To hide one tear that will not be witheld—
Yet here 'tis due from manhood—O my wife!—

South. I had forgot—Yes, Essex, I will live—
For thy dear ſake I'll make a weary pilgrimage,
To guide thy other ſelf thro' all the thorns
And mazes of the world; 'till the wiſh'd hour

By

By fate appointed comes, when we ſhall meet
To part no more.

ESSEX. Cheriſh, protect, ſupport her.

SOUTH. Ever, ever.

ESSEX. Then the great buſineſs of the world is over—
You two make all my treaſure left on earth;
Comfort each other, we ſhall meet hereafter
In happier climes—the heaven I have in view
Will not be perfect elſe—'Till then, farewell!

SOUTH. Whilſt I have ſpeech to ſay—'till then, farewell! [Exit SOUTHAMPTON.

ESSEX. Now on, my lords, and execute your office. [Exeunt CECIL and RALEIGH.

SCENE X.

Enter RUTLAND and Ladies.

RUT. Where is he? let me catch him! hold him! ſave him!
Ruſh on the ſtroke that would attempt his life!—
O ESSEX, O my lord!—

ESSEX. This is too much,
Too much for man!—I hoped—Ah cruel dear!
Were not eternity, and ſudden death,
Of weight ſufficient to a mortal nature?
And art thou come to reinforce their powers,
And weaken what was left of man about me?

RUT. The QUEEN, my love—the QUEEN permits this meeting;
And therefore grants, that we ſhall part no more.

ESSEX.

ESSEX. What doſt thou mean?—Thy looks are wild, and keen;
They pierce my ſoul—Retire, my angel—do—
Let me prevail, and recollect thy ſpirits;
But for a moment.

RUT. 'Tis impoſſible—
High Heaven doth know it is impoſſible—
I cannot leave thee—never will I leave thee!
Sure we may die together—

ESSEX. My ſoul's treaſure!
It is in vain; the hand of ſtronger fate
Compels, and we muſt part.

LIEUT. My gracious lord,
Your lateſt minute is at hand—

RUT. What's this?
An axe! an executioner!—'Tis dreadful!
I am not prepared for this—Is it a dream?
If you have pity, wake me.

ESSEX. A ſhort abſence—
No more—'Tis but to bid one dear farewell,
'Till we do meet to part no more.

RUT. Ah whither would'ſt thou?—Think not to eſcape me—
No barbarous ESSEX, thou ſhalt never part me;
I'll cling to thee in death.

ESSEX. This, this, cuts keen
And deep, beyond the ſhallow reach of ſteel;
It is the quick of ſoul that here is pierced!
Haſte, haſte, in pity as I ſtand diſpatch me—
Is there not one, one hand of friendly mercy,
To lodge a poniard here?—
Quick, drag me to the block—Help me to ſunder—

Yet

Yet, hurt her not—It is in vain—ſhe graſps me
As in the agonies of death—Loſt wretch!
And wert thou born to this? Accurs'd the hour
That gave me up to light!—Yet more accurs'd
That hour I once deem'd happieſt over all
The world calls happy, to this bleſſed flower
Tying my baleful influence—Ha! ſhe's going—
Her ſpeechleſs lip grows livid, and thoſe orbs
Wane from their peerleſs luſtre—Gently, gently—
Now looſe her hold—Support her.—

LIEUT. Now, my lord,
'Twere beſt to ſeize the occaſion—The time's paſt.
My orders are——

ESSEX. Come then, and puſh me off
Down the dark void that ſpreads upon futurity.—
O my loſt love!—
O Gem! for which the world were richly ſold!
If there's a heaven can counterpoiſe thy loſs,
It is indeed beyond imagination!
Night comes upon me—when my eyes have ta'en
Their laſt, laſt look—the bitterneſs of death
Is paſt—and the world now is nothing!

[Exeunt ESSEX, &c.

SCENE XI.

Enter QUEEN, NOTTINGHAM, Ladies and Gentlemen, &c.

QUEEN. Is he then gone?—To death?—ESSEX to death!
And by my order?—Now perhaps—this moment!—
Haſte NOTTINGHAM, diſpatch—

NOTT. What would your majesty!

QUEEN. I know not what—I am in horrors, NOTTINGHAM,
In horrors worse than death!—Does he still live?
Run, bring me word—Yet stay—Can you not save him
Without my bidding? Read it in my heart—
In my distraction read—O, sure the hand
That saved him, would be as a blest angel's
Pouring soft balm into my rankling breast.

NOTT. If it shall please your majesty to give
Express commands, I shall obey them straight—
The world will think it strange—But you are QUEEN.

QUEEN. Hard-hearted NOTTINGHAM! to arm my pride,
My shame, against my mercy.—Ha! what's here?
A sight to strike resentment dead, and rouse
Soft pity even in a barbarous breast—
It is the wife of ESSEX!
Rise RUTLAND, come to thy repentant mistress:
See, thy QUEEN bends to take thee to her bosom,
And foster thee for ever!—Rise.

RUT. Which way?
Do you not see these circling steeps?—
Not all the fathom lines that have been loos'd
To sound the bottom of the faithless main,
Could reach to draw me hence. Never was dug
A grave so deep as mine!—Help me, kind friend,
Help me to put these little bones together—
These are my messengers to yonder world,

To

To ſeek for ſome kind hand, to drop me down
A little charity.

QUEEN. Heart-breaking ſounds!

RUT. Theſe were an infant's bones—But huſh—
don't tell—
Don't tell the QUEEN—
An unborn infant's—May be, if 'tis known,
They'll ſay I murder'd it—Indeed I did not—
It was the axe—how ſtrange ſoe'er, 'tis true!
Help me to put them right, and then they'll fly—
For they are light, and not like mine, incumber'd
With limbs of marble, and a heart of lead.

QUEEN. Alas! her reaſon is diſturb'd; her eyes
Are wild, and abſent—Do you know me, RUTLAND?
Do you not know your QUEEN?

RUT. O yes, the QUEEN!—
They ſay you have power of life and death—Poor QUEEN!
They flatter you.—You can take life away,
But can you give it back? No, no, poor QUEEN!—
Look at theſe eyes—they are a widow's eyes—
Do you know that?—Perhaps indeed you'll ſay,
A widow's eyes ſhould weep, and mine are dry:
That's not my fault; tears ſhould come from the heart,
And mine is dead—I feel it cold within me,
Cold as a ſtone—But yet my brain is hot—
O fye upon this head, it is ſtark naught!
Beſeech your majeſty to cut it off,
The bloody axe is ready—Say the word,
(For none can cut off heads without your leave)

And it is done—I humbly thank your highneſs,
You look a kind conſent. I'll but juſt in
And ſay a prayer or two.
From my youth upwards I ſtill ſaid my prayers
Before I ſlept; and this is my laſt ſleep.
Indeed 'tis not thro' fear, nor to gain time—
Not your own ſoldier could meet death more bravely:
You ſhall be judge yourſelf.—We muſt make haſte—
I pray be ready—If we loſe no time,
I ſhall o'ertake and join him on the way.
[Exit RUTLAND.

QUEEN. Follow her cloſe, allure her to ſome chamber
Of privacy; there ſooth her frenzy, but
Take care ſhe go not forth. Heaven grant I may not
Require ſuch aid myſelf! for ſure I feel
A ſtrange commotion here.

SCENE XII.

Enter an OFFICER.

OFFICER. May it pleaſe your majeſty,
The earl, as he addreſt him to the block,
Requeſted but the time to write theſe lines;
And earneſtly conjured me to deliver them
Into your royal hands.

QUEEN. Quick—What is here!—Juſt heaven! Fly, take this ſignet,
Stop execution—fly with eagle's wings—
What art thou?—of this world?

NOTT.

NOTT. Ha!—I'm diſcover'd—
Then be it ſo—Your majeſty may ſpare—
QUEEN. Stop, ſtop her yell!—Hence to ſome dungeon, hence—
Deep ſunk from day! In horrid ſilence there
Let conſcience talk to thee, infix its ſtings,
Awake remorſe, and deſperate penitence;
And from the torments of thy conſcious guilt
May hell be all thy refuge!
[Exit NOTTINGHAM guarded.

SCENE XIII.

Enter CECIL, RALEIGH, &c.

CECIL. Gracious madam,
I grieve to ſay your order came too late;
We met the meſſenger on our return
From ſeeing the earl fall.
QUEEN. O fatal ſound!——
Ye bloody pair! accurs'd be your ambition,
For it was cruel.——
O RUTLAND, ſiſter, daughter, fair forlorn!
No more thy QUEEN or miſtreſs, here I vow,
To be for ever wedded to thy griefs—
A faithful partner, numbering ſigh for ſigh,
And tear for tear; till our ſad pilgrimage
Shall bear us where our ESSEX now looks down
With pity on a toiling world, and ſees
What trains of real wretchedneſs await
The dream of power and emptineſs of ſtate.

E P I L O G U E.

Written by Mr. GARRICK;

And ſpoken by Mrs. PRITCHARD, in the character of QUEEN ELIZABETH.

IF any, here, are Britons but in name,
Dead to their conntry's happineſs and fame,
Let 'em depart this moment—Let 'em fly
My awful preſence, and my ſearching eye!

No more your Queen, but upright judge I come,
To try your deeds abroad, your lives at home;
Try you in every point, from ſmall to great,
Your Wit,—-Laws,—-Faſhions,-—Valour,-—
Church and State!
Search you, as Britons ne'er were ſearch'd before—
"O tremble! for you hear the lion roar!"

Since that moſt glorious time that here I reign'd,
An age and half!—what have you loſt or gain'd?
Your Wit—whate'er your poets ſing or ſwear,
Since Shakeſpeare's time is ſomewhat worſe for wear.
Your Laws are good, your lawyers good of courſe;
The ſtreams are ſurely clear, when clear the ſource:
In greater ſtore theſe bleſſings now are ſent ye;
Where I had one attorney, you have twenty.
Faſhions, ye fair, deſerve nor praiſe nor blame,

Unleſs

Unlefs they rife as foes to fenfe or fhame:
Wear ruffs, or gauze—but let your fkill be fuch,
Rather to fhew too little, than too much.
As for your Valour—here my lips I clofe—
Let thofe who beft have proved it, fpeak—your foes.
Your Morals, Church, and State, are ftill behind—
But foft—prophetic fury fills my my mind!
I fee thro' time—behold a youthful hand,
Holding the fcepter of this happy land;
Whofe heart with juftice, love, and virtue fraught,
Born amongft Britons, and by Britons taught,
Shall make the barking tongues of faction ceafe,
And weave the garland of domeftic peace:
Long fhall he reign—no ftorms to beat his breaft;
Unruly paffions that difturb'd my reft!
Shall live, the bleffings he beftows, to fhare;
Reap all my glory, but without my care.

CONRADE:

A

FRAGMENT.

CONRADE:

A

FRAGMENT.

The SONG of The FILEA of Antient Days, PHELIN the gray-hair'd Son of the Son of Kinfadda.

WHAT do I love—what is it that mine eyes
Turn round in ſearch of—that my ſoul longs after,
But cannot quench her thirſt?—'Tis BEAUTY, PHELIN!
I ſee it wide beneath the arch of Heaven,
When the ſtars peep upon their evening hour,
And the moon riſes on the eaſtern wave,
Houſed in a cloud of gold!—I ſee it wide
In earth's autumnal teints of various landſcape,
When the firſt ray of morning tips the trees,
And fires the diſtant rock!—I hear its voice,
When thy hand ſends the ſound along the gale,
Swept from the ſilver ſtrings; or, on mine ear
Drops the ſweet ſadneſs!—At my heart I feel
Its potent graſp, I melt beneath the touch,

When

When the tale pours upon my ſenſe humane
The woes of other times!—What art thou, BEAUTY?
Thou art not colour, fancy, ſound, nor form—
Theſe but the conduits are, whence the ſoul quaffs
The liquor of its Heaven.—Whate'er thou art,
Nature, or Nature's Spirit, thou art ALL
I long for!—O, deſcend upon my Thoughts!
To thine own muſic, tune, thou Power of Grace,
The cordage of my heart! fill every ſhape
That riſes to my dream, or wakes to viſion;
And touch the threads of every mental nerve,
With all thy ſacred feelings!—

THE SUN now haſten'd down his weſtern Heaven,
And ſaw his beams reflected from the ſpires
Of fair Emania.—High, within the Hall,
With all his Heroes, names of wide renown,
With all his Sages, heads grown white in council,
With all his Bards, the ſires of ſong, around him—
CONRADE the mighty, ſate!

Wide o'er the feſtal board, in many a bowl,
The various liquor flow'd.—In various cups,
Metal, or wrought from veiny adamant,
Or of the treaſures of the pearly deep,
The ſocial pledge of health went round. Before
The King of Chiefs, the hoar and reverend brow

Of

Of Wiſdom was unbent, and every heart
Caught gladneſs from his aſpect. Near the ſeat
Of lifted Majeſty, ſtood the young bloom
Of Erin's hope, SLEMFANNON, as a ſapling
Sprouting aloft beneath the parent oak,
That overlooks the foreſt. Now, and oft,
He turn'd his face of filial ſweetneſs upward,
To catch the glance of the paternal eye,
That dropt indulgence and delight upon him:
Now, with both hands, faſt by the ſinewy wriſt,
He graſp'd the Firſt of Heroes—" O," he cried,
" Will ever, ever, your SLEMFANNON wield
" The craſhing mace, or bend the bow of ſteel,
" With ſuch an arm as this?"—He ſpoke, and rear'd
The ponderous hand on high! The ſhout of joy
Pour'd round the table!—for, in that right hand,
Lay Erin's glory, and the ſure reſource
Of nations from the waſters of the world!

Soft ſmiling, gently bending from his ſeat,
The Monarch anſwer'd—" Yes, thou pride of CONRADE,
" In whom he fondly joys to live renew'd,
" Freſh born, a dearer growth of young exiſtence—
" Thou art the veſſel that ſhall pour his fame
" On future times!—The day is yet to come,

When

" When nations, to exalt the name of CONRADE,
" Shall ſay, He was the Father of SLEMFANNON!"

" Thine arm is young, my ſon, but not inglorious;
" The Romans, from the Rhodane to the Po,
" Have felt it through their ſteel! The ear of heroes
" Liſts not to its own praiſe—yet know, thy name
" Is in the ſong of bards; and PHELIN, oft,
" To me gives up the muſic of thy deeds,
" And tunes my ſoul to joy.—But, mark, SLEMFANNON!
" The arm of Power is, ever, worthieſt ſeen
" In Preſervation—he, who ſaves, is next
" To him who gives exiſtence. O, SLEMFANNON,
" That we might ſave!—that we might ſave ALL, then,
" Without offence to Any! In this Hall,
" O, might yon length of ſword, yon ſhining mail,
" Hang indolent for ever!—and, in days
" Of ages yet to come, the Sons of Peace,
" Gazing and wondering, queſtion, with each other,
" What once had been their uſe!—Attend, my heroes!—

" Man

" Man comes into this paffing world of weak-
nefs,
" And cries for help to man! for, feeble is he,
" And many are his foes—thirft, hunger, nak-
ednefs;
" Difeafes infinite within his frame;
" Without, the inclemency and wrath of feafons,
" Famines, plagues, pefts, devouring elements,
" Earthquakes beneath, and thunders rolling
o'er him;
" Age and infirmity, on either hand;
" And Death who, lifts the certain Dart behind
him!

" Thefe we might deem (had any Pitying
Power
" Ordain'd the ways of man) were ills fufficient!
" Man thinks not fo—on his own race he turns
" The force of all his talents, exquifite
" To fhorten the fhort interval, by Art,
" Which Nature left us! Fire and fword are in
" His hand; and, in his thought, are machinations
" For fpeeding of perdition! Half the world,
" Down the fteep gulph of dark futurity,
" Pufh off their fellows—paufe upon the brink—
" And then drop after!"—

" Tell me, ye Sages, tell me, if ye can,
" Whence is the Stream of Life!—It rifes frefh

" In

8

" In ſmiling infancy; and pours along,
" Short, turbulent, and murmuring in its courſe,
" To its capacious ſea. The ſea fills not;
" The ſea, from whence it never has return'd;
" Nor ceaſes, yet, the ſtream.—Where lies the Fund,
" From whence it flows?—will it be ever, thus?—
" And to no end, no purpoſe?"—

While, thus, the Hero queſtion'd on the height
And depth of vaſt Infinitude, intent
To plumb it with his fathom; through the Hall
A ſudden Radiance broke!—All turn'd their eyes
Upon the coming Glory; for, of earth,
They did not deem the viſion!—On ſhe came,
SHULAMA, daughter of the gold-throned king
Of Scandinavia—on ſhe came, in all
Her pleaſantneſs of beauty, as the morn,
Bluſhing amidſt the brightneſs of its eaſt,
Riſes on human ſight! A train of virgins
Follow'd her ſteps; to them, twice twenty heroes,
Lords of wide lands and famed in northern fields,
Succeeded; and yet, diſtant, far behind,
Was ſeen the long retinue! Through the Hall,
Silent and ſtill, as in the noon of night,
Attention held its breath—the white hair'd Sages

Rear'd

Rear'd their ſpread hands, in wonder—and SLEM-
FANNON
Gazed, as a blind-born man endow'd with ſight,
When firſt he looks upon a new found world!

Tow'rd the gem'd throne of awful majeſty,
The Maiden bent the luſtre of her eye,
And grace of motion. Lowly, on her knee
She ſunk, imploring—"Hail, thou Firſt of Heroes,
"The conqueror of the conquerors of the world,
"King over kings uplifted!—Have I then,
"Beheld the face of CONRADE, and ſurvived it?"

"RUTHAMOR, monarch of the golden throne,
"Whoſe deeds light up the north, hath ſent
SHULAMA
"To ſeek alliance with the might of CONRADE!—
"I come from far, ambaſſadreſs of love;
"And claim a partner for my father's throne,
"Even your beloved daughter, SEGALEME,
"The witch who rolls the eyes of young enchant-
ment!"

Riſing, and ſlow deſcending from his throne,
CONRADE advanced. He rais'd the awe-ſtruck
maid,
And, to his war-imprinted boſom, claſp'd
The dangers of her beauty—"Welcome, welcome,
"Welcome,"

"Welcome," he cried, "to CONRADE, to his Erin,
"Thou daughter of delight! — for favouring Heaven
"Hath made thee in its pride of workmanſhip,
"And planted lovelineſs, as light, around thee!

"Hadſt thou, O daughter of the bleſt RUTHAMOR,
"Required a province at the hands of CONRADE,
"It had been given—or gold, and coſtly jewels;
"He would have ſtored your ſhipping with the burden,
"Till you cried, Hold!—But, here, alas, you aſk
"The only thing I covet!—SEGALEME,
"And young SLAMFANNON, are the eyes of CONRADE—
"The precious eyes, by which he guides his ſteps,
"And looks, alone, for joy! And ſhall I, then,
"Shall I ſend off the treaſure from my ſoul,
"To enrich the land of ſtrangers?—No, SHULAMA!
"Haply, when grown infirm, and dim with age,
"When I can only feel around for comfort,
"How ſhall my hands ſtretch forth to foreign climes,
"And, to my knees, draw up the little ones
"Of SEGALEME?"—While the Monarch ſpoke,

A diſtant

A diſtant portal open'd: SEGALEME
Appear'd to ſight, and fill'd the paſs with brightneſs!

As, ſhould two moons, at eaſt and weſt, ariſe
In aſpect oppoſite; and each, in other,
Behold the image of its own perfection;
So ſhone, ſo moved, ſo gazed, the Rival Lights
Of CONRADE and RUTHAMOR! They approach'd—
Their ſteps ſeem'd meaſured by the ſound of muſic;
And each had loſt the memory of herſelf,
In admiration of the other's beauty!
Silent, their arms of ivory they expand;
They fold each other to a poliſh'd boſom,
And mix their rays of brightneſs!—SEGALEME
Firſt broke the ſtillneſs in the Hall of Heroes.

"Welcome," ſhe cried, "thrice welcome to the vale
"Of Erin, that ſhall gladden in thy preſence,
"O Beam of northern hills!"—"And have I, then,
"Have I, at length, beheld thee," cried SHULAMA,
"Thou praiſe of every tongue?—mine eyes are ſatiſfied,
"And take their reſt with thee!"—"Thou art the joy,
"The ſiſter of my ſoul!" ſaid SEGALEME—

She ſpoke, and kiſs'd her forehead.—Whiſpering
ſoft,
SHULAMA then inquired—" Say, which is he,
" The force of your SLEMFANNON, ſo renown'd
" For feats of warfare in the field of Romans?
" Which is your mighty brother, SEGALEME?—
" For mine eye dare not venture in his ſearch,
" Amid the groups of Heroes that ſurround us."

" There, there he grows, the flower of Erin's
garden,
" Faſt by the royal pillar of the land!—
" There ſtands the young SLEMFANNON, in his
ſweetneſs!"

Full on the youth, the Maid of Scandinavia
Roll'd the young lightning of the glance of beauty—
His eyes met hers; and down they ſunk abaſh'd,
As caught in ſome tranſgreſſion.—

" Ah, thou deceiver, beauteous witch of Erin,"
Rejoin'd SHULAMA, " this is not thy brother!—
" I ween'd to meet ſome giant, as in tales
" Of old renown, and terrible to fight!
" But here, I view the Infant of the Spring,
" Like one of us, who pale to look on blood,
" And, o'er the dying ſongſter of the cage,
" Shed tears of mourning!"—SEGALEME ſmiled;
And from the dimpling of her radiant cheek

A glory went abroad!—Forth, by the hand,
She led the lovely Stranger to her bower.

Mean-ſeaſon, to the Peers of Scandinavia
The Monarch bow'd benevolent, and ſaid—
" Welcome, ye Heroes of the ſky-topt hills!
" Thrice welcome all, though each had been an hundred—
" For Plenty dwells upon the vales of Erin,
" And CONRADE's palace is the Home of Strangers!
" The night deſcends—light up my many halls;
" Spread wide the boards; pour plenteous, to the brim,
" The juice of every region!"—It was done.
By hundreds, and by fifties, ſat the Chiefs
Commix'd with Bards and Sages; while the voice
Of feſtal joy was heard throughout Emania.

But, far within, in regal majeſty,
Sat Erin's Strength! SLEMFANNON bleſt his ſide;
And, full in view, he placed the high-born maids,
And fed his ſoul upon the work of Beauty.

PHELIN, the ſeer and ſong of antient days,
The ſage inſtructor of his loved SLEMFANNON,
Was ſeated here—and here, again, Siffrenna,
The white hair'd guardian of SHULAMA's beauties.

Soon as the board lay lighten'd of the banquet,
Fair boys and maidens, into chryſtal cups,

Pour'd the rich vintage of the Greekiſh iſles
Of Archipelago. The joy went round;
The wiſh of pleaſing, and the ſweets of converſe!

"SLEMFANNON," ſaid the Monarch, "take the harp—
"Thou arm of CONRADE, take the ſtrings of ſtory,
"And, to the ear of Erin's lovely Gueſt,
"Tune ſome of thine adventures, when thou ſtood'ſt,
"In ſouthern climates, by the ſide of CONRADE,
"Then, like a glimpſe of lightning, ſhot abroad,
"And overturn'd the foe!"—Yet ſtill obedient
To the high call, the bluſhing Youth replied:
"I turn'd, and ſhelter'd me behind your buckler,
"As though behind the walls of Ariſphellan!"

Old PHELIN from its chain releas'd the lyre,
And gave it, ſmiling.—O'er the ſilver ſtrings
Light flew the fingers of the ſhamefaced Boy,
Scarce audible.—At length the tale began;

Our tent was pitch'd amid the field of Narbon—
The dead lay wide around—the night came down,
To veil their ghaſtlineſs—no ſtar appear'd—
And the moon, ſickening at the ſight of blood,
Had ſhrowded up her viſage!—Through the gloom,
Mine ear was ſtricken with the voice of wailing,

Sad

Sad as a thousand sighs, when the dark winds
Sob through the yews that stand amid the graves
Of Arnel!—Forth I went to seek the mourner.

Through the night's glimpse, that struck upon his mail,
I saw a warrior, tall and fair of stature.
Upon his strenuous arm, he, lightly, bore
The corse of his companion. On a bank
He laid the body down, and sunk beside it.

"Art thou then gone," he cried? "for ever gone,
"Companion of my soul! in whom I lived,
"The dearer self of desolated HUGON!
"Wilt thou no more arise, like light, upon me?
"Nor give the smile of friendship to mine eyes?
"Nor cheer my spirit with thy voice of music?

"Why didst thou step before me in the battle?
"Wast thou not safe, behind my wheeling sword,
"As in the fort of Delma?—That my breast,
"O, that my naked breast had met the dart,
"That slew my brother!—Thou hast left me, BERITH,
"With Grief, alone, companion'd.—O, stern Grief,
"Sad is thy fellowship! I will not bide it.—
"I will o'ertake thee, BERITH!—We will live,

"Perchance, in happier climes; or, in one grave,
"Silent lie down, and sleep in peace together!

"Look not, my mother, from the wonted pride
"Of thine high battlements, to see thy son
"Returning, in the front of all his trophies!—
"Mistake not Arden's forest for his flags;
"Nor the wind's western clangor for his trumpets!—
"Thou shalt look upward, with a tearful eye,
"And sigh to see, how empty is his armour!—
"Thy hall, it shall be hung around with black,
"And one lone lamp shall light thee!"

Straight, by the accent of the Hero's tongue,
I knew him for an enemy to Conrade:
But well I knew, that Conrade was the friend
Of humankind!—With gentle voice, the voice,
As of a brother, I the Chief accosted:

"My heart, O Warrior! takes a kindred share
"In all thy sufferings.—In the field, indeed,
"My faulchion rises in my country's quarrel;
"But my soul knows no warfare with the Brave,
"The Good, or the Unhappy!—Know, great Hugon,
"That the Distress'd are held as Sons and Brothers
"To Conrade and Slemfannon! Near at hand,
"Extends our camp—whate'er of friendly aid

"Can

"Can there be given, is thine!" He anſwer'd not;
But, with a grateful and aſſenting claſp,
Confined me to his boſom—while our ſouls,
Mingling their friendſhips, coaleſced together.

Attendants ſtraight I call'd; then to my tent
Convey'd the corſe, and gently on a bed
Reclined, and ſoon the ſteely mail unbraced—
When, ſtrange to tell! upon the aſtoniſh'd ſight
Roſe two twin-orbs of beauty!—Back, abaſh'd,
Starting I turn'd, and ſent the female-train;
Then ſought where HUGON, all involv'd in grief,
Sat with my Sire. In panting haſte I told
The wondrous tale.—The Hero cried, "'Tis ſhe,
"'Tis ſhe herſelf!—it muſt be ELIPHENE!—
"My heart confeſs'd her, though my eyes refuſed
"Its atteſtation, turning Love's fierce ardours
"To Friendſhip's gentler flame!"—At once they roſe,
And follow'd, where the beauteous body lay,
Decent, in virgin ſheets.—We ſent in haſte,
And call'd ELPHENOR, ſovereign of all herbs
And arts for healing—He the deadly wound
E'er long diſcovered; for it ſtill oozed crimſon,
Like a roſe ſpringing midſt a bed of lilies!
The vital heat, unwilling to forego
Its lovely manſion, feebly held the center;

And ſtill a thread of life gave faint pulſation!
From his elixir'd chryſtal, drop by drop,
Thro' the pale lips, the cautious Sage infuſed
The potent cordial.—Thus, while doubtful life
Hung, fearfully ſuſpended, generous HUGON
Addreſs'd my Sire—

O CONRADE, cried the Chief,
Thou Dread of Tyrants; hateful to Oppreſſors,
But, to the Feeble and Oppreſs'd, a name
Of ſure Aſylum—loved of all the Valiant!—
Yes, HUGON ſwears the Valiant love thee, CONRADE,
Even while, as foes, they draw the ſword againſt thee!—
O Monarch, lend the ear of thy compaſſion;
Thine ear, ſtill open to the tale of mourning,
Lend it a while to HUGON!—He's a Tuſcan,
By clime and birth thine enemy—although
His kindred ſpirit long has held the dear,
Even with the deareſt.—Hear then, hear my tale
Of ſad diſtreſs!—That lovely, hapleſs Maid,
Of nobleſt lineage, to my guardian care,
Was by her parents left.—She was addreſt
By all the potentates, whoſe ſtation warranted
To lift an eye ſo lofty.—I was, then,
In foreign climes, on travel—I return'd.

Upon

Upon a ſtated feſtival, the chiefs
And princes of the land, with princely dames,
Convened, a galaxy!—I too was there;
And there was Eliphene, as the ſtar
Of beauty, regent, midſt the ſmaller ſparklers!
With fond attraction ſhe compell'd me to her,
As the touch'd needle to the frozen north;
For ſo I did miſdeem it.—From that day,
Amidſt the nobleſt of her princely ſuitors,
I too preferr'd my claim.—She firſt receiv'd me
With ſmiling, kind, encouraging complacence:
But ſoon her looks grew more conſtrain'd—whene'er
Her eyes met mine, ſhe bluſh'd and turn'd aſide,
As wiſhing to avoid me.—To all others,
She look'd an elegance of eaſe, and ſpoke
In terms as free as air—to me, her ſpeech,
Unfrequent, was abrupt and cautious.—Stung
With ſcorpion'd jealouſy, I, to my ſoul,
Thus ſpoke indignant—"What have theſe to boaſt,
"Theſe favour'd rivals, o'er rejected Hugon!
"Does their pre-eminence conſiſt in ſhape,
"Or feature?—eyes, that are not Eliphene's,
"Will anſwer, No.—And, as to feats of proweſs,
"Compared with me, they're nameleſs!—O ſhame, ſhame,

"Shame

" Shame on this weakneſs, this degrading paſſion!
" Henceforth, I will wage war on my own heart—
" And conquer it, or periſh!"

At the time,
The tidings of your dread invaſion reach'd us.
Quick, at the name of CONRADE, my whole ſoul
Kindled to generous rivalſhip—" Yes, yes,
" Thou ſhalt be met, thou mighty one!" I cried,
" Thou ſhalt be met—thy beſt eſteemer ſhall
" Oppoſe thee, front to front!—I aſk of Heaven
" No boon, no other bounty, than to have
" My death ennobled by the arm of CONRADE!"

Straight I addreſs'd for war; but Love, uncall'd,
Obtruded, whiſpering to my ſecret ſoul,
" Firſt take thy laſt adieu of ELIPHENE!"
Pride, haughty champion, roſe, with ſtern rebuke
Againſt the gentler Power. He frown'd, and cried,
" What, are we not, as yet, enough debaſed?—
" Shall we add further forces to the foe;
" And furniſh arms, againſt our nobleneſs,
" To the tried ſcorn and inſolence of Beauty?"

Dire was the conteſt—Love long kept his ground;
But Pride, at laſt, was prevalent—I rent,

I tore myself away from my Beloved,
From my true Lover—
As a self-murderer, desperate of his state,
Makes a divorce betwixt his soul and body!

I lay encamp'd, my legions tented round me,
When word was brought me of a youthful warrior,
Of graceful mein, and more than matchless beauty,
Who ask'd admission.—To my presence led
He bow'd submiss; and, blushing, pray'd the grace
Of being privileged to do me service.

My heart straight took acquaintance with his aspect—
Some strange similitude fond memory found
'Twixt him and ELIPHENE!—but, my soul
Conceiv'd no thought, that she her tender frame
Should vest in steel—should seek the man she hated—
Should trace her HUGON into death and dangers!

Instant, our hearts commenced a friendship, tender,
Fondly inviolate, as caught together
By hooks of golden grappling.—I, no more,
Sought CONRADE on the perilous edge of conflict;
I now had one to care for! and my eye,
My guardian eye pursued and watch'd his motions,
On this side, and on that.—In this day's battle,
I charged him, on his duty, on his love,

To

To hold him rearward.—Still I turn'd, and turn'd;
Even as a timid deer accompanied
By her loved fawn, to ſee if he was near—
But yet, alas, in fear of loſing fame,
I led my Friend too deeply into dangers!

At length, toward eve—for who can cope with
CONRADE?—
Your hoſt prevail'd!—Indignant I oppoſed,
And would have reinforced the fight—when, lo,
A random ſhaft ruſh'd, rudely, through the mail,
The light framed mail of my beloved Companion,
And ting'd his arms with blood! Upon the inſtant,
Our legions ſounded a retreat. Then, then—
Muſt I confeſs that HUGON trembled?—Straight
Into my arms I caught my beſt beloved,
And fled the hindmoſt: night came on apace,
And parted all affray—Upon a bank
I laid her down, and, to the pitying moon,
Whoſe doubtful glimpſes thro' the darkneſs broke,
Utter'd my wailings.—Then, our loved SLEM-
FANNON
Came, provident of comforts, to conſole;
And did conſole, by ſhewing, that, on earth,
Such Virtue ſtill was extant!—Here, the Hero
Cloſed his ſad narrative!

Meantime, ELPHENOR, pendent o'er the corſe,
Still plied his tender offices. At length,

The

The beauteous Form began to move—each heart
Bounded with expectation—when her eyes
Open'd their faint refulgence to the light,
Look'd wild around her with a sickly gleam,
And closed their orbs for ever!—Then ELPHENOR:
"By death's cold hand this Rose of Beauty cropt,
"Fades, and shall bloom no more—except in Heaven!"

Meantime astonish'd, o'er the lifeless corse,
The Hero speechless stood—then, all at once,
As some high cliff, far jutting o'er its base,
Disparts and dashes on the sea-beat shore,
Bereft of sense he fell—bless'd pause of being!
But O, how fearfully to be succeeded
By anguishings unutterable!—Long,
Long lay he tranced—I thought, I wish'd him dead—
For what had life, midst all its stores of bliss,
For him, save misery extreme?—At length,
He waked to all the pangs of mental feeling!

Five days, and five soul-torturing nights, he lay
By the embalm'd Remains—in all which time,
Nor food, nor word of utterance, past his lips;
Nor word of consolation to his ear

Obtain'd

Obtain'd admiſſion—By his ſide faſt laid,
I preſs'd his hand in mine, and on it dropt
The tear of ſad condolence! Through the camp,
Sudden I heard the ſhout of joint laments—
I roſe, and iſſued forth.—

FINIS.

www.ingramcontent.com/pod-product-compliance
Lightning Source LLC
Chambersburg PA
CBHW021110270326
41929CB00009B/812
9783744677868